CHASING
the
WHITE DOG

AN AMATEUR OUTLAW'S
ADVENTURES IN MOONSHINE

MAX WATMAN

SIMON & SCHUSTER

NEW YORK   LONDON   TORONTO   SYDNEY

Simon & Schuster
1230 Avenue of the Americas
New York, NY 10020

First Simon & Schuster hardcover edition February 2010

SIMON & SCHUSTER and colophon are registered trademarks
of Simon & Schuster, Inc.

For information about special discounts for bulk purchases,
please contact Simon & Schuster Special Sales at
1-866-506-1949 or business@simonandschuster.com.

The Simon & Schuster Speakers Bureau can bring authors
to your live event. For more information or to book an event
contact the Simon & Schuster Speakers Bureau at
1-866-248-3049 or visit our website at www.simonspeakers.com.

Designed by Kyoko Watanabe

Manufactured in the United States of America

1   3   5   7   9   10   8   6   4   2

Library of Congress Cataloging-in-Publication Data

Watman, Max.
Chasing the white dog : an amateur outlaw's adventures in moonshine / Max Watman.
p.   cm.
1. Distilling, Illicit—United States—History.   2. Brewing—Social aspects—United
States—History.   3. Liquors—Social aspects—United States—History.   I. Title.
HJ5021.W38 2010
363.4'1092—dc22   2009024657
ISBN 978-1-4165-7178-0

For my mom,
who undoubtedly had something better in mind.

Contents

CONTENTS

CHASING
the
WHITE DOG

On Top of Old Smoky

The manufacture of illicit whiskey in the mountains is not dead. Far from it.

—THE FOXFIRE BOOK, VOL. 1

THE FIRST TIME I SAW RENÉ WITH A JAR OF MOONSHINE, WE were having a beer in an empty bar and gazing at the sun-dappled trees of Tompkins Square Park. It was a quiet afternoon at Doc Holliday's, a honky-tonk in downtown New York City with David Allen Coe on the jukebox, cowboy boots nailed to the ceiling, and cheap PBR. These bars, of which there were maybe half a dozen throughout the city, were headed toward a weird pinnacle of noxious renown: It was 1999, and there were already stories circulating about beautiful celebrities dancing on the bar while the bartenders (gorgeous, wild) poured flaming booze and screamed for their tips through megaphones.

René is the kid brother of a dear old friend, and in my imagination he is permanently fourteen. His beard, in fact his whole outdoorsy, laid-back, good-looking adult person, surprises me every time. He has wrenched motorcycles and hiked the Appalachian Trail, and he had spent his first paycheck from the Smoky Mountain forestry service to come visit.

He reached into his knapsack but stopped with his hand in the bag.

"Can I?" he asked, his eyes alight.

His brother shrugged.

Out came a Mason jar of clear liquid. This was years before I saw white lightning drip from a still in my own kitchen—in 1999, a jar of bootleg was a surprise. We took searing sips and shared it with the bartender.

Years later I took a break from the archives of Appalachian State University to call René and arrange our Labor Day visit in Sylva, North Carolina. He had been trying to line up a series of moonshiners for me to meet, and he had been excited at the prospect of cruising the country roads, meeting the locals, and drinking the legendary "charred liquor" of the hills. He seemed disappointed with what he'd managed. He hadn't found any charred, and all the moonshiners had stopped returning phone calls, as moonshiners are wont to do. We would drive up the mountain to his friend Larry's house—he might have some liquor—and have a barbecue. It was a fine way to spend Labor Day, I assured him. I could tell he felt that he'd failed.

I followed René up the mountain past small pastures and little homesteads nestled in leafy trees. At about 3,600 feet, we took a left onto a gravel driveway canopied by old-growth forest. A stream crossed the driveway at a ford, and we splashed through it.

Larry's unassuming rancher is surrounded by bedded plantings. He's built fences of driftwood and strung bottles along them. Arrayed about the property are benches he's cut from entire trees. One of them overlooks his two little ponds—one for swimming, one for fish (his teenage son Wesley announced there were twenty-six of them). Up the hill, rows of Christmas trees awaited harvest. He took us into the woods, to a spot on a creek where magnolias grew like mangroves and a small, beautiful waterfall rushed. We talked about recipes for the perfect margarita.

Larry has tricked out a little wooden barn with a gigantic Peavey PA system, a bar, and a lava lamp. He opened the freezer door and said, "Sheeat! Look in here, there's a jar of water that doesn't freeze!"

A neighbor showed up with some shucked oysters from her home in South Carolina.

We listened to Steve Earle, Ralph Stanley, and AC/DC and poured moonshine over the oysters and shot them with Tabasco.

Larry mentioned a friend with stovetop still, and praised the famous Smoky Mountain charred.

I sipped Larry's good corn whiskey—and that's what it was, there was no doubt about it—and smiled at them and told them this was perfect. A late summer day spent high in the Smokies drinking good white lightning is pretty satisfying.

It was on this trip that I went in search of famed moonshiner Popcorn Sutton.

Popcorn Sutton has made a career out of moonshine, but not, or not wholly, in the usual way. Rather than rely upon actually selling jugs of the stuff, he authored the perpetually out-of-print and consistently in demand book *Me and My Likker* and set out on a mission of bizarre celebrity. He spent a lot of time driving around in a Model A Ford and being interviewed for local news footage about the "old ways."

On Willie Nelson's Web site, you can see Willie with his arm around Popcorn. Willie is dressed nonchalantly in black—hoodie, trousers, sneakers, t-shirt, cowboy hat. Popcorn, in contrast, is attired in his usual costume: overalls, a flannel shirt, and a greasy leather fedora. He's hunched, his wild beard radiating down to his chest from drawn cheeks. He can't be an inch over 5 feet 6, and I'd be amazed to learn that he weighs more than two cases of beer. He is somewhere between 45 and 105 years old—apparently it's a bad idea to ask him. He looks as if he clips Snuffy Smith cartoons to his bathroom mirror.

Lana Nelson (Willie's daughter) captioned the photo: "Somewhere in the Great Smoky Mountains near Cherokee, N.C., world renowned moonshiner and literary giant, Popcorn Sutton, visits Dr. Booger Nelson [Willie's nickname is Booger Red] at a top-secret, undisclosed location. Popcorn brews corn liquor for thousands of thirsty customers in the dry county, and received a standing ovation when Dad introduced him at the sold-out Harrah's concert."

Popcorn never figured out how to monetize his celebrity. He gets hauled up on stage and smiles out into an exultant crowd, but he doesn't get any more bills to stuff in his mattress. He has sold at least one Model A, and he doesn't have the few thousand dollars it would take to get another print run of his book, although the thing is practically a home run, guaranteed to sell out while still warm from the printing press.

I had figured that his moonshine was all postmodernism, more about performance and presentation than liquor. Certainly, he doesn't actually make liquor for thousands of thirsty customers. He speaks at folk-life festivals. I thought of him as the Andy Warhol of hooch. Just another example of how something that had once been purely American and real had transformed, for purposes of display, into something else.

The truth turned out to be much weirder.

Authenticity is evasive and hard to understand in America. Why were there half a dozen honky-tonk beer joints in New York City at the turn of the century? I don't know what to make of the Inner Harbor of Baltimore, Fisherman's Wharf in San Francisco, or the French Quarter in New Orleans. For that matter, I don't know what to make of my own town, in which the historical review board insists that the houses continue to be built as if it were the middle of the nineteenth century, to maintain an authentic cohesion, without stopping to consider that nothing is more artificial than building nineteenth-century houses in the twenty-first century.

It's a slippery thing. There is no denying that the French Quarter really is the French Quarter or that Fisherman's Wharf is built on the quays. These places have found themselves, due to the pressures of commerce or culture, in a state of aggravated self-consciousness, compelled to emulate and replicate their salient features until artifice overtakes authenticity.

This shift happens to people, too. My suspicions about Popcorn's artifice were only further underscored by one of the two places he lives, a vacation hub called Maggie Valley, his perfect correlative.

West of Lake Junaluska in North Carolina, I drove Route 19 between Hard Ridge and Utah Mountain. The asphalt rolled flat for a short stretch between the many hills and became Soco Road. I drove through miles of restaurants, bars, hotels, and gift shops. Maggie Valley, according to the 2000 census, is a town of 607 people. On the five-mile stretch of Soco Road, I counted about thirty restaurants.

Today every slope is a housing development—for vacationers, I assume—named, as is the mode for developments, for the very things the bulldozers took from the landscape: Walnut Hills, the Meadows, Wild Acres. The one I explored was a cluster of gray, particleboard-paneled houses stacked like playing cards.

Whatever Maggie Valley once was, it no longer is.

The town has commodified itself, just as Popcorn has. I got the feeling that everything I touched, everything I saw, was being done for the benefit of tourists. That feeling is enhanced by the breathtaking tally of the roadside gift shops. Finally, at the edge of town, a gigantic sign in yellow and black announced that I'd found the most photographed vista of the Smokies.

Certainly, this place was perfect for books about backwoods distilling, for stoneware jugs, for metamoonshine.

But there was one last contradiction: Popcorn had been busted.

The headline had read, "Fire Call Leads to Moonshine Bust: Firefighters Responding to a Cocke County Fire on Tuesday Discovered Much More than They Expected."

On property belonging to Marvin "Popcorn" Sutton, they found everything needed to make moonshine, as well as dozens of jugs of the finished product. Three large stills were in operation, and a building on the property was on fire.

Sutton now faces two charges stemming from Tuesday's bust. Before his arrest, Sutton had gained a certain notoriety for his popular books and videos teaching others how to make moonshine.

According to one of Popcorn Sutton's videos, he's gotten in trouble for moonshining before—in 1974, and again in 1998.

He's expected to appear before a judge on these most recent charges on May 9.

Popcorn's shack in Maggie Valley is at the top of a hill, and at the bottom of that hill is the Misty Mountain Ranch, a bed-and-breakfast with a few cabins arrayed around a gravel parking lot. Karen and Peter, originally from Chicago, own the place. They, being garrulous and good-natured folks, befriended Popcorn, and he eventually became a mascot for the B&B. They bought one of his Model A's and dropped it in the yard, where it sits with a copper still bolted onto the back and some stickers, one of which reads DON'T LET THE TRUTH GET IN THE WAY OF A GOOD STORY.

It was here that I lurked and waited for Popcorn, and things got strange.

"Oh, I wish you'd called ahead," said Karen, "but it's okay, he's coming here today, anyway. Do you have his cell phone number?"

His what?

When the local news did a segment on him, the whole thing was framed by the idea that Maggie Valley is a beautiful place where people can see life "the way it used to be." The local news writers held that the more folks wanted to see the old ways, the more they crowded them out. The old culture died. What's left of the old ways, they claimed, throbs in Popcorn's breast. This sort of thing suits Popcorn fine; it's exactly the line he sells about himself.

I hadn't begun by looking for inconsistencies, but once I started paying attention—once, in other words, someone offered up a self-proclaimed mountain man's cell phone number—they began to leap out at me like mice from a kitchen drawer.

I went back and watched the clip of that local news report again. The camera is on Popcorn in his cabin, ostensibly a mountain shack, heated by just a woodstove. He says, "I can cook right here on top of it just as good as you can on an electric stove, downtown." In the left margin of the screen there is an electric stove.

That's not fair—perhaps it's gas.

Karen told me that Popcorn was not well, he'd fallen off of his front porch and hurt his back. He was seeing a chiropractor, and that was making it worse. "He's taking codeine," she said, "but maybe he'll want to meet you."

So I waited around.

I gave Karen $35 for Popcorn's DVD, mendaciously and manipulatively titled *This Is the Last Dam Run of Likker I'll Ever Make*, and put it on back in my cabin.

The documentary is fun: Popcorn drives around in his old Ford, looks for a good spot, and rambles on about himself.

Popcorn finds a stream with good water and shows the camera some "water weeds," which he claims prove the water will make good liquor. He's 10 yards ahead of the camera, and he climbs over a rock or two to come back toward the cameraman. He bitches about how hard of a job it is. It's rough stuff, in rough country, and he's old and tired.

The camera follows him as he walks, and we see that the car is on the side of the road, which is maybe 10 yards away—quite a hike.

I wandered back up to the house, fed the ducks, and drank a beer with my hosts until a gold Toyota pulled down the driveway. It was Popcorn. He was too tired to talk, in too much pain, and too foggy from the codeine.

He's tiny.

That was the end of me and Popcorn, but it wasn't the end of Popcorn's story. After the fire at his home led to being busted, he proceeded to sell moonshine to a federal undercover agent, who ramped him up until they were dealing in volume. Popcorn sold him 300 gallons, and promised him another 500. The feds raided him, and found "three large stills with capacities up to 1,000 gallons, over 850 gallons of moonshine, and hundreds of gallons of mash, materials and ingredients used to manufacture moonshine, and firearms and ammunition." He pled guilty, and received his sentence on January 26, 2009. He got eighteen months in the federal penitentiary.*

On March 16, a few days before he was to report to prison, Popcorn hooked a pipe up from the exhaust of his Ford Fairlane—his three-jug car, he called it, because he'd traded three jugs of liquor for it—and asphyxiated himself.

---

* How to Be a Criminal, Item 1: Do not, while on probation or having recently come to the attention of the law, engage in large-scale felonies with strangers.

Bringing It
All Back Home

It is a way I have of driving off the spleen, and regulating the circulation. Whenever I find myself growing grim about the mouth; whenever it is a damp, drizzly November in my soul; whenever I find myself involuntarily pausing before coffin warehouses, and bringing up the rear of every funeral I meet; and especially whenever my hypos get such an upper hand of me, that it requires a strong moral principle to prevent me from deliberately stepping into the street, and methodically knocking people's hats off—then, I account it high time to get to sea as soon as I can.

—HERMAN MELVILLE, MOBY DICK

IN PURSUIT OF THE WHITE DOG, I DREW UP MY LIST OF INGREdients and found a dusty little shop hidden away in the winter woods in upstate New York to fill the bill. The shelves were piled floor-to-ceiling with mysterious ingredients: crystal 6-row malted barley, torrefied wheat, Maris Otter, Belgian candy sugar, flaked maize, amylase enzymes. On the back wall hummed a refrigerator full of yeast. Fermometers, hydrometers, double-level cappers, spargers, wort chillers, scales, stainless-steel pots, vitamin bottles of isinglass and peach flavor, empty bottles, tubing.

To the side was a kitchen of sorts, with a big blackened Vulcan stove and a rough table covered in winemaking supplies. Every inch of wall was festooned with posters of beer festivals, red-nosed beer drinkers announcing a favorite brand, pictures of hop and barley varieties, and everywhere bottles of beer—most of them empty.

The dusty, molasses smell of sweet feed lingered.

Bella—not her real name—was on the phone when I got there, repeating herself. She couldn't help the guy on the other end.

"Don't have any . . . don't know who does . . . yeah, well, maybe earlier in the year, but by now everyone's thrown that all out . . . yeah, I can't really think of anyone . . . no, I don't have any . . . don't know who does . . . yeah, well . . ." and so on while I wandered around the shop, soaking up the atmosphere and fingering the odd tools while my son squirmed in my arms and looked excitedly around.

She hung up fifteen minutes later and rolled her eyes.

"Can I ask you something?"

I nodded.

"This guy," she said dismissively, "I know him, he's a customer, but he wants the used-up little grapes"—she scrunched her face like a used-up grape and held her two fingers up to indicate the tiny size—"after you make wine."

I've seen, in the basement of a neighbor's house, the cloudy, blooming, yeasty mess that is that pile of wine leftovers, and I can't imagine desiring it for anything.

"He wants to make cookies. Says they give the cookies a texture."

I thought that sounded disgusting and I told her so.

"Good, I'm glad you agree. Ugh. Some people. What an idea. Anyway . . ." She had moved out from behind her counter and was standing across from me at the butcher block that ran down the middle of the store, with trays of apothecary bottles stacked on one end and a grain mill bolted on at the other. "What can I get for you?" she asked.

I held my son to my chest with one arm while with my other hand I took a folded sheet of paper from my back pocket: I have a list . . .

The first recipe I used to make whiskey was the same one that George Washington's farm manager, a Scot named James Anderson, developed and used at the Mount Vernon Distillery. Anderson knew a lot about whiskey, and he convinced Washington that distilling the farm's grain would help Mount Vernon make money. The instructions are clear, but Washington's distillery was a commercial interest (in 1799 it produced over 10,000 gallons of whiskey) and operated on a scale I cannot match. To make a hogshead of mash, the script calls for 40 pounds each of rye and corn, 10 pounds of malted barley, 41 gallons of boiling water, 4 gallons of lukewarm water, and approximately 5 gallons more cool water to finish the mix off at the end of the mash-making process, to bring it down to a comfortable 70 degrees. I divided the whole thing by 40, so I'd have a recipe based on 1 pound of corn and 1 pound of rye. My new recipe called for just about a gallon of water. For my first batch I doubled it, hoping to get about 3 gallons of mash.

I figured that if I matched the output of moonshiners, and got 10 percent out of the mash, I'd have a quart of high-proof alcohol. I'd learned at bourbon distilleries that when they uncask their whiskey they add water to bring it down to a drinkable 80 proof, and I planned to do the same.

Walker Percy proclaimed that he never understood an enthusiasm for overproof whiskey, as it only meant one had to drink less. He wanted four glasses of bourbon everyday, and if the bourbon were stronger, he would have to limit himself to three, and that didn't sound like a good deal to him. I've always liked the thought. I would cut my whiskey down, and I'd walk away with two quarts or so of good 80- or 90-proof white dog.

I began: I need some . . . corn . . . some rye.

I enjoy mischief and misdemeanors as much as the next guy—

perhaps more—but standing there I was struck by the illegality of what I was up to. Bella would certainly know what I was doing. It's her job to understand all these ingredients. She is the keeper of these many strange tools, she knows their magical, alchemical qualities, their tastes, their by-products. If she knows what isinglass is for, she would figure me for sure.

I spoke in starts. I laugh when I'm nervous—. . . and some . . . malted . . . barley.

"Aha"—a sly smile snuck to the corner of her mouth. "What are you trying to make?"

Might as well have been dressed up like Cary Grant in *To Catch a Thief*, standing around on a second-story balcony smoking and flipping a half-dollar.

Hesitating, I kept a close watch on my shoes and tried to hide behind my son, who was still squirming in my arms and pointing at everything in the store, asking "Dat? Dat?"

The label read "Crystal 6-Row Malted Barley," and I told him that was what he was pointing at. He pointed at a row of 3- and 5-gallon glass jars—"Dat!"—and I told him they were called carboys. I turned my attention back to Bella and asked her how many of her friends were agents for the Bureau of Alcohol, Tobacco, and Firearms.

"I have some customers who do what you're trying to do," she said. She continued that turn of phrase throughout our conversation, trying to avoid calling what I was doing by name, as if the FBI had a parabolic mike fixed on the place, or I was wearing a wire. I don't think it would have done her any good at the grand jury; her prefatory statement more or less incriminated her: "If someone walks in the door, I'm going to start talking about how to make your own soda. I know my customers, and there are some we just can't have this conversation in front of. I have police officers, state troopers, that come in here. So if I change the topic abruptly, that's what's going on. Some people are cool. Some people are not."

I agreed, and we began an impromptu lesson on the qualities of various grains. Some of them would make a mush like Quaker oatmeal, and I'd have a hard time getting the liquid out. It was a good idea to separate the liquid from the solids before distilling. (This is often not done in moonshining, but it is done in commercial distilleries, where the leftover grains are sold as feed for livestock.)

"I assume you have some sort of apparatus?"

I said that I did, and after I'd described it, Bella said, "Oh, so we're talking about very small quantities."

My heart sank. I muttered something that wouldn't qualify as actual disagreement.

"Like, just a little." She held up her fingers to indicate maybe a shot's worth. I didn't think she was right, but I didn't want to argue. What, after all, do I know? What's more, I was reassured—if I was making a third of a cup of moonshine at a time, who would care?

As if reading my mind, Bella started on a tear about how people think that it's okay to distill if they only do a little. "People think it's not really illegal. People think that it's okay with the state. The state? I tell them not to worry about the state. Who's worried about them? This is against federal law. This is the feds you're dealing with. Feds trump everything."

When her husband, whom I'll call Bruce, came back from lunch, she said, "Oh, good, this guy has some questions about distilling."

"We don't do that," he deadpanned with a small flare of the eyes. Then he corrected my choice of malt. (Barley comes in 2-row and 6-row varieties, which refers to the number of rows of kernels on the head. Six-row malt is higher in the enzymes necessary for the conversion of starch to fermentable sugars.)

Maybe the joint was bugged. Maybe I was in over my head; maybe they were just paranoid; but regardless, it was at that moment that I decided to stop telling people what I was doing, and further, to tell most of the folks who already knew that I had changed my mind and decided not to do it. It had truly dawned upon me that I was breaking the law, or at least intending to, and that I wasn't flirting with the local cops or a speeding ticket or even an open-container summons. I was flirting with real consequences, breaking laws that were not only enforced by local and state agencies, but also by the sort of federal bureaus better known by acronyms.

Bella told me a story about a guy she had supplied who was selling moonshine to his neighbors. He left the door to his garage open and stood there making liquor in the light of day until a state trooper drove by (in an unlikely coincidence that to my ear calls the whole story into question, Bella knew the trooper, too). When they raided him, the guy had 80 gallons of the stuff sitting around. All his neighbors testified that they'd bought some from him. He got fifteen years in the state house.

I left the shop with flaked maize, Briess 6-row pale malted barley, Briess flaked rye, Weyermann rye malt, a 3-gallon carboy, three packets of Pasteur Champagne yeast, a hydrometer, and a thermometer. When I paid, Bella assured me that she wasn't going to enter me in the computer. "You were never here. I don't know you."

George Washington's Recipe	My Approximation	
9 gal. boiling water	28.8 oz.	
40 lb. corn	1 lb.	agitate, and let stand 2 hr.
12 gal. boiling water	38.4 oz.	stir briskly, and let stand 15 min.
4 gal. lukewarm water 10 lb. malt	12.8 oz. .25 lb.	lukewarm water poured malt gently poured (so as not to mix) let stand 30 min.
14 gal. boiling water	44.8 oz.	let stand 1 hr.
40 lb. rye	1 lb	work well let stand 2–4 hr.
		add cool water till 70°
pitch yeast	pitch yeast	let ferment until fit for still
	124.8 oz. water = .97 gal.—which I think means that if I double it, I'll get about 3 gal. of mash.	

On a Saturday morning I mixed 2 pounds of the flaked maize with roughly 57.6 ounces of boiling water. The maize was excellent and smelled delicious—fresher and with more flavor than any cornmeal

I've ever cooked with. The next time I make polenta, I am using flaked maize from the brewers' supply. Of course, polenta was more or less what I had made, and as it thickened in the bottom of the lobster pot I was using as a mash tun, I began to get nervous about how I was going to pour it.

By ten o'clock the mix was like dried cement.

At eleven I attempted to "stir briskly" and recalled the heavy, clodding feeling of trying to run through a muddy field. I had a flash of insight while considering what this would be like if I'd used the full recipe, for stirring 40 pounds of mushed-up, cemented corn at the bottom of a pot while adding boiling water to it must have been incredibly hard work.

But of course it was work that would have been done by slaves. I know it's chump talk—me standing in my own house, freely pursuing an activity that is only a shade away from recreation—but I felt a real throb of empathy for the plight of the enslaved.

When I added the malt to my mash, it made my kitchen smell dusty and sweet—the same barn bouquet I had picked up on in the brew shop. As the rye woke up in the water, it tossed off an aroma of whiskey. Only a few hours in, and already my house reeked like a distillery. I was gaining confidence and getting excited, but the first real hurdle was yet to come. The mash was forming amoebic clouds in the water. Had the conversion worked? Had the enzymes in the malt converted the carbohydrates to sugar? Would my yeast have anything to eat?

I brought the temperature down to about 70 degrees, floating my thermometer in the lobster pot and double-checking with a meat thermometer because it's faster. I poured in the yeast, diluted in a quarter-cup of warm water, and I tried to be patient.

I snuck down to the kitchen at 2 A.M. and looked in the pot, to find it bubbling and foaming like witches' brew. The mashed grain would stay on the counter for seven days, during which I would entertain a raft of fears.

First, I feared that perhaps I'd made vinegar.

Yeast eats sugar and converts it to carbon dioxide and alcohol, and ideally the process stops there. Alcohol, in turn, can be converted into acetic acid—vinegar—by bacteria called acetobacter. Acetobacter is everywhere, and keeping it out of your mix when you're brewing beer or making wine is one of the reasons you put an airlock on the top of a carboy.

There are other bacteria floating around that are best avoided as well. Foreign, wild yeast brings with it crazy flavors—garden hose, dirt, garbage, worse. The week passed, and with every sniff of the mash I was assured. It was tangy, as it should be, but not overly acidic. And anyway, if it was turned to vinegar, so what? It'd be horrible, and I'd start over again. No harm done, and some malt vinegar for fish and chips to boot.

My next anxiety was of a more serious nature. Rye is where ergot blossoms.

Ergot is a parasitic fungus that grows on grasses, and it likes rye most of all. Simply put, ergot will mess you up. I was flirting, I suddenly feared, with turning an amusing cocktail hour into a mind-bending, agonizing horror show. I would be able to tell if I'd made vinegar; how could I tell if I'd made poison? Ergotism used to be called "St. Anthony's Fire," and aside from simple symptoms like gangrene and death, it can cause psychosis, hallucination, and seizures. There is speculation that ergot-infected bread caused the Salem Witch Trials. A whole town in France went haywire in 1951 due to the stuff.

In *The Alaskan Bootlegger's Bible*, I read: "Do not try mashing or malting your own rye! The ergot fungus poses a very real hazard to the beginner. Ergot causes a violent deviant sexual behavior. In the incident cited above, peaceful peasants went on a rampage of rape and murder. When armed troops got involved, it was hellish." Most of the paragraph is italicized in the book.

I allayed my fears as best I could with a crash course on ergot. Food-grade rye is ergot-free. No more chance of poisoning than if I'd made bread. Still, I vowed that the first drink I'd drink alone, and that I'd tell my wife what some of my symptoms might be if I was afflicted with St. Anthony's Fire, and leave her a number for the exorcist.

I hunched in my basement to avoid banging my head on the exposed pipes or shattering one of the bare bulbs. The hunch fit, an appropriate posture for a mad scientist. On my stainless-steel table I'd gathered a 5-liter Erlenmeyer flask and some glass tubing I found on eBay, a single-coil electric burner I bought at Kmart, and a heat-diffuser gadget of the type long loved by grandmas simmering soups. The key to my ad hoc distillery is the worm coil an old friend from the Shenandoah Valley made for me years ago. It's about the size of a coffee can, with copper tubing poking out at the top and bottom.

The basic plan of every still is as follows: fermented material is boiled in a pot, and since alcohol boils at a lower temperature than water (alcohol at about 173 degrees and water at 212), the alcohol boils off first. The alcohol vapor is captured and run through a condenser, which cools it down and turns it back into a liquid. The famed alchemist Jabir ibn Hayyan, also known as Geber, who lived from 721 to 815, observed that heated wine released a flammable vapor—"of little use, but of great importance to science"—and he invented the alembic to capture it. Surprisingly few real advancements have been made since. Various small refinements have been added, such as a thump keg to double-distill in one run and a slobber box to catch the mash that boils over, but there have been only two major revisions. The "reflux still" or "column still" distills at a higher purity for commercial distilling by making the alcohol vapor travel through a column before it gets to the worm; the continuous column still distills mash nonstop (rather than one charge at a time in a pot); and the "submarine still" allows moonshiners to up their production because the mash ferments in the same container in which it is boiled. This streamlines the process; moving 800 gallons of mash in the woods is difficult.

My first setup mirrored the simplest pot still, and my technique did not differ greatly from Geber's, or for that matter, from most Scotch whiskey makers, who use a simple, inefficient pot still because it carries the most flavor from the mash into the beverage. If you distill very purely, you get neutral grain spirits. To get whiskey, you want the flavor of the grains.

Although it might have been easier to set up my still in the kitchen, next to the lobster pot full of whiskey mash bubbling and fizzing away on the counter, my stove is powered by propane, and I feared that the glass might break, the still might slip or leak, or that I'd simply knock something over and spill it. Vaporized alcohol is extremely flammable, and I didn't want to distill over an open flame. I thought I could minimize the risk with an electric burner over the concrete floor of my basement.

One week had passed since I briskly stirred the cemented polenta of my mash, and I'd pieced together my lab equipment in a clumsy sort of hackneyed arrangement: a snare-drum stand held the coil in place, and an old Igloo cooler elevated the catch jar.

The finished mash remained on the kitchen counter, and my plan was to siphon the liquid out of the lobster pot and into the flask in two batches, and then bring the flask back down to the basement and fit it to the worm coil. Problems began immediately. The mash was thick. The gelatinous, glossy, half-digested grain clogged the tube and I couldn't get the siphon to flow.

The disturbed mash, which had formed a discomfiting filmy bloom on its surface, belched a miasmic sour smell into the kitchen, as if some kind of horrible sourdough had been left alone for far too long. I tried to pour the mash out of the lobster pot and strain it into another vessel, but clumps of grain fell and splashed, and soon there was stinking, glistening grain meal everywhere. It was on the wall, on the backsplash, on the floor, on my butcher block. The mash was far more viscous and much nastier than I expected. This was a glutinous, fetid porridge. I could see why someone might want to make moonshine in the woods, but I didn't see how it was something you could hide very well. The smell would give you away.

When all was in place—and the kitchen given a cursory hosing down—I took the filled flask back down to the basement and hooked the pieces together. A led to B led to C, but immediately I understood that my plan for a floating thermometer in the glass flask would not work—the liquid was too opaque and I'd never see the reading. Temperature is important because the very first thing boiled off is at best wretched-tasting and at worst poison. With a thermometer you can see easily when you're getting alcohol (at just over 173 degrees); without one, I'd have to rely on the old hill-country method to gather what distillers call the foreshots. The still sputters. A steady stream starts flowing. The still sputters again, and then starts streaming alcohol. You toss what you get first.

As I cranked the knob to power up the burner, I imagined myself sitting, feet up, sipping from a Ball jar of white dog. The flask was holding about a gallon of liquid, so I was expecting to get one-tenth of that, which I'd cut back up to almost a fifth with water. I could already taste it.

For a long, long time, nothing happened. I was trying to heat it slowly; fast distillation lands weird stuff in the catch jar, but hours were going by and I hadn't even gotten to a simmer. Every time it seemed to get close, the burner would cool off due to some seemingly random safety gauge the manufacturer had built into it. I began to think about how thin the glass of the Erlenmeyer flask was, and how it must be releasing heat. Is it possible, given a weak, irregular heat source and a container that disburses heat, that a liquid might never boil?

Finally, I removed the heat disburser and put the flask directly on the burner. I was concerned that the flask would shatter. But I was resigned; I figured it wouldn't matter, since I would only be breaking something that didn't work.

The flask didn't break.

The mash began boiling.

The boil gained vigor until the bubbles that rose up the neck looked about to blow off the top and spill. Condensation beaded inside the glass tube leading to the coil. My first steam. Here came the foreshots. I gathered the crazy chemicals in a tin cup, and when the stream flagged, I slipped my Mason jar under the catch spout.

Then things went haywire.

The ice in the cooling tank was already melted, and the cooling water was steaming. The flask was boiling so vigorously that all the fittings were separating, steam was shooting out of the sides of the stopper, and liquid was sputtering out of the gap and spilling down the side of the flask. Steam was erupting where the glass met the copper. Since the coil was no longer cold, vaporized alcohol was traveling all the way through the condenser without condensing and shooting out like steam blowing a whistle.

It was chaos, but a thin trickle of something clear was making it into my Mason jar, and I ran my finger through it. It was unmistakable.

Moonshine whiskey.

I got 2 ounces.

It tasted horrible.

A River of Whiskey

I'm drowning in a Whiskey River.

—WILLIE NELSON

FRANKLIN COUNTY, VIRGINIA, IS LOUSY WITH WHISKEY stills. There's one behind the Historical Society in Rocky Mount, the county seat. There are a few at the Blue Ridge Institute in Ferrum. There's a clutch of them not too far away at Tim Smith's farm in Climax, where he runs an annual festival of moonshine culture called the Moonshiner's Jamboree—"culture" here meaning everything but the liquor, everything inside the law. Model stills are ubiquitous; little turnip-shaped things built of copper and mounted onto a varnished plank with miniature dollhouse campfires under their boilers. There's a picture that shows up all over town of what had been, in 1973, the largest raid ever—twenty-three black pot submarine stills, each with an 800-gallon capacity. It hangs in the dining room of Hema's restaurant on Main Street in Rocky Mount.

Whitey Taylor mounted a sign by the road to his speedway in Callaway, Virginia, which read WHITEY TAYLOR WELCOMES YOU TO FRANKLIN CO., MOONSHINE CAPITAL USA.

The place is in love with hooch.

There are hot rod shows where prizes are awarded for the car that most accurately depicts a vehicle in which liquor might have been run. (And occasionally one of the cars in the show is, in fact, a car in which liquor was run.) In the winter of 2006, the Blue Ridge Institute at Ferrum College put on an exhibit, and they parked a bootlegging truck in the lobby of the museum and displayed a wealth of collected distilling equipment. The Historical Society, as well as having a still out back, has a few examples arrayed inside with all the tools of the trade: mash forks, proofing bottles, Mason jars, kegs, etc. They also sell books and recipes, and give an annual tour.

This county-wide celebration of illegal liquor is prevalent, but it is not without controversy. That sign by the speedway, for instance: the county asked Whitey to take it down. The residents of Franklin County are proud of their heritage, and they paint a picture of gentle folk, hardworkers who distill a little to make ends meet, or just for the craft and love of it. They'll tell you about the coppersmith who built the stills by hand, and how much his pieces were valued.

But sepia-toned celebrations of moonshine's history do not tell the whole story. Backwoods distilling did not fade away with leaded gasoline and AM radio; it transformed.

Over the years, moonshine has become a booming business, and hooch is produced and sold at a surprising clip, in surprising places. Just a dozen blocks or so north of Philadelphia's Chinatown you find yourself as far as can be from the glorious statue of William Penn atop City Hall while still, so to speak, in its shadow. The city turns grim and dismal, and what vibrancy is on display is not inviting. Thuggish men slow-roll down the middle of the street, glowering. Sullen girls stand alone in rubble-strewn lots. There are corner stores with Newport ads and rowhouses in heavy disrepair. On many blocks more houses are deserted than occupied.

This is as far from stereotypical moonshine country as it is from Franklin County. Moonshine in songs and movies is almost exclusively a pastime and product of poor whites. The people of North Philly are poor blacks. Nonetheless, this is the biggest market for moonshine in America. This is where the vast majority of illicit hooch is sold.

On a May evening in 2002, an immense explosion set the shoe fruit swinging on the telephone wires. It had come from North Uber Street, near Montgomery Avenue. A low brick warehouse stood across from a row of houses, some with plywood hinged onto the doorframe to serve as an entrance, others just shells.

The whole block seemed to be waiting for an explosion, and perhaps the residents, hearing the blast and the clunk and tumble of falling bricks, thought that the city fathers had succeeded in one of their constant motions to flatten and rebuild.

But if you had turned the corner onto North Uber from Montgomery, you'd have looked up at a gaping hole in the third story—this was no demolition job. There were no workers there, no caution tape. As the evening peace reasserted itself—plastic grocery bags swirled into the soft breeze coming to rest again in the skinny branches of sooty trees—you'd catch a whiff of something strange, as if the explosion had uncovered a bakery and the blast had sprayed the air with donut batter and turned the breeze sour, yeasty, and sweet. Then you'd notice a higher smell, a pervasive and fiery odor, familiar, but out of context and hard to recognize.

Alcohol.

The street, the sidewalk, the porches across the street, the tumble of bricks all over the place, everything was moist with viscous, stinking, slick syrup. The block had been bathed in unprocessed sugar jack moonshine.

Through the hole could be seen huge steel vats and a maze of piping, all well organized and put together, with HVAC systems and drainage, boilers, and tubs.

The plant that exploded that evening in North Philadelphia had a processing capacity of 3,000 gallons. Using the rough rule of thumb that one gets about a tenth of whatever you put into the boiler out as distillate, 3,000 gallons means this operation was producing 300 gallons of alcohol at a time, which would add up to 600 gallons of

100-proof white lightning. No one sets up a still of that magnitude and complexity—HVAC! Drainage!—so they can run it as a hobby on Saturday afternoons. This is not a pastime. This is business. One run a day would produce 4,200 gallons of illegal liquor a week. That's roughly 179,200 one-dollar, 3-ounce shots a week, with a year-end value of $9,318,400.

Of course, it's not all sold by the shot. Shine is moved by the gallon and the quart out of the trunks of cars in blackmarket streetlight deals more reminiscent of a drug score than a trip to the liquor store. But the numbers indicate that Philadelphia is drinking well over 10 million shots of moonshine per year, because this can't be the only game in town.

In Virginia, the *Roanoke Times* wrote up the story and quoted Sergeant Stacey Marshall of the Pennsylvania State Police Bureau of Liquor Enforcement: "This is huge. We're talking about an extremely sophisticated operation," he said. "I guess there must be a lot of people with a taste for this stuff." And then, overlooking the recent explosion to make a point, he continued: "There are legal microbreweries that are not as well-put-together as this place."

Mark Chait, the ATF assistant special agent in charge of the Philadelphia office, was at the scene. "It appears to be a fairly well-organized still," Chait said. "We don't uncover these very often, especially inside the city limits. It's the kind of thing you usually see in remote areas."

"I was always under the impression that it came up from the South," agreed Sergeant Marshall.

Although moonshine is low on the Philadelphia legal radar—this story vanished as quickly as the dust settled—Sergeant Marshall wasn't surprised about the presence of, or market for, 16,800 gallons of moonshine a month. Sergeant Marshall was simply surprised that it was being made there. Surprised, because the millions of shots of moonshine that Philadelphia drinks every year are trucked up the highway from the border of Virginia and North Carolina. Philly is the moonshine-drinking capital of the world, and Franklin County is

the moonshine-making capital of the world, and the interstate high-
ways that connect the two (81 north to 66 east to 95) are like a pipeline.

The stills had had to move, at least for the time being, and mostly
because of the effort of Jimmy Beheler and the agents who worked
with him on the Illegal Whiskey Task Force of Virginia's Alcohol Control Board (ABC).

I met Beheler at a Mexican restaurant called El Rodeo on the out-
skirts of Rocky Mount, Virginia. I was anxious as I drove Route 40
through the shaley, steep bit of country, where the hills are close like
the bellows of an accordion. It was a mild December day, the day
before Christmas Eve. As I drove, I caught brief glimpses into tiny
shaded hollows; here a few dozen square feet back in the crook, there
a quarter-acre of flat land with a couple of trailers or a little cabin
chugging woodsmoke into the gray winter air. "Horizon" in Franklin County becomes an unimaginable abstraction. Your eye never fo-
cuses on anything more than 400 yards away.

It must have been hard work chasing moonshiners here.

There were plenty of them to chase. The whiskey rebels followed
these mountains down from western Pennsylvania, no doubt wishing
to continue their lives apace, as if the Whiskey Rebellion—and the
whiskey tax—had never happened. They must have looked upon the
country with the same gleam that a cattle rancher displays looking
out upon an endless, sagey stretch of open range. There are plenty of
places to hide.

Beheler is a tall, strong-looking man with light brown hair and
a brushy mustache, and when I met him, he was in blue jeans and
a button-down oxford with a patch designed after the Sun Records
seal. He waited for me in the parking lot, smoking a cigarette in his
big Ford pickup.

"Nobody ever did like Jimmy," I'd heard. "Now they hate him."

Most of this is the simple animosity generated by Beheler's
twenty-four years of enforcing laws that the majority of the county

would rather see ignored. Many citizens don't want Franklin County associated with moonshine, and an odd but prevalent logic has it that the reporting and arresting of moonshiners outweighs the impact of the moonshine itself.

Beheler was a great violator of a hill country omerta. He betrayed the gentleman's agreement that moonshiners would not get arrested unless agents caught them red-handed. He'd gone to high school here, grown up here, but he'd refused to play along.

While some would find it understandably awkward to arrest former classmates, Beheler had reconciled: "If you don't want to get arrested, stay out of the liquor business."

Beheler also refused to be bribed.

"One of the biggest bootleggers in the county, he approached me about Christmastime '91 or '92. He was walking around with a couple of people, laughing. He walked by me and said, 'Jim, how you doing?' 'Pretty good, Bobby Joe, how 'bout you?' "

They made some small talk, said Merry Christmas, and shook hands.

"There was five hundred dollars there in the palm of my hand. I said, 'Bobby Joe, uh-uh. No. You can't do that.' "

Beheler said they stood for what felt like fifteen minutes passing the money back and forth.

"You don't owe me that," Beheler told him.

He tried to get something done about the attempted bribe.

"It was a joke, it was a fucking joke. For six months I went to the commonwealth attorney. Finally, I went to one of the state police investigators."

Together they put on a sting operation. Beheler would play along.

"I walked up to his truck. I had a tape recorder. We talked for a couple of minutes and I said, 'Bobby Joe, Whattayou want from me?' Just point-blank. He said, 'I don't care about anybody else, but whenever you haul up close to where I'm at, I want to know about it. I'm not doing a lot now, but in the spring I'll get started up pretty big. Right now I'll give you five hundred a month, and in the spring, we can talk about it, and I can do a lot better.' . . . And then, for the next five or six months, first of the month, he'd call me, and I'd go meet him. And then a couple of times he'd call late at night, and I didn't know, I was a little uneasy."

Beheler gave me the impression that he never knew who was on which side of the law, that he never knew who might tell Bobby Joe that he was being set up. Beheler always told someone where he was going and who he was meeting.

I pointed out that that wouldn't have kept him from getting shot.

"Least they would have an idea who did it," he countered.

They kept up the charade until it got repetitious.

"I'd just get the money, and I'd give him information, meaningless shit, you know, I never told him anything that would amount to nothing."

What Jimmy wanted most of all was insight into who else had been bribed.

"I mean, for him to walk up to me and just stick five hundred dollars in my hand, he had done that before. We wanted to know who he had paid in the past."

When they arrested Bobby Joe, he said he'd snitch, but a couple of days later he changed his tune. He'd been thinking about it, and he wanted to go to court.

"He pled guilty to five or six counts of bribery," said Jimmy, "and one count of manufacturing. He got fifty-five years, I believe. He pulled about two years up here in the local jail. I mean, shit. Sent him on home." Jimmy shrugged. "That's the way it works."

People in Franklin County, thinks Beheler, just fail to see moonshining as a big deal.

The justice system, it seemed, reflected an attitude more suited to the nostalgic recollections of moonshine's past than to the bustling, million-dollar business it had become. Those who were not bribed, it seems, were simply complicit because they don't see moonshine as a crime. As a result, the laws went mostly unenforced.

"For so many years, the stakes were very minimal. Year after year after year, you caught the same people. I've arrested people and seized their vehicles, and the commonwealth attorney was calling me before I got back to the office to do the paperwork, and they wanted to bond their trucks back out. We've seized the same trucks over and over and over again. And of course it's in someone else's name, and of course they get it right back. The first time, I can understand that. The second time? No. Third, fourth, fifth? No. It's not your wife's truck."

When Franklin County moonshiners were arrested in the past, they were represented by local lawyer William Davis, and they were tried in the county court. If they did a turn in lockup, they were treated nicely. Not only were their trucks out of impound quickly, but their farms were never seized, their bank accounts never frozen. In one famous example, a moonshiner was let out every afternoon to feed his cows.

"It's a bit of nudge and wink. They think, oh well, he might be making liquor, but you know, it's just a little bit."

It wasn't a sideline misdemeanor. Shine was business, and Beheler began to treat it that way.

The Racketeer Influenced and Corrupt Organizations statute, the RICO Act, is usually used as a tool for the prosecution of organized crime, because under it, if you conspire to break the law, it's as if you'd broken that law yourself. RICO spreads out the responsibility for criminal activities. To oversimplify the thing, if you are the head of an organized-crime family and murders happen on your watch, you can be tried for the murders. No longer will the chain of subordinates protect you. No one would be able to hide behind still hands; no one would skate.

Perhaps more important, Beheler had successfully courted the feds and was sending cases to federal court, which meant different judges, different lawyers, and different rules. Property would be seized, bank accounts frozen—people wouldn't be getting their trucks back, and they wouldn't be let out of jail to do chores. This was the big time.

I had seen a series of photographs that recorded a bust in the 1980s, and the image that had struck me as most interesting, I told Beheler, was the one that depicted the busted moonshiners sitting in the grass. The sun was shining on their shoulders and they looked at ease, if not downright jovial, with their elbows resting on their crooked knees and open cans of Budweiser at their feet. They didn't look like folks who were under arrest.

That seems, I said, like a very friendly bust.

"Oh, well, yeah, I mean, you know, you never mistreated anybody."

And vice versa?

"Exactly. There's a line here. And you don't cross it."

And as the stakes got higher, did that line change?

"Yeah. That changed."

The Crossroads:
Jefferson, Hamilton, and
the Golden Age of Whiskey

We are already obliged to strain the impost till it produces
clamor, and will produce evasion, & war on our own citizens
to collect it: and even to resort to an Excise law, of odious
character with the people, partial in its operation, unproduc-
tive unless enforced by arbitrary and vexatious means, and
committing the authority of the government in parts where
resistance is most probable, & coercion least practicable.

**—THOMAS JEFFERSON, IN A LETTER TO GEORGE
WASHINGTON, 1792**

MY VERSION OF GEORGE WASHINGTON'S WHISKEY WAS
vile, brutal stuff with a nose like paint thinner and a finish like a wire
brush. Nonetheless, I raised my Ball jar and managed a small toast to
the outlaws. Drunk and armed, they'd gathered in Monongahela to
protest the Whiskey Tax of 1791, loathed since it was levied. George

Washington and Alexander Hamilton mustered 13,000 troops and led them to Pennsylvania to put the rebellion down, but by the time they arrived, the rebels were gone. America's first moonshiners had packed up their stills and moved on. Here, at the Whiskey Rebellion, begins the split: the legal distilling industry on one side, black-marketeering on the other.

There had been no such thing as moonshine in America. Distilling, at any level, was legal and untaxed. Farmers didn't register their stills any more than they registered their plows, for distilling a harvest of grain was simply good farming. There are three key reasons for this. First, a couple of bushels of rye, each of which weighs 56 pounds, can be converted to 5 gallons of whiskey. Forty bushels of grain would equal two barrels of whiskey. It's easier to transport grain that is stored as whiskey than it is to transport the raw product. Second, grain spoils, whiskey doesn't. Third, whiskey is always worth more than the grain that went into making it.

As if that weren't enough, let us not forget the bonus: you can drink the whiskey.

For these reasons, farmhouse stills were common, and they were an integral part of the cultures the early settlers brought with them to America. This country was founded by distillers. The bedrock of America's idealized notion of itself, the buffalo shooters, the deerskin-clad men who battled and befriended nature and the Cherokee to survive, held kin and autonomy paramount, and they held whiskey a close third. The first Finns to hit these shores, the so-called "axe-wielders," were slash-and-burn farmers who threw their improvised hunting shanties together from felled trees and torched the rest of the timber so they could plant rye in the ashes, which they would then distill. The religious Germans were distillers for whom whiskey was a sort of legal tender. The passion for distilling held in the breast of the Scots-Irish makes the previous two ethnic groups look like Sunday painters. All of these early settlers cooked up batches of rough, raw whiskey to trade with each other and the Indians, and to drink.

Marshaling these settlers was the first task set to our young nation. In what way would they be organized into a cohesive whole? What shape would the nation take? The United States of America needed to be more than a loose aggregate of isolated settlements, it needed to be one land and one people. There were two core visions of how this might be achieved, two men at the blueprints, drawing the architectural sketch for the structure of the nation. They did not agree.

In one corner stood Alexander Hamilton, a Federalist, a self-made man, a champion of industry, a friend to the creditor, a man of finance. In the other corner, Thomas Jefferson, Republican, a wealthy aristocrat with his head full of noble visions in which the yeoman farmer heroically toiled at small-scale agriculture. Would America become a financial empire? Or would it grow into a loose system of cooperating individuals? Would the bedrock of our nation's wealth be built upon commerce or agriculture? In the building of any economy, advantages must fall either to the corporation or to the individual, where would our nation aim its sympathies?

When Alexander Hamilton envisioned a design for America, he saw a machine built to enrich the few.

Certainly, Jefferson and his family had been the beneficiaries of aristocratic privilege. Jefferson's father died when the future president was just fourteen, and his inheritance included 5,000 acres and enough slaves to work them. Jefferson struggled with the conundrum, the paradoxical nature of his position and his life. His heart was with the farmer. Jefferson was the ur-proponent of radical chic. His design for America did not include consolidation, grand incorporation, or debt. He exulted in the local economies of early America, and longed to keep the nation decentralized.

It would be a lengthy and desperate fight, and in many ways it was a fight over whiskey.

Jefferson, unable to suffer his disagreements with Alexander Hamilton, left George Washington's cabinet and climbed his mountain to Monticello where he busied himself with his corn, his peas, his nailery, and his unremitting opposition to Hamilton's plans for the young America. He wrote to James Madison on October 30, 1794, that he wished "much to see the speech." The speech in question was Washington's, forthcoming on November 19, in which he would justify calling the militia to arms to quell the whiskey rebels. He wanted to know "how such an armament against people at their ploughs, will be represented, and an appeal to arms justified before that to the law had been tried and *proved* ineffectual."

He wrote to James Monroe, this time motivated by the movement to ban the assembly of political clubs, but still with the Rebellion on his mind:

> Hence too the example of employing military force for civil purposes, when it has been impossible to produce a single fact of insurrection, unless that term be entirely confounded with occasional riots, and when the ordinary process of law had been resisted indeed in a few special cases, but by no means generally, nor had its effect been truly tried. But it answered the favorite purposes of strengthening government and increasing the public debt; and therefore an insurrection was announced and armed against, and marched against, but could never be found.

From Jefferson, too, comes a report of the action against the Whiskey Rebels that differs from the official copy. He wrote to James Madison on December 28, 1794:

> The excise-law is an infernal one. The first error was to admit it to the constitution. The 2d. to act on that admission. The 3d. and last will be to make it the instrument of dismembering the Union, and setting us all afloat to chuse which part of it we will adhere to. The information of our militia returned from the Westward is uniform that tho the people there let them pass quietly, they were objects of their laughter, not of their fear, that 100 men could have cut

off their whole force in a thousand places in the Alleganey, that their detestation of the excise law is universal, and has now associated to it a detestation of the government, and that separation perhaps was a very distant and problematical event, is now near, and certain and determined in the mind of every man. I expected to have seen some justification of arming one part of the society against another, of declaring a civil war the moment before the meeting of that body which has the sole right of declaring war, of being so patient of the kicks and scoffs of our enemies, and rising at a feather against our friends, of adding a million to the public debt and deriding us with recommendations to pay it if we can, &c. &c..

Hamilton, the excise tax, and the federal action against the Pennsylvania farmers offended the very foundation of Jefferson's ideals.

Putting down the Whiskey Rebellion was an indication of what Hamilton intended—strong central government, direct taxes, weak states, a nation siding with the creditors rather than the debtors, with industry rather than individual. Just as the aristocracy gets rich on the labors of hoi polloi, the new American upper class would be the beneficiary of America's labor and plenty. They would rule according to noblesse oblige, and their wealth would shape the nation.

The zenith of the Federalists' ascension was the Alien and Sedition Acts, which muzzled the press. Historian Susan Dunn wrote: "Not just the shocking abrogation of Americans' constitutional rights or the anachronistic infringement on a free press, the Sedition Act represented one of the last mean gasps of the Federalists' political philosophy—a philosophy that was still rooted in their belief in their social and intellectual superiority, their old sense of their entitlement to govern, their reverence for hierarchy. The new law, charged the Boston *Independent Chronicle*, was the final breath of an 'expiring Aristocracy.'"

It wouldn't expire on its own, however. The Virginian came down off his hill to do it in. Against the Sedition Act he had written that "were it left to me to decide whether we should have a government without newspapers or newspapers without a government, I should not hesitate a moment to prefer the latter."

Perhaps he'd been plotting it all along; many seem to think his retreat to Monticello was calculated. Perhaps he wanted to lay off and gather strength, to look like a fresh face and a symbol of change. This much we know: In the next election Jefferson would not lack resolve as he had in 1796. In the election of 1800 he came out swinging.

Washington had served two terms and John Adams one. The government was now hotly divided into two parties for the first time. On the side of the incumbent John Adams (at least in the beginning) were the Federalists, and with Jefferson, the Republicans.

The campaign was adversarial, and all across the country openly partisan printers cranked out screeds supporting their side. It was the first competitive election, and it was fought by propaganda. This was the dawn of the sound bite. Susan Dunn wrote of a contemporary critic of this new style of public address who accused the Republicans of having a quiver of words at their fingertips, ready to fire at any time. The words were "British influence, standing army, direct taxes, funding system, expensive navy, and aristocracy." It's worth noting that "funding system," "standing army," and "expensive navy" all add up to "direct taxes." I would further suggest that "British influence" and "aristocracy" ring the same bell. Which means we're down to two central ideas hurled at the Hamiltonian Federalists: they are elitist and they raise taxes.

In the *Vermont Gazette*, we find more of the same in a published prayer called "The Republican Litany."

> *From a burial place for American nobility*
> > *Good lord deliver us*
> *From a direct tax*
> > *Good lord deliver us*
> *From Jay's treaty . . . and from a war with the French Republican*
> > *Good lord deliver us*

From all old Tories; from aristocrats
    Good lord deliver us
From heavy taxes, expensive salaries
    Good lord deliver us
From the alien act; from the sedition act, and from all other evil acts
    Good lord deliver us

Of course, the cornerstone of the direct tax, the most egregious of all the taxations, was the tax on spirits distilled from American grain. The Whiskey Rebels hadn't actually vanished, of course; they had simply moved. They'd rolled down the mountain range and found themselves pockets of wild country where they might be left alone. They settled along the western slopes of the Blue Ridge, they settled in the Smoky Mountains, and they settled in Kentucky.

In the election of 1800, Jefferson and the Republicans didn't do so well in New England, but they took New York. New Jersey sided with the Federalists; Pennsylvania went slightly to the Republican side. Maryland was split. Below Maryland: a Republican landslide. Historian John Ferling wrote of the "sun-seared back country and the Piedmont" that "Jefferson had been popular all along among the smaller farmers who inhabited those regions, men who viscerally disliked the Bank of the United States, had never cottoned to the notion of a strong national government, and were outraged by what would come to be known simply as ''98,' the year of Federalist repression and heavy taxes."

Jefferson's victory was a peaceful revolution against direct taxes, and the most obvious and painful of those taxes was the Whiskey Tax. The promise of its repeal had been a solid plank of Jefferson's platform.

Jefferson's time in the White House must have been fun. He introduced "pell mell" seating, which eschewed class and rank distinction at state dinners—worthies clamored for seats in a great chaotic rush to the feed bag. Many dignitaries were horrified and insulted. Stories—perhaps apocryphal—indicate that the president wandered the halls of the White House dressed in a bathrobe and moccasins. It wasn't all foolishness: he made the Louisiana Purchase, and sent

Lewis and Clark off to explore the continent, for dreams of empire were not foreign to Jefferson, despite the inherent contradictions.

Most important for us, here, he made good on his promises and repealed the Whiskey Tax.

For whiskey, the first few decades of the nineteenth century were the boom time.

The industry expanded from Pennsylvania and Maryland into Kentucky and Illinois, which would become distilling hubs. According to William L. Downard's *Dictionary of the History of the American Brewing and Distilling Industries,* there were 2,000 stills in Kentucky in 1810, producing 2.2 million gallons of whiskey. There were another 3,594 stills in Pennsylvania, producing over 6 million gallons. Downard writes: "The total number of distilleries in the nation was approximately 14,000 in 1810." (There are, as of this writing, well over 150 small-scale distilleries in America, and perhaps 20 big ones.) Among those 14,000, small distilleries with tiny annual productions of 3 to 15 barrels were common. If the excise tax had not been repealed, these small distilleries would not have been viable.

This is the beginning of bourbon. Jefferson had, as governor of Virginia years before, offered land grants of 60 acres in Kentucky to anyone who promised to grow corn on the land. You can't eat 60 acres of corn—you've got to drink it. Those folks were no doubt tired of hiding their stills from the excise man, and now they no longer had to. Jefferson's plan had worked, and the hills were planted heavily with golden maize. Bourbon luminaries Evan Williams, the Reverend Elijah Craig, Jacob Spears, and Jacob Myers were making a nascent version of the product in the decades leading up to the turn of the century. Soon, bourbon would become the specific spirit that it is today, with a grain bill that is 51 percent corn, mixed with good limestone water and aged in new charred barrels. The Samuels family—who today run Maker's Mark—were already there, and already distilling, first as farmer-distillers, and later commercially. Jacob Beam sold his first whiskey in 1795, and the family is still expanding the business today. Dr. James Crow immigrated to Kentucky and applied his considerable scientific knowledge to Colonel Willis Field's distillery, where Crow is credited with discovering the importance of limestone water and inventing the sour mash process.

Technological advances abounded. This is the moment of transformation in distilling, where it moves from a mysterious backyard art form to a full-blown, carefully controlled science. There had not been many technological advances since Geber first made his flammable vapor centuries ago, but Americans bent their industrious heads to the task.

Wayne Curtis, in his history of rum, wrote: "Between 1802 and 1815, more than a hundred patents were granted by the government for distillation devices—or about one in every twenty patents issued. Printers published articles and pamphlets to aid journeyman distillers, with titles like the 1824 'Essay on the Importance and the Best Mode of Converting Grain into Spirit.' "

The continuous still was invented. No longer had the distiller to empty and clean the pot after every batch; he could just keep pumping the wash right through. This made large-scale distilling possible. About 1826, Aeneas Coffey further advanced the process by inventing the Coffey still, which distills at very high proofs and allows more control over the product. The rough, harsh whiskey of the frontier was morphing into something more palatable and more consistent.

These were the wettest decades of our history; from the moment Mr. Jefferson lifted the tax, we were awash in ardent spirits. The commonly bandied statistic is that Americans drank 5 gallons of absolute alcohol per year. Which at first doesn't seem like all *that* much: 19 liters per capita per year? 360 milliliters a week? That's downright rationing, that's a drought.

First of all, that's absolute alcohol, which means 195 proof, which means that for our purposes we should more than double that amount to get to a product we can understand. So that's a 750-milliliter bottle, the standard one you find in the liquor store, every week. Actually, that's not that much either. There are only sixteen drinks in one of those bottles, and that's if you're a light pour (in my house, they only come with about ten drinks in them, and sometimes I swear the liquor company is shorting me). That's two drinks a day, more or less, which is hardly bingeing—that's doctor-prescribed!

How then our reputation? For Americans were famously sozzled at the dawn of the nineteenth century. Travelers were constantly mentioning how much everyone drank.

In answer, W. J. Rorabaugh wrote in *The Alcoholic Republic:*

> So the typical American was drinking heartily, but not all Americans drank their share. It is impossible to obtain an exact accounting, but the American Temperance Society estimated that during each year of the late 1820s nine million women and children drank 12 million gallons of distilled sprits; three million men, 60 million gallons. At this high point the average adult male was imbibing nearly a half pint a day. Few, however, were average. It was calculated that half of the men drank 2 ounces a day; one-quarter ("habitual temperate drinkers"), 6 ounces; one-eighth ("regular topers, and occasional drunkards"), 12 ounces; and another eighth ("confirmed drunkards") 24 ounces. Thus half of the adult males—one eighth of the total population—were drinking two thirds of all the distilled spirits consumed.

To put this in more dramatic terms, of the aforementioned 3 million men in the nation, 375,000 of them were drinking like Hemingway every single day. Twenty-four ounces of whiskey is sixteen drinks. Dylan Thomas famously said, "I've just had 18 straight whiskeys. I think that's the record." He clearly didn't know his history.

Slowly, an organic pattern of consolidation emerged. The nation was drinking, and the distillers were cranking out the booze. Bigger distillers put out more product. Improvements in technology continued and transportation made it less necessary for farmers to do their own distilling. Liquor was becoming an industry—not at the insistence of the clerks in Washington, but organically.

Then came war.

White Dog Is Dead

I hate small towns because once you've seen the cannon in
the park there's nothing else to do.

—LENNY BRUCE

MORRIS HAD WRITTEN A STORY ABOUT A DEAD DOG.

I sat in an old, shot chair at a battered desk in the offices of the
Franklin News-Post with musty archival binding open flat in front of
me, and I heard him say "It's gonna be the human interest story of
the year."

He managed to talk it on to the front page, and one of the suggested titles was "White Dog Is Dead."

I didn't think I'd told Morris the title of my book, and they don't
call moonshine "white dog" in Franklin County. (They don't really
call it anything. Sometimes, to outsiders, "moonshine," but mostly
they'll just say liquor.) Certainly, many of the residents of Franklin
County, Morris included, would very much like me to believe that
white liquor was dead, but to go and put it on the front page, well,
that seemed a bit much. In fact, White Dog turned out to be an actual
dog. The shepherd-lab mix had shown up at the landfill seventeen

years ago and had been its unofficial mascot ever since. That Monday, he'd been run over by a truck.

For decades, they chugged out copies of the *Franklin News-Post* right across from the courthouse on Main Street in Rocky Mount, Virginia, until the printing machine abraded a smooth, shallow shadow into the concrete floor where it stood beneath fluorescent tubes. These are different times; the printing room where I sat and read from the archives was mostly empty. I read amid disused computers, old lamps, and a palette of grocery store inserts. Sound bounced around in there, slapping off the tall walls.

The archive goes back to the forties, when local newspapers were still the record of the day. Locals followed the progress of the boys they had sent off to fight the Germans by reading this newspaper. The day after an election, it was the *News-Post* headline that told folks who had won.

Morris Stephenson came to work for the paper in the summer of 1964. By then the news had gone local. People would get their national and international knowledge elsewhere, while the *News-Post* reported on local politics, car accidents, and high school sports.

"Oh, that was a fun one," said Morris. On the front page was a picture from the Brookside Swimming Club pool, the kind of thing a small-town paper runs to commiserate about a hot spell. Three wet-haired boys have crooked their elbows on the concrete edge. In the foreground, vertically scissoring the picture is a gorgeous, fleshy pair of legs that culminate in a ripe, 1964 boy-short bathing suit bottom. The boys are ogling the girl—or a part of her, anyway—all crew cuts and dopey looks.

Laughing, Morris says: "Yeah. I had to take that picture a lot, you know what I mean? Had to get her to put her foot just so."

Morris put his hands to his chest as if he were holding an old medium-format camera and looking down into the range finder.

"Do that again, honey! I don't know if I got it! Okay! Stand there for a minute!"

In fact, her foot *is* just so, her arch up off the concrete of the pool's edge, taut, her back leg flexing. It's a very good picture. This is one of the core truths about Morris. He's a kidder. He was a lush—a twelve-pack a day, at least, until he quit drinking after a spectacular bender landed him in the hospital. His publisher says that when they met, Morris reminded him of Dennis Hopper. But Morris is a newsman to the core. He's an excellent photographer, and he's got a natural feeling for news, and a seamless, professional writing style that makes the Franklin County paper read like it's written by a Pulitzer-winning senior correspondent. He's supposed to be retired, working part time selling ads, but he can't stay off the street. He can't quit.

In the swimming-pool picture of 1964, the young boy on the left, staring right up at the girl's ass and perhaps licking his lips, is retired ABC Special Agent in Charge Jimmy Beheler. This is the kind of coincidental crossed path that happens over and over again in southwest Virginia, or in any small town. Sometimes it seemed to me that all the crossed paths of Franklin County cross Morris. He verges on being the nexus of the place—not the center, but the connection.

"I can't even come back here, don't even want to look, it's just too much," Morris said, shaking his head at the archive and leaning back against a strapping machine. Morris was the only photographer and the only reporter at the paper, and flipping through the archives is really flipping through his book of clips.

Morris's penny loafers were polished (and penniless). His slacks had a sharp crease, even though it was four o'clock in the afternoon and oppressively hot outside. He wears a beard and I've never seen him hatless. On his breast there is typically pinned a tiny Energizer Bunny, beating his drum and going, going, going. Morris keeps a pack of cigarettes tucked into his sock.

While I read, Morris would walk into the room with a "Hey, Dude!" and look over my shoulder just long enough to glance at the paper. Then he'd pace a semicircle around me, gesticulating and telling me adventure stories.

He sounds like mountain-and-river country. He sounds like a hell-raiser, a coon hunter, all throaty and sparkling with enthusiasm.

I learned to trust his stories. He never forgot that I wanted to talk about moonshine, although he'd often take his time winding up.

He'd just start reminiscing about the Golden Knights parachute squad, and how they'd landed on the football field at the high school with their smoke streamers, the whole squad touching down on the fifty-yard line like they had simply walked up to it. Morris and the paper had organized a party for the boys, but Morris was late because he'd had to take a picture of a school board meeting or someone had wrecked their car on Route 220.

He'd gotten the jumpers some moonshine; they'd begged him for it, especially one from Massachusetts named Moose, who seemed obsessed.

"Are you sure there's gonna be moonshine there?" Moose asked Morris. "Really?"

"It's done," answered Morris.

When Morris arrived with a jar, he couldn't find Moose anywhere. Someone else had brought some of Franklin County's finest to the party, it seemed. Moose had bravely declared that he'd never met a liquor that didn't agree with him, poured himself a tall jelly jar of the stuff, and sucked it down. Morris found him passed out in the back of a station wagon.

After he told me the story, he gave me a copy of the edition with the White Dog story on the front page, which was, like every one of his stories that I picked out of the paper over the years, exceptionally well written and perfectly sympathetic.

Sympathetic, even, with a man named William Philpott.

"I'm good friends with William, and Jaybird's other boy, too," said Morris. He gave a sideways grin.

Any good journalist makes enemies, and Morris was the only journalist in town for decades, so it goes to figure that he'd have had opportunity to piss off a fair number of folks. Morris's relationship with Jaybird Philpott, however, was exceptional.

Jaybird was a moonshiner, alleged murderer, and a bigamist, and he was, at one time, a serious and very real threat to Morris's well-being.

Morris frequently doubled as a crime scene photographer, and as such was often called to the site of a still about to be destroyed, even if it wasn't particularly newsworthy. One afternoon in the mid-1960s the revenuers were busting up a still site on Jaybird Philpott's farm, and they were going to dynamite it, but they'd left the dynamite back at the office. They told Morris they'd be right back, and he stuck around to get his shots.

"I was finished, and I was walking back up to my car," said Morris. "Jaybird came up on me and told me I was trespassing. I said: 'I ain't trespassing, I'm working, and now I'm leaving.' I told him he should take it up with the agents."

In a display of classic country storytelling Morris skips over the ensuing conversation—whatever hustle Morris laid on him to convince him that they should be acting like friends—and picks up the thread with the two of them sitting on a diesel tank back at Philpott's barn, shooting the breeze. Jaybird related to him that he'd been in Georgia, and he'd been caught up in a big moonshine bust down there. He'd come back home. (It's worth noting that the masthead of the *Franklin News-Post* carries the logo "covering the land between the lakes" and has two squiggly outlines of the local bodies of water. The one on the right is Smith Mountain Lake, and the one on the left is Philpott Lake. When Jaybird Philpott said "home," he meant it.)

He had thought he was through with running stills, but when he got back to Franklin County, a few prominent members of the town had begged him to start up. They wanted his liquor. In May of 1966, Jaybird pled guilty to two counts of liquor violations (he got a three-year suspended sentence on the first count, and a $2,000 fine on the second, payable by installments). Morris wrote in the paper that Jaybird had claimed that he wasn't making liquor for "fast money, but rather for some of his 'friends,' big wheels and lawyers."

Morris didn't have to spell it out. The implication was that Jaybird received a light sentence because the judge was a client of his. Jaybird had neglected to suggest that this conversation be off the record, and Morris printed it.

The next time they saw each other, Jaybird said Morris was going to pay for that.

Animosity from Jaybird Philpott was not a thing one took lightly. In 1968, Philpott's first wife had disappeared and was found in the woods after an exhaustive search, partially decomposed and ripped into more than one piece. Morris took the forensic photographs of that crime scene.

No charges were ever filed.

The new Mrs. Philpott was still married, and soon enough Jaybird Philpott was marched to the courthouse in handcuffs.

Morris got the perp-walk shot, of course, and the classic lurching-man-in-handcuffs shot must have done nothing to ameliorate their relationship. Sheriff Overton gave Morris a .25-caliber pistol that he had seized. Morris walked around with it shoved in his pants, thinking he was going to shoot himself in the ass every time he sat down.

Jaybird's next sensational turmoil would be his last. Jaybird had been having some problems with people putting sugar in the gas tanks of his farm equipment, and when he found two kids who had made the horrible decision to use his farm as a lovers' lane, he stabbed the boy to death. The girl got away, but Jaybird had threatened to kill her since she was a witness to his killing of her boyfriend. Her father, B. B. Willis, didn't wait around to see if he meant it. B.B. put the word out and soon enough got a tip. As I've heard it told, he drove straight to the loading dock of the Southern States farm store and shot Jaybird dead. B.B. served about thirty days; the jury deemed it a justifiable homicide.

Morris was off the hook.

In general, Morris's relation with the outlaw classes has been much smoother.

When the Hell's Angels came to bury a member in Rocky Mount, it was Morris who ended up acting as an emissary between the one-percenters and the law.

The Angels were at the funeral home, and Sheriff Overton was with a concerned group of citizens on the steps of a church about 100 yards away, up a hill. Morris was attending the funeral, taking pictures and notes for the paper. It's amusing that the town—this town—was concerned about their well-being. Given the general lawlessness of the county, I'd have been more worried for the Hell's Angels. And perhaps that's what the leader of the cyclists was hinting at when he called Morris aside, gestured up the hill, and said, "What's with that guy?"

"That's the sheriff."

Overton was a snappy dresser. "And this was the seventies, you know. He had on a leisure suit, I think it was maroon, and a big collar out to here."

"That guy?" asked the Hell's Angel, incredulous. "What's he doing?"

Morris explained that they were afraid, like all small towns are afraid, that the Angels were going to riot, or burn something down, or rape everyone, or whatever it is that Angels do when they are burying someone.

"Go up there and tell him we're here for a funeral."

So Morris ran up the hill and told the sheriff that the Angels had no plans for mayhem.

The sheriff said to Morris: "Good. Go back down there and tell them that I appreciate that, and that I'll escort them to the cemetery if they like, and have deputies block off the intersections for them."

Morris ran down the hill.

"Tell the sheriff thank you. Tell him we're not going to wear our helmets on the ride from the funeral home to the cemetery."

Up the hill.

"Tell him that's okay, but that when they leave the cemetery, they better have them on. I'll be right there, and anyone who rides out without a helmet on is breaking the law."

Down the hill.

The head guy of the Angels said to tell the sheriff that was fine. "But man, I was tired of running up and down that hill, so I just turned around and waved my hands in the air to the sheriff, you know"—Morris demonstrated—"and I gave him the big thumbs up. One of those guys came up and gave the leader a brown paper bag with a green bottle in it, and he passed it to me. I looked up at the sheriff. Fuck him, you know?" Morris mimed shrugging in the direction of Overton, turning his back on him, and taking a pull from an imaginary bottle. "God. That was the best stuff I have *ever* tasted. Don't know what it was, but it was smooth."

Morris doesn't drink alcohol anymore. Hasn't touched it in twenty years. He owned the *Franklin News-Post* twice, and after he sold it the first time, he went wild. He was partying with another motorcycle gang up in an apple orchard in the rain. He told someone he didn't feel right and wandered off. He doesn't remember what happened, but they tell him he was picked up wandering down Route 40 and taken to the hospital. He had a fever of 108, and he spent twenty-eight days unconscious in the ICU. He says he died three times.

"The Lord must have a plan. I don't know what it is. But as long as I can get out on the river, it's okay with me."

He keeps two canoes tied to the top of his 4Runner.

"I got nowhere else to put them." Which must be true, because they were tied to the top of his truck in the middle of winter.

Morris is the only reporter to ever have been taken to a still in Franklin County while it was operating. Not for show, for real. In all my reading for this book, I have never found a similar story.

Morris had developed a good relationship with many moonshiners, in part because his editor, Red, loved to splash pictures of busted stills across the front page of the paper.

"The moonshiners were coming in, asking if I'd make prints for them. Well, hell, I made prints for 'em. Sometimes I'd get some liquor." Morris chuckled. "One day the secretary comes back to my desk, and she tells me there are a couple of really rough-looking dudes out front that want to talk to me—send 'em on back!"

They told Morris, "Come on, let's go get drunk."

"Boys, it's one o'clock in the afternoon, I got work to do, I can't be going off and getting drunk with you."

"You've been goin' 'round town, talkin' about how you want to go off and get drunk—well, we're fixing to."

And he realized what they meant.

"I had begged and begged and begged. Because I had never heard the sound of it running, I'd never smelt it, I'd never watched a still work."

Morris asked them when and where. They told him to meet them out at a Boones Mill beer joint called the Raceway Restaurant. They'd have a few beers, and then they'd go.

He'd told the special agent in charge of the ABC agents in Franklin County at the time, Kenny Strohman, that he was trying to get someone to take him to a still, and that he was going to call and tell him, just in case the still got raided while he was there. They'd realized that it was likely that the moonshiners might be with him when he made the call, so they'd established a code. Morris was to call and say he was going to Roanoke.

Coming from anyone else, of course, this might not have flown, but Morris's uncle had been close with Kenny, back when they both lived in Wythe County.* After they discovered the connection, when Morris first moved to Franklin County, Kenny took Morris under his wing.

"So I called his house, and his wife answers the phone. He wasn't there! 'He's out on a stake out, Morris, he's going to be gone all night.'" So not only could he not get word to him, but he now feared that the very still he was going to was being watched.

"Look, when you see him, just tell him I went to Roanoke."

"Was he supposed to go with you, Morris? Because I don't think he's going to be back in time."

---

* The Illegal Whiskey Task Force agents had told me a story about another writer who had told them that he was looking for moonshine stills. They told him—and by implication, me—that if they found him at a still, they'd arrest him.

"No, no, no. I know. It's okay. Just give him that message. Tell him *I'm going to Roanoke.*"

And with that, Morris suited up and got himself ready.

"I don't know why, but I thought we were going to be outdoors. And it was cold, so I've got a t-shirt, a thermal shirt, a flannel shirt, and an honest-to-god Army flak jacket on. I've got my combat boots on, and blue jeans, and a hat, the whole nine yards." He figured he'd be standing in the woods for hours.

After they'd had a few beers at the Raceway, they made him lie down in the back of the car. He paid attention—they made a turn, another turn, they hit a gravel road—and he was able to go back and find the still site later.

"There was a big apple orchard up there at Boones Mill, and come to find out this was one of their storage buildings." There were three pots in that little building. They'd already run one of the pots, but the other two were ready to go.

As he tells the story, his eyes light up. He leans in.

"I watched them start-to-finish, you know? They put the paste on the still. They turned it on. They had propane. They had a fork made out of pipes, little holes in it. It was hooked up to a little hose. God, when they turned that thing on, Max, *RHRHRHRHRHRHRHRHRHRH*, it was just roaring. It was hot as hell in there. I had all that shit on, too. I don't know why I'd thought we were gonna be outside. One of them started stirring it, to keep the mash from sticking. That's work. The other one went to sleep while the thing was cooking. I heard the thumper get going." Here he made a noise like a bull-frog and pumped his fist in the air. "I watched the first stream come out. I drank the water from the cooling box. I watched *everything*. I wanted to drink it when it first came out. They said, 'No, no, no, that's 200-proof, you can't drink that!' I tasted it anyway, burnt the shit out of my mouth. We made 160 gallons, and we left it outside. Except for a few half-gallon jars"—he pauses and grins—"which I kept."

That's the kind of story that makes Morris rock back on his heels and announce that he's had a hell of a life. "And I've never lost the thrill."

In a region to which he is so inexorably linked on every side of the law, I cannot expect him to turn on it and lead me to the liquor, but I can point out the resistance he's thrown up.

Morris took the picture that hangs in Hema's restaurant of the biggest still busted in Virginia (until it was superceded in 1993), and he gave me a big, beautiful print. It was twenty-six black pot stills. They suspected the setup was owned by Bobby Joe Whitlock (the same Bobby Joe who had tried to bribe Jimmy Beheler), but they never proved it. Across the back of the photo Morris wrote with a Sharpie: "To Max Watman: Days like this are gone forever!"

"Just last week a fellow asked me, he said, 'Hey, Morris, you know everybody around here, you been everywhere, you know where I can get a half-gallon of liquor?' And I told him I don't. There might be one guy, here or there, making a little bit for his friends, but the big stuff is gone. There's nobody getting arrested. There's no liquor. If Jimmy Beheler thinks they're still making liquor around here, he's full of shit."

One afternoon at the Lynchburg branch office of the ABC, I mentioned this idea to the Illegal Whiskey Task Force.

Morris says he doesn't know where any liquor is, says he couldn't find any if he tried.

They fell about the room, fifty-year-old men in convulsions of laughter, chorusing:

"He told you that?"

"Morris!?"

"Yeah, right!"

Applejack

Burglar 1 (Legs): What does this applejack remind you of?

Burglar 2 (Willie the Weasel): It reminds me of the old
　　Orland Social Club. Remember how Saturday night we
　　used to get plastered on applejack, and what we used
　　to sing?

Legs: "On the banks of the Wabash, far away . . ."

(They sing)

Oh, the moonlight spreads the night upon the Wabash . . .

Through the fields has come the breath of new mown
　　hay . . . of new mown ha-ay . . .

—W. C. FIELDS, *MAN ON THE FLYING TRAPEZE*
(PARAMOUNT PICTURES, 1935)

HORRIBLE THINGS CAN HAPPEN WHEN YOU BEGIN TRYING
to create strong inebriants at home. I've heard stories of people living in the forest for weeks while they shake off the blinding poison of jimsonweed. You start with a simple thought, making or harvesting the thing that gets you high, and you are found streaked with the juice of wild berries, dancing around inside a magic circle of stolen lawn

ornaments. The more up-to-date version is that you order some "research psychedelic" off of eBay, pop four of them, and end up dead.

My misadventures, in other words, were not so awful.

Here's the upside: I had not poisoned myself. I had not been struck with ergotism and been found capering about the lawn deep into St. Vitus's Dance. I hadn't rubbed the sleep out of my eyes and found myself in jail. I hadn't burnt anything down.

Further, something resembling liquor had come out of my contraption. I'd built a bridge between grain and booze: rickety, unreliable, rough-hewn, but a bridge nonetheless.

The downside: I didn't get enough liquor out of my still. The liquor I got was terrible.

With some ceremony and superstition I recorded my questions in my distilling log: "How to get more?" "How to get better flavor?" Although those two simple questions represent pretty much all the problems available to a distiller, written down, they seemed manageable.

Equipment improvements were necessary. Steam found every unsealed crevice and badly sealed joint and shot from these openings, threatening to turn the still into some sort of omnidirectional flamethrower. Could it actually blow up? Further, with all those leaks, I was bound to lose a lot of liquor.

Like a visit from a ghost in a sitcom that long ago jumped the shark, I heard Morris's drawl in my imagination, recounting his trip to the apple house with the moonshiners. "I watched them do everything. They put the paste on the still . . ."

Moonshiners use a paste made with rye flour to seal the joints of the still. The idea is that it's solid enough to hold the joints together and weak enough to blow apart before the still explodes.

I made my paste and sealed my joints. I didn't use rye. I used stone ground whole-wheat flour, because that was what I had. It was a tractable paste, but sticky, and I ended up with bulbous, badly shaped loaves cemented around tiny glass tubes. Ugly and odd, but it seemed like it would hold.

A gallon or so of George Washington's mash remained. I strained it very carefully, through cheese cloth, and got out every solid I could, until I ended up with about 2 liters in the Erlenmeyer flask.

I decided to do the run upstairs, in the kitchen, where I had good light and a stool. I drew the blinds.

I skipped the heat disburser, and the wash was up to temperature very quickly. My log says that I cranked it up at 11:05 P.M., and that by 11:25 I was collecting foreshots. At 11:40 the run was done, and I had 125 milliliters in a Ball jar.

Four ounces.

Four ounces from half as much wash. Technically, that meant that I'd quadrupled my output! It would be a long time before I was passing out jars at Christmastime with a wink and a don't-ask-me, but there was no arguing with the fact that 4 ounces from 1 gallon was a big step up from 2 ounces out of 2 gallons.

I held my jar up to the kitchen light. It was clear as a lens. Swirled around, clingy rivulets streaked the glass, which in wine tasting indicates that there's a lot of alcohol. I assumed it was the same. (There are other things, I realize now, that might cling to the side of a glass. I wonder what gasoline looks like if you swirl it in a Riedel burgundy goblet?)

I cautiously perched my nose on the edge. No repulsion, no gag reflex, no dizziness. It was almost as if the fluid smelled like nothing at all. I moved in closer and took a deeper whiff, and still got almost no nose. A very deep draw revealed a faint astringency. It was not inviting to smell, but nor was it horrible. With my nose buried in the glass, breathing deeply, I detected in the far background a semipleasant scent of baked goods, such as one finds in the nose of certain champagnes, but not as alluring.

I took a cautious swig. It was like nothing I'd ever tasted.

On the front of the tongue the whiskey was very watery, and spread out into distinct, disconnected flavors. There was no fabric or context to the taste. I discerned dough and water, separately, as if I'd dissolved a piece of baguette into a glass of ice water. I could still taste the baguette, and I could still taste the water; each had been ruined by the other, but they had not blended. If I held the whiskey in the front of my mouth, there was no alcohol taste to it at all, and no burn whatsoever.

At the throat, the burn began. It was strong, but not in a familiar way. The burn was very sharp, more like a hundred tiny pin pricks than a fiery glow.

I breathed out over it and the burn vanished—even 80-proof whiskey typically lingers and smolders. I tasted cocoa powder. When I set the glass back down on the table, the taste of wet bread lingered on my palette.

After three sips, my mouth was numb.

I read until my head hurt. I concerned myself with pH levels, with yeast nutrients, with different strains of yeast. My eyes moved across pages and pages of distilling advice in books and on the Web, and it all blurred together in a potage of scientific information out of which I could barely glean a morsel of anything I'd call knowledge. Distilling is art and science both, and I'm not very strong at kitchen science. I'm improvisational in the kitchen. I don't measure. I don't keep a recipe near. It goes without saying that I'm not much of a baker. I like to know a principle. Salt, for instance, will move through a permeable membrane to equalize the saline content of a given two things. This is how salt gets into a joint of pig and makes ham. I love that fact, and I put it to use curing my own duck breasts and eye rounds of beef. But "Permeable Membrane" is about as deep into the science books as I go, and, six sentences into a tract on the theory of fermentation, I found myself a little dizzy.

I struggled on, muddling toward a greater purpose. I read online forums dominated by highly technical home-distilling whiskey geeks. But something in me doubted my tack. Something didn't feel right. What about the famed still in the basement of the apple-processing plant in Winchester, Virginia? That place made the best apple brandy in the Shenandoah Valley. I guarantee you the folks sweeping the crushed apples up off the floor and fermenting them didn't have science. They didn't measure pH, or shop for esoteric yeasts. They had apples.

As anyone who has driven by an orchard at the right time of year can attest, fruit turns to alcohol if you leave it alone. Then all the sensible woodchucks come out of the woods and gorge themselves on your grassy *eau de vie*.

Rather than cajole whiskey out of grains, why not simply play along with fruit? If cornmeal unadulterated remains cornmeal, and apples unadulterated become alcohol, then perhaps apples would be a better jumping off point.

I headed to the farmers' market and came home with two gallons of apple cider.

This technique was not going to land me in the annals of artisanal spirits production, I'm aware. There are two schools of eau de vie making, and they fall roughly into the camps of Old School and Slow Food. For those makers who fall in with the latter set, real eau de vie is the product of fresh, ripe fruit. Those folks want their raw material to look as if it were nestled in a straw basket being sold for $18 a pound at some luxe market. Old School eau de vie is often made from fruit that is well on its way to rotten.

I reassured myself that this was, after all, only my second attempt at fermentation. I wasn't experienced enough to worry over these sorts of details. Considering the fruits of my initial labors, I was in no position to gas about artisanal anything. I just wanted to make some hooch, something drinkable.

Things started going well. I boiled water with an equal amount of sugar to make simple syrup, and by the time the sugar had dissolved and the syrup was clear, the whole setup was ready to go. I poured the syrup into the carboy with the cider (again, adding sugar is a cheat; I'm not making any friends among the craft-distillers with this method). I threw in a package of champagne yeast, air-locked the carboy, and left it. The air lock is a plastic doohickey that lets the CO_2 escape but doesn't let air in. This would prevent the aceto bacterias from getting in there and turning my mash into apple cider vinegar, and it would keep out undesirable yeasts as well. Maybe I'd limit the funky tastes.

One of the key measurements in all fermentation is the relative measurement of the initial specific gravity in relation to the final specific gravity, as measured with a hydrometer. Water with sugar mixed in is denser than water without sugar, and the hydrometer measures the specific gravity and relates it to a potential alcohol content. As the yeast eats the sugar and converts it into alcohol, there will be less sugar in the fluid and the so-called "gravity" will go down.

I had 1.08, which means that if the yeast did its job and ate all the sugar and I ended with a specific gravity of 1.00, I'd have a batch with 11.8 percent alcohol. I didn't see vigorous fermentation, no bubbles, no churning, but the next day I took a hydrometer reading and saw that the sugar was down to 1.03. It was working! By Sunday the gravity was down to 1.015 and the cider was fizzy and smelled sharp.

After much scribbling and head scratching—and a series of different answers to the same bit of arithmetic—I decided that there was enough alcohol inside the cider to make about 3.3 liters of 80-proof booze. Three liters! Who would I invite over to drink it? Would I ever have to go to the liquor store again? This would be fantastic! Three liters!

At midnight I pasted the still together, put half of my wash in the flask, and set a 1.75-liter liquor bottle (I'd been saving them—embarrassing how quickly they add up when you put your mind to it) under the spout. If I stopped just shy of filling it up, I'd have gotten the right amount of alcohol out of the half batch, and we'd be off to the races, because I'd have another half to go!

My run yielded a pint of liquor.

With the optimistic resolve of a thoroughbred owner, I chanted to myself that a pint is 16 ounces, and last time I only got 4.

I'd quadrupled my output yet again.

I took a deep, sighing breath, and encouraged myself that I was on my way. On my way.

But then there was the pint itself, which was not pretty. It still smelled like cider, not at all like liquor. And there were amoebic flourishes of apple floating in the distillate. What was it? Was it even liquor? Had I simply moved fluid from one place to another via some overly complicated, heated siphon?

I was again faced with a bottle of something I didn't want to put in my mouth, and again I labeled it and stacked it on the pantry shelf. The Ball jars were adding up, and it was beginning to look less like a collection of experiments and results, and more like a collection of failures.

It was a cold February evening, and the trees were cast in the chilly glow of moonlight reflected up off of snow. At the end of a gravel driveway with deep snowbanks on either side, the square windows of the little brew shop twinkled with a light the color of honey. Woodsmoke tinged the air. There were a few cars parked askew before the door.

Inside the shop I discovered half a dozen people leaning on tables and chatting over small goblets of beer. The side kitchen looked recently used, there were quarter kegs arranged on the floor, and kettles and cauldrons atop the old, blackened Vulcan stove.

I'd interrupted a home-brew club meeting. They were rosy-faced and cheerful, all beaming broad smiles at me as I entered. I tried to cover my panic—I didn't need a bunch of folks hanging around watching me purchase supplies for my moonshine outfit. Surely, the proprietor would recognize me. I could rely on his discretion. He and Bella had taken the whole thing so seriously, after all.

But he flashed me a stoned smile and garrulously shouted out, "Welcome! What can I help you with?" He didn't recognize me, it was clear.

"Want to try my saison?" said a young woman with long brown hair. I said I'd love to, and she delivered a small cup full of spicy, floral beer.

I sipped.

"I screwed it up," announced the Saison Girl. "What do you think?"

I told her I thought it was good.

(I later looked up "saison," and found that it was the French farm-house ale, like Dupont, which is a beer I love. I read that it was often "phenolic." I looked up "phenolic" and read that "a molecule containing an aromatic ring that bears one or more hydroxyl groups is referred to as 'phenolic.' Examples include flavonoids, isoflavonoids, and lignans. The word comes from 'phenol,' the name for the structure below which has one hydroxyl group attached to the ring." Delicious, huh?)

"I was drunk when I spiced it, and forgot, so I did it twice."

Everyone laughed and I told her I thought it had worked out well.

"Do you think so? Really?"

I was nodding—she was obviously worried about this, and wanted reassurance. I thought that I could use the conversation as a pick-and-roll-type distraction—if everyone would just keep talking about her spicy phenolics, I could browse without revealing myself.

But she turned on me: "What are you making?"

All eyes were on us. Was she yelling?

I answered: Cider. Ha-ha-ha. But I haven't gotten one I like; I don't really know what I'm doing; ha-ha. My brother-in-law is the brewer. He's in charge! Just do what I'm told! Test batches, you know? Experimenting. Ha!

My smokescreens failed to slow the pursuit. They all loved cider.

I'd left my wife and son in the car, since he'd fallen asleep on the ride, and suddenly, my saviors, they burst loudly through the door.

"Want to try my saison?" said the young woman with long brown hair.

Bruce offered some advice, and if I'd been any other customer, his detailed description of his cider-making adventures would have been exactly what I needed. But I couldn't talk about what I was doing. If he'd only remembered me, we could have talked in code. Or he could have let me know that everyone was cool, and we could have all talked about it. I suspect that it was a safe crowd, but you never know. Cops brew their own beer, too. As it was, his probably useful suggestions about potassium sorbate and arrested fermentation were met with a sullen, nervous chuckle.

Some of what I was there to buy (cleaning agents, a spigot) were innocent enough, but among the goods I finally laid on his table were five more packets of champagne yeast and a proofing hydrometer, which instead of measuring the specific gravity of sugar in water, measures the density of alcohol and gives you a percentage. Dead giveaway.

"Let's see here," he said, moving his fingers over the merchandise. "This is a proof/trane hydrometer, you know."

I nodded.

He noticed the champagne yeast.

"I'm not going to ask, I don't even want to know."

I slid him the money and slipped out the door, vowing that I'd never go back. I was an outlaw, and outlaws have to know when a place goes wrong and when to cut loose. Collusion relies upon good memory. Stoners make horrible con men.* If you're going to break the law, the people in on it need to be reliable. I'd miss the little shop in the woods. As I drove away, hopped up on adrenaline as if I'd just robbed a gas station, I knew it was over.

I ran through a few of batches of cider in quick succession, and except for some silly missteps stemming mostly from overconfidence—paste spattered all over the kitchen, simple syrup sluicing across the kitchen tiles—each run was more successful than the last. I was getting better, but I wasn't breaking through. My applejack was not quite right, and I had yet to make anything I wanted to drink.

How much time would I spend making booze and drinking store-bought on the rocks? I started to feel that I'd moved a lot of fermented materials around my kitchen, and stored a lot of things in the basement, and spent a fair bit of money, put myself at legal risk, and

---

* How to Be a Criminal, Item 2: Surprisingly, drugs and crime don't mix. Stoners will forget what they have to remember, crackheads are unreliable, meth heads are crazy. Even drunks—they'll either get pulled over for driving drunk or they'll get in a fight.

all I had to show for it was a shelf of sample jars, each dated, labeled, and utterly undrinkable.

I wanted a cocktail hour. I wanted to settle into a chair, put my feet up, and take a swig of something I'd made myself, but this goal began to seem unattainable.

Then I found the secret, my turning point, the biggest step in my distilling education thus far. I was reading the schedule for a workshop taught at the Cornell Extension Department of Food Science and Technology, which had been overbooked. I had learned about it late, and hadn't gotten a slot in the class, so I was looking over the syllabus and seeing what I would have learned if I'd gone. I read that they would, among other things, distill a wash into head, heart, and tail cuts, and then examine those cuts using "sensory evaluation," which is excellent fancy-speak for "drinking."

The class is a kind of traveling educational advertisement for Christian Carl pot stills, and Rex Halfpenny had attended one weekend at Michigan State University. In Bill Owens's newsletter for the American Distilling Institute, Halfpenny wrote:

> Of course, not all of the resulting distillate was the good stuff. The distillate, which was captured into 0.5-liter cuts, was diluted to 40 percent alcohol. We were then allowed to sensory-evaluate the results. The first five cuts were determined to be heads, full of higher alcohols and in most cases disposed of. The next nine were the hearts and represented the best of the batch—the secret of distillation. The last 18 were the tails, which can be saved and re-distilled.

These were much bigger cuts off the front and the back than I'd imagined, and it had never occurred to me to distill into a series of smaller vessels so I could preserve the purity of the middle. (This, though successful, was not without its own comedy. While "sensory-evaluating" the middle part of the run, I must have sipped something close to 170 proof, and let me tell you, that will light you up.)

Within a day I had a quart of excellent applejack. With my new proofing hydrometer I saw that on my second run through the still (I was distilling the applejack twice now) I'd achieved 145 proof. At 145, it was very strong. I knocked it down and tasted it. Still slightly too strong at 100. I had a flash of funny insight, proofed it down to 44 percent alcohol and scrawled "Rocket 88, Apple" on a piece of masking tape.

With great anticipation I put ice in a tumbler and poured myself a drink. I sat down in a comfortable chair in the living room and took a slow, careful sip.

Finally.

Delicious.

The Moonshine Man

Shipwrecks are apropos of nothing. If men could only train for them ...

—STEPHEN CRANE

IN 1860 THE LIQUOR BUSINESS WAS BOOMING. THE NATION produced almost 90 million gallons of spirits each year. Whiskey was cheap—24 cents a gallon in New York, 14 cents a gallon in Ohio—and none of it was taxed. The lush life would not last, for war devours goods. Grain, horses, man hours, warehouses, the majority of efforts north and south were turned to belligerent ends. Many states stopped, or attempted to stop, whiskey production in an attempt to conserve food.

There was still whiskey. Kentucky—divided even after its short-lived neutrality—provided spirits to both armies. Small distillers supplied an intermittent stream of booze. The spirits ration in the U.S. Navy was abolished, but sailors managed to find a drink here and there. The Union soldiers purchased drink as they marched through Pennsylvania. But whiskey was now expensive. In 1864, whiskey in the South was fetching an astronomical $60 per gallon. Although I'm sure many folks would have liked a drink, it became increasingly difficult to get one.

I grew up on the battlefields where the Civil War was waged, but I was twenty before the war became in any way palpable, made real by a famous photograph. On May 3, 1863, in the immediate aftermath of the Second Battle of Fredericksburg, a photographer stood behind the stone wall along Sunken Road, where Brigadier General William Barksdale's Mississippi Brigade had defended Marye's Hill against an overwhelming force under the command of Union General John Sedgwick, and took a wrenching, stunning photograph. Barksdale had been augmenting Jubal Early's corps in a failed attempt to keep Sedgwick from marching south toward Richmond. They'd defended this very hill five months earlier against General Burnside. This time they were profoundly outnumbered. In the photo, bodies are twisted and slumped into a ditch. Rifles are scattered across the dirt. The ground is littered with hats, bandannas, torn bits of cloth. Although it is May, there isn't a leaf to be seen; the trees are denuded and shattered.

I had a girlfriend who lived in the upstairs apartment of a brick house at the intersection of Sunken Road and William Street in Fredericksburg, Virginia. I walked Sunken Road to reach the library of Mary Washington University. Although I don't think that the battle stretched to that part of Sunken Road, as I looked out her window and watched for her walking home from class, I would imagine the narrow street strewn with discarded rifles and the air filled with the moans of the dying.

When I was a child, the folks who lived in my Shenandoah Valley town treated the Confederacy as if it were their team. The Confederacy existed not in any sort of real way, but only as a system of symbols and stickers and t-shirts that brought a group of folks together, rallied them under one flag, and granted them a few catchy phrases ("The South Will Rise Again!") without anyone having given any consideration to the significance of their nostalgic allegiance or the meaning of what they were celebrating. With complete disregard for the violence inherent in the symbol or the impropriety of celebrating the death of so many, the battle flag of the Confederacy was to my high school what the Che t-shirt was to the campus of my graduate school.[*]

I rooted for the other team.

My understanding of the Civil War was simple, on the one side was Good, and on the other Evil. Bigoted Southerners had owned slaves. The North brought justice and freedom to a bunch of backward rednecks. I remember explaining—horrified—to my parents that my grade school had retained strange, old textbooks which were brought out when it came time to study the War Between the States, and that the Confederacy was treated in those dusty volumes heroically, and not at all condemned for their obvious failings. In my young mind Confederates were correlative with Nazis.

One cannot live in the Sweet Sunny South for as long as I did without slowly reevaluating the terms of the war, and allowing, at least, that it might have been a complicated, multifaceted conflict. I used to play croquet in a park on top of a hill in Richmond that had been a field hospital. On hot summer days after our game we'd fall out onto the grass, twirling our mallets and sipping our cold beers. As idyllic as the moment was, one cannot forever escape. Eventually, with the sun beating down and the air as thick as soup, you try to envision the meadow soaked in blood.

I came to see the Civil War for what it was, horrific in a way that defies description. Wont as we are to tout the nobility of the Lost Cause, or to wrap a cloak of emancipation and justice around the Union, we must remember, first and foremost, that the Civil War was an awful holocaust. We must separate the reality from the per-

---

[*] I've always cut the kids of the Shenandoah Valley some slack. Many people assume that there is a racist undertone to the confederate flag decals and the rebel yells, but I found, growing up, that there was no undertone to it at all. There was no intention behind the symbols. That's not to say that racists and bigots don't also adopt those symbols, or that racism didn't exist—it did, dramatically and obviously—but the confederate battle flag was no more a symbol of racial oppression to the kids in my high school than their Christmas trees were totems of a pagan religion.

ceived nobility of the thing. We may love the brass-buttoned general riding at the head of his troops, waving his saber and spurring his frothy mount while his long hair flashes in the wind like a banner, but we must remember the war as a tragic, bloody half-decade that cost America close to 700,000 lives.

The South was devastated. Looking at the picture of Sunken Road, one does not see the plush grass, the thick trees, the settled rock wall, and the rolling hills. Just outside that picture, it's easy to assume that cattle lay dead and buildings were burning.

The war was costly.

The Union government had put the mechanism by which the cost would be recovered into action on July 1, 1862.

> Be it enacted by the Senate and house of Representatives of the United States of America in Congress assembled, That, for the purpose of superintending the collection of internal duties, stamp duties, licenses, or taxes imposed by this act, or which may be hereafter imposed, and of assessing the same, an office is hereby created in the Treasury department to be called the office of the Commissioner of Internal Revenue; and the President of the United States is hereby authorized to nominate, and, with the advice and consent of the Senate, appoint, a commissioner of Internal Revenue, with an annual salary of four thousand dollars . . .

The first commissioner was George Boutwell; he described the Bureau of Internal Revenue as the largest government department ever organized. The bureau taxed everything, enacting licensing fees, stamp taxes, taxes on processed food, taxes on manufactured goods, and gains taxes on interest and dividends. There were sin taxes on tobacco and playing cards, and luxury taxes on carriages and jewelry. Income tax had been instated at the onset of the war, to pay for the interest on war bonds.

On March 3, 1863, the commissioner was joined by a deputy. Joseph Dabney wrote in *Mountain Spirits* that it was at this moment that three detectives "were authorized to help deter, detect, and punish tax evaders. Their job, in other words, was to 'protect the revenue'—thus they became 'revenuers.'"

In 1862 the tax on liquor amounted to 20 cents per proof gallon. By the close of the war the tax was increased to $2 per proof gallon.

The moonshiner burst forth into the world fully formed, midwifed by the stroke of Lincoln's pen. Just like the Whiskey Rebels, who were his literal and figurative ancestors, it was not he who had changed, but the law. He became a criminal out of his unwillingness, or inability, to adopt new laws as his own.

At the close of the war a new battle began: the battle for the revenue.

In Georgia the moonshiners so despised the government that the period of their resistance is called the Georgia Moonshine Wars. The vast majority of federal court cases in postbellum Georgia, 80 percent by some estimates, were liquor trials. Bruce Stewart wrote in *The New Georgia Encyclopedia* that "moonshiners attacked revenuers and intimidated local residents who might otherwise be tempted to help revenuers identify lawbreakers. In the early 1870s the Ku Klux Klan joined forces with them to combat the IRS." In North Carolina, moonshiners also allied with the Ku Klux Klan, brought together by their shared hatred for the Republican government. (This got out of hand, and Alamance County and Caswell County were both declared in a state of insurrection and put under martial law.)

Jess Carr wrote in *The Second Oldest Profession* that

> In 1867 it became necessary to send a detachment of marines to Philadelphia to aid the civil forces attempting to destroy illicit distilleries. In 1869, in Brooklyn, New York, the opposition of the illicit distillers was so great that a marine detachment attempting to destroy illicit stills was beaten off by a mob. A charge with fixed bayonets was finally required to finish the job.

Despite the ubiquity of the violations (all sorts of people in all sorts of places were making booze), our national imagination took up the idea of the Moonshine Man about this time, and he was a very narrow character.

The Appalachian myth of the drunken hillbilly, the violent redneck, the families caught up in multigenerational feuds, the sexual deviance, was built in the years following the Civil War, during which the Appalachian people came to be stereotyped, as Bruce Stewart wrote in his dissertation-cum-book, as "eccentric, illiterate, lazy, and hard-drinking." Stewart's work insists that these "misconceptions were not based on evidence," but were, rather, lurid inventions. It suited some—writers, missionaries—to have discovered a lost tribe in America, an isolated group that had not been smoothed and civilized and educated, and had not experienced the explosion of technology and industry that had so swept the rest of the country.

Our moonshine man shuffles onto the stage, a cragged and bent mountaineer with a greasy hat and an old gun. In the October 22, 1877, number of *Harper's Weekly*, readers were presented with "The Moonshine Man: A Peep into His Habit and Hiding Places." It began, "Chief among the number phases of lawlessness which first attracted attention in the South at the close of the Civil War was that of producing what government officials are wont to denominate illicit whiskey." The article is sensational and purple. The author rides out into the backwoods mountain country of Kentucky with some officers. Together they brandish their guns, threaten laughably dimwitted locals, and bust a couple of stills. The landscape is bleak, the people they accost are ignorant and menacing, though feeble before the quick-witted and well-armed officers.

> Though brave and bold at home the moonshiner in a large city is as wild-looking a man as is ever seen. The sudden change from horseback to a seat in the cars, on which nine-tenths of them have never

ridden until captured, and the startling effect produced by sudden entry into a city after long years of life in rural regions so overcome the illicit distiller that his appearance on the streets would picture him to the observer as meek and mild-mannered in the extreme. Clad in garments of butternut, sometimes yellow, oft-times brown, and occasionally blue jeans, and always homespun, with hands in pockets, an old slouch hat shaped in the semi-Continental style and pulled partly over the forehead, the moonshiner on arriving in Louisville, where all of his kind are brought after their capture, waddles awkwardly through the streets, with an expression upon his features, if not of awe, most certainly astonishment of the deepest dye.

So it was that the myth was born.

It wasn't, of course, entirely the work of flatlanders and foreigners. Some locals capitalized on the hillbilly's perceived "outsider" status. For various reasons—because they'd been intimidated by moonshiners, or because they resented the bigotry and belligerence of the KKK—these locals marginalized the moonshiner deliberately, insisting that their own company was nothing like that, that the moonshiner was a fringe element.

The moonshine myth wasn't an accurate depiction of Appalachia, and it wasn't an accurate depiction of distillers. Stewart tells the story of Bluford McGee, who "wrote an autobiography of his early life in Wilkes County" that painted a very genteel picture of North Carolina distilling.

McGee remembered that his father made the "best" apple brandy in Wilkes County. Residents anxiously waited to taste the elder McGee's first batch of brandy each season. McGee recalled that his father would "go out in front of the still house and blow" on the still cap "as loud as he could" to signal that a run, or batch, of brandy was complete. People from miles around heard this noise and, knowing what it meant, headed off to the still to enjoy the first run of the season. McGee's teacher was a brandy connoisseur who canceled class upon hearing the high-pitched sound. "The school house was as quiet as a tomb," McGee remembered, "when all of a sudden a deafening blast from my father's still cap came crashing in at the door." McGee saw the corners of his teacher's mouth begin "to twitch and glow with radiance, till they spread from ear to ear in a broad smile." The teacher dismissed class, put on his hat, and walked out, "leaving a clear streak of sunshine behind him that made the heart feel glad."

McGee's autobiography reveals that antebellum mountain distillers were not hillbillies or marginalized criminals, as journalists and local colorists would label them after the Civil War. Most were small farmers who augmented their income by manufacturing excess yields of corn, apples, and peaches into alcohol and selling it to neighbors or merchants. These distillers were also respected members of the community. Wilkes County residents, for instance, viewed the elder McGee's liquor enterprise as a legitimate business. In fact, his first run of the season provided citizens with an opportunity to strengthen kinship and community bonds. Farmers and schoolteachers alike congregated near McGee's still to drink, gossip, and debate politics.

The question is not, of course, whether or not moonshine was being made or taxes evaded—it was, they were.

Jess Carr wrote in his informal history of moonshining that Southern moonshiners demonstrated an "unwavering contempt for government authority."

Revenue agents and collectors were resented for more reasons than interference with whiskey-making activity. Southerners looked upon the presence of federal officials as a continuing device for tyrannizing over a defeated people and upon the whiskey tax as a federal, and hence a "foreign," monopoly.

This attitude was not limited to the mountaineers. Consider the words of George H. T. Greer (progenitor of the author of the *The Great*

Moonshine Conspiracy of 1935) delivered in a campaign speech for the Virginia House of Delegates in 1869. "The carpetbaggers, bringing with them no knowledge of our habits and customs, and being men who were the scum of society at home, will prove incompetent and inefficient if nothing more . . ."

The 1878 annual report of the commissioner of the Internal Revenue outlined a scene of rampant disregard for the law.

> It is with extreme regret that I find it my duty to report the great difficulties that have been and still are encountered in many of the Southern States in the enforcement of the laws. In the mountain regions of West Virginia, Virginia, Kentucky, Tennessee, North Carolina, South Carolina, Georgia, and Alabama, and in some portions of Missouri, Arkansas, and Texas, the illicit manufacture of spirits has been carried on for a number of years, and I am satisfied that the annual loss to the government from this source has been very nearly if not quite equal to the annual appropriation for the collection of the internal revenue tax throughout the whole country. In the regions of the country named there are known to exist about five thousand copper stills, many of which at certain times are lawfully used in the production of brandy from apples and peaches but I am convinced that a large portion of these stills have been and are used in the illicit manufacture of spirits. Part of the spirits thus produced has been consumed in the immediate neighborhood; the balance has been distributed and sold throughout the adjacent districts. This nefarious business has been carried on, as a rule, by a determined set of men, who in their various neighborhoods league together for defense against the officers of the law, and at a given signal are ready to come together with arms in their hands to drive the officers of the internal revenue out of the country.

What we see is that where it was convenient to illustrate a pattern of lawlessness in the South, the hillbilly character was invoked. Likewise, Southerners utilized the same caricature to distance themselves from elements of their own society with which they were losing sympathy. The fact remains, revenue evasion was by no means geographically limited, and liquor violations were not exclusively the territory of the popular Moonshine Man.

John D. Sanborn was one of three private tax collectors hired by the Internal Revenue in 1872. He set his sights on distillers and liquor retailers, and collected $427,000 that year. The whiskey conspiracy he broke up was in New York City.

Sanborn went mad with greed; he worked on commission and kept half of what he collected. He wrote out a roll of 760 delinquent taxpayers and soon appended another 2,000 names. In the summer of 1873, Sanborn urged department officials to add 592 railroad companies to his roster. The transparent problem with the suggestion was that his list was, according to congressional investigators "substantially the entire list of railroads within the United States." Sanborn had simply transcribed a published guide to the railroad industry.

Sanborn was indicted but never convicted, since it turned out that he hadn't actually broken a law. In the fallout, Treasury Secretary William A. Richardson had to step down. (Grant, loyal to a fault, got him a gig on the Massachusetts Court of Claims.)

Richardson's replacement would be very bad news for the biggest bootlegger of all time.

The biggest outfit ever run was not Southern, nor was it Appalachian. It was an inside job, and when the case finally broke and the grand jury handed out the indictments, one landed squarely in the office of the president of the United States, on the desk of Orville Babcock, private secretary to Ulysses S. Grant.

The Whiskey Ring of St. Louis played hard, and when their outfit was really cooking, it took home astonishing amounts of money— 2 billion a year in today's dollars.

Running the show was a man named Johnny McDonald.

Johnny was a handsome, dashing man, with an officer's beard like Buffalo Bill's. Johnny was no hillbilly. The word "cavalier" might have been invented for him, for he fits every angle of its multiplicity. He was soldierly, flip, and intense about the defense of his honor, even when the smirch was well deserved or the fault his own.

He fought for, and befriended, Grant, and was a brevetted brigadier general by the close of the war.

After the war: "In the years 1868–69 I was engaged in Washington City collecting war claims against the Government and buying up Quartermaster's informal vouchers. I conducted this business with much success."

Many who had made sacrifices in the war—or had those sacrifices foisted upon them—were left with an IOU. Some had donated cotton or had their cotton fields torn apart by camping soldiers. Barns were occupied, shelled, and burned; fields were trampled; cattle was slaughtered; hogs were eaten; bacon disappeared from smokehouses; cordwood was burned to warm the troops; carriages, buggies, and horses were requisitioned. In theory, these folks (as long as they had been loyal to the Union) could make claims to the government and be reimbursed for their troubles, but these claims were hard to realize. There arose an arbitrage market. Someone like Johnny would approach a fellow with a claim and offer him 10 cents on the dollar, cash on the barrelhead. This must have looked like an okay offer—the poor guy had no recourse: his barn was in cinders and soldiers had eaten or shot all his cattle. Johnny would then take the claim back to Washington, where his chances of seeing the note honored were enhanced by his position and his rank. This was widespread, and Citadel professor and author of *Sacred Debts* Kyle Sinisi told me that nineteenth-century Americans would have described this as simple speculation. "Agents of all stripes bought the claims at a reduced rate in the hopes of redeeming them at their face value. Needless to say, the speculators often lost their shirts in the game." For there was no certainty that a claim was valid or that the government would reimburse the expense.

Johnny McDonald was on the No. 3 Express out of Jersey City on July 14, 1869. He must have been feeling flush.* He had a stack of claims in a trunk with a face value of $9,000,000, for which he'd paid $300,000. The No. 3 barreled through the night, going full steam across Pennsylvania. Just before midnight the train was approaching the Mast Hope station, where a westbound freight train was put on a siding, waiting for the express to pass. Engineer Charles Coffey blew his whistle, signaling that the train would not stop at Mast Hope. James Griffin, the engineer on the freight, was asleep at the stick. The whistle startled him awake, and in a dream fog he started his engine, pulling his freight train out on to the main line, right into the path of the express. The two locomotives collided, and Coffey's jackknifed, scattering burning coal. The engine was next to a passenger car, and the car caught fire. The fire spread to the depot. The Reverend Benjamin B. Halleck was trapped under a bent seat, seemingly unhurt by the crash, but surrounded by fire. His brother worked to save him. By reports, the reverend gave calm instruction to those working to free him until the end, and died without a whimper. Nine were killed, and another ten injured. The *New York Times* described a "spectacle of fathers and mothers and children crushed together in a burning mass of ruin, with their cries and prayers borne to heaven on the midnight air, amid flames that would have paled the fires of Smithfield . . . little children bruised to jelly, clasped to the bosoms of mothers whose hair and clothing were adding fuel to fires that had quenched the cries and seared the gaping wounds of their kindred."

McDonald was not injured, but his trunk burned. It was a tight spot, but he was not one to let life get him down.

"That is not my style. I am neither exalted by good fortune, nor cast down by bad," he would tell a reporter a few years hence. "By God, mine is a heart for any fate."

---

* He wrote that it was in September, but he was ill when he wrote his memoirs, and prone to mendacity, which calls doubt on everything, of course . . .

Johnny McDonald met a wealthy cotton merchant known to us only as "Mr. R." in St. Louis, while Mr. R. was on his way to Washington. He traveled there twice a year to collect payment for a mail contract he had with the government. Johnny made a bit of a spiel to Mr. R., it seems, speaking in hushed tones, and going so far as to suggest that he was a relation to Sir John Macdonald, then the prime minister of Canada. Perhaps Mr. R. would need some assistance? Perhaps there was, ahhh, business to be done?

Mr. R. shrugged it off.

Johnny suggested that he'd come visit Mr. R. in Arkansas, and that he looked forward to cementing their friendship.

Superficial courtesy, thought Mr. R., nothing more than politesse.

On a beautiful December evening in 1870, Mr. R. was idling away the evening with a friend on the porch of his plantation house in Ashley County, Arkansas, when they spied a curious figure approaching. He rode a fiery, coal-black steed. The traveler was dressed in a tight, tailored, water-proof suit, and his high boots were topped with red cuffs. His beard was short and thick, and he was well armed.

It was Johnny McDonald.

"What could have induced a man of his style to abandon, even temporarily, the luxuries of St. Louis, and undergo the considerable hardship of several days' difficult travel on horseback, through a wilderness of canebrake and heavy forests, out of the way of railroads?" wondered his host and his friend.

Their wonder was soon answered, for it was the very isolation of the place that piqued Johnny's interest. The government knew little of these environs, he told them, but that it produced abundant cotton. His pitch was that he and Mr. R. would corrupt some officials and conspire to manufacture a false claim against the government. Mr. R. was well respected by the Union government, as was General Johnny; they would claim that Union Soldiers had destroyed $1.5 million worth of cotton. It would be the work of a moment, assured Johnny, to get the payment.

Mr. R. didn't bite, but Johnny gave the scam a go anyway.

He worked for nine months generating false claims. No one colluded with him (or no one admitted it), but he stepped on enough toes while amassing these claims that a citizen of the county took it upon himself to inform the Treasury Department of the impending fraud. Johnny had, by this time, amassed about a million dollars in fraudulent claims, but he hadn't acted to cash any of them. The Treasury Department investigated, and discovered, of course, that all the claimants were invented and that no Union soldier had come anywhere near the place.

Someone in the Treasury tipped off Johnny that the jig was up, and he didn't press the claims.

The story makes the next phase of Johnny's life almost impossible to believe.

For obvious reasons, Johnny skips the Arkansas story in his own retelling of his life, and says that directly after the Mast Hope disaster, he approached his old general, President Grant, to beg a letter of introduction to Jim Fisk and Jay Gould, who were then the manager and president, respectively, of the Erie Railroad Company. He thought they might at least agree to make up for the personal investment lost in the wreck of their train. In what must have been a kind of fit of clear thinking—to which a casual reading of history implies he was not normally disposed—Grant refused him.

By Johnny's telling of the meeting, he simply moved on and asked President Grant for a job. A lot of Johnny's friends, it seems, thought that he might make a good supervisor. He'd been thinking about the Bureau of Internal Revenue. Johnny's whitewash of the conversation is ludicrous, but he got the job.

He made short work of having his territory expanded to include his hometown, and set himself up in St. Louis. He took on his friend John A. Joyce as his private secretary.

Joyce was a man much given to poetry and epic thinking. When the slaves of the West Indies were freed, there was a great parade and much fanfare in St. Louis, and Joyce gave a rousing speech, full of the choruses of angels and the chimes of freedom. He had been twice interned at the insane asylum in Lexington, Kentucky—first for a few months when he was nineteen, and then again a few years later for a "considerable period." He sent a poem titled "First Love!" to a newspaper, and they printed it. It begins as if it were a limerick: "In the month of November, the day I remember; / Now gazing o'er mountain and plain," but soon crescendoes into maudlin, bathetic doggerel:

> How glorious and bright, were the stars of the night,
> And the whipporwhill tuning its song
> When our hearts were so true, and I loved only you,
> In that multitude rushing along.

It wasn't all poetry. Their first order of business was the investigation of a revenue collector named C. W. Ford.

In the investigation I prosecuted at Ulrici's distillery (formerly run by Card & Lawrence, as referred to in Simpson's letter of information) a most glaring fraud was unearthed, viz. the discovery of 48,000 bushels of grain, which had been used for distillation and unaccounted for to the Government. The magnitude of this fraud was equal to stealing directly from the Government the sum of $117,600, and I at once accused Mr. Ford of guilty knowledge in the disposition of that money. After a season of skillful evasion Mr. Ford admitted the frauds, and exhibited the deepest humility and remorse of conscience.

To find a spread of $117,600 between the collected and the uncollected tax must have put a spark in Johnny's eyes. One of Johnny's favorite ideas, after all, was "stealing directly from the Government." It's impossible to know at which point the larceny in his blood was piqued, but from that moment, the federal revenue must have seemed to Johnny but a bag of oranges waiting to be squeezed. A cursory look around town revealed that most of the distilleries were shut down due to revenue infractions, which meant two things: (1) the distillers were corrupt or corruptible, and (2) unrealized revenue was everywhere.

St. Louis was a gold mine.

After a distiller made whiskey, he'd typically put it in 40-gallon barrels and ship it to a rectifier, who would filter it, proof it down, and put it into smaller containers, such as 10-gallon barrels, to be sold wholesale. The distiller was supposed to pay a tax on each barrel shipped to the rectifier, who in turn was supposed to pay tax on each barrel he sold.

The first step in building a whiskey ring is to convince the rectifier and the distiller to only report a fraction of production. Since there's money in it for them, I assume they'd agree, but if they resist, you bribe them. If they resist further, and you happen to be the head of the revenue for the region, you fine them. It was within McDonald's power to shut a distillery down for revenue infractions, and the great trick of the ring rests in exactly that: the revenuers would punish a distiller for *not* breaking the law. Eventually, everyone played along.

The next step is to buy or bludgeon the gauger, who measures the whiskey production. According to Mary Seematter, in her essay "The St. Louis Whiskey Ring,"

> It was the gauger's responsibility to measure the spirits. If he did his job honestly, fraud was impossible. But in the whiskey ring operations the gauger might, for example, report four thousand gallons in four hundred packages of ten gallons each, when in reality there were four hundred packages of eighty gallons each. In other words, 32,000 gallons were produced and sold, but tax paid on only 4,000.
>
> Another method the rings used was to have the gaugers certify that the distiller's tax paid stamps were removed from the barrels and destroyed, as federal law required, when they reached the rectifier. In fact, gaugers rarely destroyed the stamps, but either

removed and sent them back to the distillers for reuse, or sent whole barrels with uncanceled tax stamps for reuse.

Simple but excellent tricks were developed, such as writing repeating serial numbers on barrels. A distiller would produce twenty barrels of whiskey, write only the numbers one through four on them, send them off in five directions, and claim he'd only produced four barrels. It would be very hard to catch this as long as you don't ship two barrels with the same number. Who would catch you, anyway? Understand: this conspiracy isn't with the agreement of the revenuers, it is at their behest. Tax collectors aren't turning a blind eye, they are running the show.

The Whiskey Ring was not motivated by avarice alone, but also by politics. It is suspected—though it doesn't seem to have been exactly proved—that large chunks of the money went into the Republican war chest in local elections and in Washington.

McDonald recounts a visit to Washington: "At the appointed hour we visited the White House, when, after saluting Mrs. Grant, in company with the President we retired to the Blue Room and spent a long while thoroughly canvassing the political issues in the West, and particularly our scheme for creating a campaign fund."

Timothy Rives is an archivist in the National Archives at Kansas City, and his findings there led him to author an excellent article for *Prologue.* Of the beginnings of the Whiskey Ring, he wrote: "From November 1871 to November 1872, the five principal members of the Ring received between $45,000 and $60,000 each. Four participating distilleries received the same amount. It was a profitable venture. Coincidentally, perhaps, Grant won reelection in 1872."

But they had just gotten started. The salad days were ahead of them, and they defrauded the government of $1.5 million a year from 1873 to 1875.

Much of McDonald's *Secrets* concerns the efforts made by the author and his sidekick John Joyce to keep the sailing smooth. The history is a litany of bribes and intrigue, and one is struck by how unbelievably tedious a life of crime can be. (Criminals spend more time robbing convenience stores and passing bad checks then they do stealing paintings from hotels in Monte Carlo, after all. A criminal's life is one of nickels and dimes.) Throughout McDonald's stories of the Whiskey Ring, one is subjected to the pedestrian details of what it takes to keep a syndicate going. Letters were mailed and wires were wired. Looming threats were averted by manipulation or influence. Palms were greased with gusto. Slip a 4-carat diamond shirt stud into the right hand and Bob's your uncle.

A million and a half dollars a year is something like 2.3 billion dollars, using the relative share of the gross domestic product. Use another form of measurement and you can whittle that number down to a couple of hundred million. Either way, there was lucre to be spread, and spread it they did.

As Rives wisely wrote, "It operated as long as Treasury Department officials ignored it."

The Sanborn Scandal tipped the boat for the St. Louis boys. After Secretary of the Treasury Richardson stepped down and lit out for Massachusetts, he was replaced by Benjamin Bristow, and it wasn't long before this incredible headline (the whole thing is a headline, a piece of newspaper wonder) was splashed across the top of the *Chicago Tribune*:

GIGANTIC FRAUD: Secretary Bristow Grapples the Whisky Ring. And Successfully Exposes a Vast Conspiracy. Thirty-two Distilleries and Rectifying Establishments Seized Yesterday. Five of the Former and Three of the Latter Belong to Chicago, The Wide Ramifications of the Ring Laid Bare to the World. Revenue Officials of Every Grade in Collusion with the Ring. The Government Beaten Out of $1,200,000 Annually. Its Servants "Stand In" for Forty Per Cent of the Robbery. Fifty Thousand Barrels of Whisky Escape the Tax in St. Louis. Exposure of the Methods of Perpetrating the Frauds. Valuable Assistance Rendered by Two St. Louis Editors. Splendid Work Performed by Bluford Wilson and Elmer Washburn. The Removal of Commissioner Douglass Explained.

Hundreds were indicted, but here's the intro to the meatiest indictment returned:

> The Grand Jury of the United States of America, duly impaneled, sworn, and charged to inquire in and for the Eastern District of Missouri, on their oaths, present that Orville E. Babcock and John A. Joyce, late of said district, on the first day of January in the year of our Lord one thousand eight hundred and seventy-four, at the said district, did conspire, combine, confederate, and agree together among themselves, and with John McDonald, Joseph M. Fitzroy, Alfred Bevis, Edward B. Frazer, Rudolph W. Ulrici, Louis Tenscher, John Busby, Gordon B. Bingham, and with certain other persons to the Grand Jurors aforesaid unknown, to defraud the United States of Internal Revenue tax of seventy cents, then and there imposed by law upon each and every proof gallon of a large quantity, to wit: 1,000,000 proof gallons of distilled spirits thereafter to be produced at certain distilleries then and there situated in the City of St. Louis . . .

Orville E. Babcock was Grant's right hand. He'd served gallantly in The Battle of the Wilderness. He'd run the communications between Grant and Sherman. In the course of the war, he had been brevetted up to brigadier-general. He was Grant's private secretary. To indict Babcock was to imply an indictment of Grant, as well.

Grant had been very enthusiastic about the prosecution of the ring, which is cited as an indicator of his innocence, but I think it was a Hobson's choice. What else is he supposed to have said? Let them go?

Still, when the prosecution reached Babcock, Grant wanted to defend his friend. He first planned to go to St. Louis and testify on his behalf, a plan the level headed Hamilton Fish discouraged. Timothy Rives wrote that "a sitting President had never before—and has not since—testified voluntarily as a defense witness in a criminal trial. For Grant to do so, in person no less, was more than his cabinet would bear." Fish's argument amounted to reminding the President that in a case titled "The United States versus . . ." *he himself* was the highest manifest representation of the United States. A "voluntary offering of himself as a witness for the defense in a criminal prosecution instituted by the government, of which the President is the representative and embodiment" would be beyond imprudent, it would "place him in the attitude of volunteering as a witness to defeat the prosecution, which the law made it his duty to enforce." Rives wrote that "Fish prevailed, up to a point. Grant would testify for Babcock, but there would be no trip to St. Louis, no crowds in the street, no dramatic courtroom entrance, just a deposition taken in the quiet, controllable confines of the White House."

"Perhaps you are aware, General," asked Major Lucien Eaton, representing the United States, "that the Whiskey Ring have persistently tried to fix the origins of that ring in the necessity for funds to carry on political campaigns. Did you ever have intimation from General Babcock, or anyone else in any manner, directly or indirectly, that any funds for political purposes were being raised by any improper methods?"

Grant answered: "I have seen since these trials intimations of that sort in the newspapers, but never before."

It is, of course, impossible to prove with the available evidence whether or not Grant knew of the Whiskey Ring (though as the eight ball says, "All signs point to 'yes' "), but it's pretty clear from the above answer that he knew his way around a prosecutor. All he really says is that he never saw anything in the paper about improper political fund raising before the trials started. A very sharp or aggressive prosecutor might have dogged him, but the Treasury had received a wire that morning that read "tell Eaton that he must show on cross-examination that the President had no knowledge of the secret correspondence of Babcock with Joyce and McDonald." Eaton obeyed.

All of the indicted were convicted, save one. Grant's deposition worked its magic, and it took the jury only two hours to return a verdict of not guilty for Babcock.

A party ensued at the Lindell Hotel, where the jurors celebrated Babcock's acquittal with a crowd of swells and, according to Rives, he was serenaded.

It was only a short while until Babcock was again implicated in a scandal, the Safe Burglary, that cost him his desk at the White House. Grant, loyal Grant, got him a gig as chief inspector of lighthouses. Babcock met his fate aboard the *Pharos,* a seaworthy, two-masted schooner. A few years later, she would rescue the ship *Sybil* when that one encountered a severe hurricane near Dog Rock, off the Florida Keys on November 12, 1857. The *Sybil,* according to the *New York Times* of December 1, "was ran inside and anchored" to prevent her from going ashore, but "she would not bring up, [and] the three masts were cut away." The ship and crew weathered a day like that, but on the thirteenth the wind shifted, rounding to the east. The anchor wouldn't hold, and the crew let go the chain. Improvising a mast, they tried for shore. She was seen by the *Pharos,* "who went to her assistance and succeeded in getting inside the reef." The *Sybil* was towed into port on the fifteenth "totally dismasted and without anchor or chains."

On June 3, 1885, the *Pharos* was under the command of Captain Anderson. She was lying off of Mosquito Inlet, near Daytona, where Stephen Crane clung to a lifeboat after the *Commodore* went down on her way to Cuba (a story he fictionalized in "The Open Boat"). It was a treacherous spot, and the seas that night were very high.

Chief Lighthouse Engineer Orville E. Babcock was aboard, overseeing the building of a lighthouse that would fill an especially long gap on the coast between Cape Canaveral and St. Petersburg. The shores of Mosquito Inlet had seen the smashed bits of over seventy hulls, and the beacon would make it safer.

No one seems to have recorded why, exactly, General Babcock so urgently wanted off of that boat. He should have known how to keep a cool head, and how to comport himself in the face of danger.

I can only imagine he had some pressing matter ashore, and that it was either assignation or ill-gotten gain.* The captain told him to sit tight, but Babcock repelled the advice and insisted on calling a surf boat out to meet them.

The boat struggled to the schooner, and the captain again attempted to divert Babcock, feeling that he and his party were going to their death.

Babcock laughed, told the captain he'd landed in rougher places than this, and got in the boat with his friend Dr. B. F. Sutter and one Mr. Levi P. Luckey of the Lighthouse Department. The small boat was out of sight amid heaving breakers within moments.

Captain Anderson seems to have waited until the water was very safe to go out looking for them. The crew of the boat was never found, but several days after they'd launched toward the shore Anderson found Babcock, Sutter, and Luckey half buried in the sand on the beach. Dr. Sutter's legs had been bitten off by sharks.

President Ulysses S. Grant said, in eulogy, that "General Babcock was a very able man, and a brave and good soldier."

McDonald was first incarcerated in the local jail, where his cell was "freshly painted, and the walls were decorated with choice oil paintings and flowers." He subscribed to magazines, and his meals were cooked to order. He entertained hundreds of visitors and plied them with wine, cigars, and liquor. His cell was so full of flowers that it resembled the basket in which the beautiful Cleopatra died, and he likens his own activity in the clink to that of an editor at a major metropolitan newspaper.

His cell was not locked, and when the other prisoners took to the

---

* One of the most damning pieces of evidence in the case against him in the Whiskey Fraud proceedings was a telegraph signed "Sylph." McDonald suggests that Sylph was a real woman who caught Babcock's eye, and goes so far as to give us a portrait of her and describe the circumstances of a tryst. It has been suggested, convincingly, that Sylph was simply a pseudonym, probably for Joyce. Regardless of the truth, Babcock's proclivities would seem to divide into women and larceny.

corridor for exercise, he "remained on the balustrade fronting my cell door, and generally amused myself throwing apples or candies among the crowd of prisoners to watch them scramble."

Pleasant enough, but he wouldn't have it for long. He was moved to the penitentiary in Jefferson City, where he describes a sort of hell of gray stone and the tortured cries of the abused prisoner. He became ill while there, and a newspaper account of a visit with him paints a grim picture of a sallow, wan, and fading man. He stayed imprisoned for eighteen months.

After Grant won reelection, he pardoned Johnny.

Johnny would spend the rest of his days in ill health, narrating his memoirs, clipping items from the newspaper, and shooting off letters to the editor in defense of his honor.

Beauty and Damnation

Seligman had ... set himself up for this, early—making the fatal mistake of everyone who chooses a business involving many, many tiny things and objects and their collision with people who want but can't understand them—the madness and doom of stationers and hardware men.

—TODD MCEWAN, WHO SLEEPS WITH KATZ

HUNDREDS OF DUSTY, SCUFFED CARTONS WERE SHELVED tightly together before me, a dizzying wall of bright copper couplings, fittings, reducers, unions, and tubes of all imaginable sizes. There were T-joints, elbows, valves, and bushings. Brass that had been threaded to fit hoses, to fit sinks, to fit irrigation, to fit gas lines. I had no idea what I was looking at—or what I was looking *for*—and there was no "Moonshine Still" section. The longer I stood there, the taller the wall seemed to reach, the farther it stretched out in either direction, like some sort of cosmic obstacle you hear about people confronting in an ayahuasca trance.

My kitchen experiments had surged forward after the success of the applejack. Having a cocktail of my own making had been a milestone, a kind of a bar exam, if you'll pardon the pun. Perhaps I was more confident, certainly I'd learned, and things started to swing right.

First came the turbo yeast—a miracle in a sack of golden foil that I bought from Mile Hi Distilling, a home-brew shop in Colorado. Champagne yeast comes in a small packet just like baking yeast from the grocery. One dose of pale brown turbo yeast, however, comes in a sack the size of a pocket paperback, and measures about a cup and a half. On the label there was pictured a snow-peaked mountaintop, and in big blue letters: "48 Hour Turbo Yeast. Dual Purpose. 14% in 48 hours, 20% in 5 days. Ingredients: High Alcohol Distiller's Yeast, Yeast Nutrients."

There are three tricks to turbo yeast. The first is the sheer volume of yeast per packet. The second is the strain of that yeast, selected and bred for strength and resistance to alcohol. The third is the most important of the three: each bit of genetically engineered, superhybridized, bionic-rugby-player yeast has been caked in a little shell of nutrient and pH adjuster. You don't have to screw around with measuring the pH, or find the right combination of citric acid and nitrogen and whatever else yeast wants by way of invigoration. All the adjustments that need to be made will be made by the pale brown nodes in the packet. It's a one-stop shop, like a Betty Crocker cake mix, with instructions right on the bag. "To make 6.5 U.S. gallons (25L) pour 5.5 gallons (21L) of warm water (104°F/40°C) into your fermenter. Add 13 lbs (6 kg) sugar to make 14% alc./vol. in 2 days, or 18 lb (8 kg) to make 20% alc./vol. in 5 days. Mix well until sugar is completely dissolved. Add the Turbo Yeast package contents and stir for one minute. Leave to ferment between 75–85°F(21–30°C) until fermentation ceases. Complete fermentation times are temperature dependent. *Important: Do not airlock fermenter.*"

This puzzling insistence on repeating every measurement in metric reminded me of the strange pomposity of insurance men and Old School clerks who write numerals next to the word for the number because it makes them feel diligent and official. ("Please find here three

(3) copies of form 27b/6, as per your request.") Turbo yeast is not an aesthetically sensitive product. Genetically engineered superyeast is more suitable for the production of fuel than it is for the production of drink. It's made to get the most alcohol out of the least wash, and that alcohol is meant for a column still—as opposed to a pot—which would strip it to a high level of purity. There's nothing gentle, or artisanal, or tasteful, about it. This is the yeast you'd use if you wanted to make pure alcohol. (Which, it turns out, a lot of people do.)

I also didn't like that bit about "temperature dependent." It seemed a red flag: they didn't want to hear about it when the promises made on this golden bag failed to come true. If you can't make sure your house is between 75 and 85 degrees, that's *your* problem. Don't call us complaining about your 6 gallons of unfermented simple syrup.

I had my doubts entering the turbo yeast experiment, but I figured it was worth a shot. I fiddled with the recipe. In conversation with a distiller from a rum company—a notable, venerable rum company with its product on the back bar of virtually every bar in America—I'd learned that rum manufacturers sometimes substitute brown sugar for molasses, because it is, after all, the same thing. I also had learned that rum ages well, and quickly. If you lay it down on wood for two months, it's legitimately on its way.

I filled my trusty lobster pot with 2.75 gallons of water and stirred in 6 pounds of brown sugar, took its temperature, and pitched in the sack of yeast. My hydrometer told me that I had specific gravity right around 1.100, which promises a potential alcohol of 13 percent in the wash.

Within three hours the pot was bubbling and roiling like mad.

I began to calculate output: 13 percent of 3 gallons = 1.47 liters. If I took 3.5 liters off on the first run, I'd be right around 40 percent.

Two days later I was pleasantly surprised to see that I had full fermentation: Specific gravity was down to zero. The wash even smelled good, like rum-soaked molasses cookies.

I divided the wash into gallon batches and prepared to start distilling.

As the yeast begins to die of alcohol poisoning in the wash, it settles to the bottom and the wash clears. I didn't know this yet, so I grabbed a yeasty gallon and shoved it through the still. It came out tasting wrong, sharp, and filthy.

However, I'd gotten 100 proof on my first run, and for once my calculations had proved to be correct. I had almost a liter.

I looked around and read about turbo yeast distilling, and discovered a line somewhere in an online forum about not distilling with yeast in the wash. You're supposed to let the yeast settle, and then either distill it or move it into another container, which people call "racking." So I let the yeast settle and returned the following day to find a beautiful, clear, brown rum wash with a layer of khaki-colored sediment about an eighth of an inch thick on the bottom of the Lexan container.

When I ran another gallon, I got another liter, which I then double-distilled to 140 proof. I proofed it down with some bottled water to a drinkable 44 percent alcohol: Rocket 88 Rum.

Most interestingly, I was no longer shooting in the dark, because immediate comparison was possible. Up until now I'd had no analogue for my output, since I had no apple brandy on hand and I hadn't scored any corn liquor yet, but I had a bottle of Myers white rum in the liquor cabinet. Side by side, the two had more in common than not.

What I'd made tasted like rum.

Bad rum.

Blended with a bit of solvent.

But it was clearly headed in the right direction. I was getting somewhere.

Bursting with confidence, I made another grain mash, this time mostly of barley malt. I got a pint of whiskey. The nose was still redolent of paint thinner, but once you got past that, it smelled sweet and grainy. What's more, it actually tasted like whiskey. Young and hot, raw as hell, but focused, and undeniably *whiskey*. It felt clean and clear in my mouth, and had a rock-candy flavor running strong through the center of the taste. It seemed to cry out for the vanilla that would come from time spent in oak, it wanted to go rest in a barrel for a few years and become something recognizable and good. But there was so little of it—just a scant pint.

I made a couple of daiquiris for the curious with my own homemade rum. I gave out some tastes of the whiskey. People weren't recoiling. They were nodding approvingly. You had to really *like* whiskey to see the whiskey in what I'd made and where a good white rum will blend into limes and sugar and become almost invisible, mine stuck around and didn't hide as well as a white rum should. The approval I got from my guinea pigs was tentative, there were raised eyebrows and shrugs, but it was approval.

Then I'd hit them with a new batch of the Rocket 88 Applejack. The applejack was a smash.

"That's delicious."

"That's like poire!"

"You made that?"

Something was happening.

The telephone rang on a chilly autumn afternoon, and my brother-in-law asked me if I'd be interested in getting hold of some cider. He had met an orchard keeper who used to make hard cider and had a special blend from the dozens of varietals around the orchard. He'd give us 12 gallons for $20.

It came in two 6-gallon carboys, and it was the most delicious cider I've ever drunk. It was unpasteurized and untreated, fresh and so bright-tasting that it seemed effervescent. I'd never had anything like it. Crisp and clean, it was a clear autumn sky reflected in a glass. The cider they sell at the store, even the cider at the farmer's market, seemed like dusty, stringy stuff by comparison.

Anyone who has ever been passionate about food knows the excitement of a first-rate product. When a rack of really good elk chops hit your board, when you caught the fish, when a *real* tomato arrives, the thrill is tangible. Good product is the basis of good food, and good product demands to be treated with respect, with subtlety. This was the best I could ask for, and I had a lot of it.

I went back to the books and the boards, and I read about yeasts. The sugar content wasn't all that high, potential alcohol of about 6.5 percent. I didn't need a powerful yeast; I needed the right one. I wanted to respect this cider. I wasn't going to adulterate it with sugar to bump up the alcohol.

After asking around, I settled on White Lab English cider yeast.

White Lab makes you think you are playing for real.

White Lab's WLP775 comes in a test tube with a heavy black screw top. Inside the test tube is a slurry the color of light mud. The package looks as if it might explode if mishandled, or like it's meant to poison the water supply of a major metropolitan area. It certainly doesn't look like something that belongs in your kitchen, or something that you should carry through a New York City airport. I didn't know that. I'd never seen the stuff before. My wife picked it up in a home-brew shop while she was out of town, and her bags came home with a note inside, indicating that they'd been searched. Why whoever searched her bags didn't take the yeast, I can't imagine. It doesn't look any more reassuring upon closer investigation, although it does have the following printed on the label:

> WLP775 English Cider Yeast: Classic cider yeast. Ferments dry, but retains flavor from apples. Sulfur is produced during fermentation, but will disappear in first two weeks of aging. Can also be used for wine and high gravity beers.

In addition to new yeast, I tightened up the rest of my proverbial ship, and purchased some better airlocks to keep out those acetobacteria. I tried to figure out what everyone was talking about when they called for the wash to be "aerated" (and failed).

I should have gathered that I was ready for a fall from grace, and I should have sensed it coming when I "sterilized" one of the airlocks by melting it into useless bit of warped plastic. But I was blind with zeal. I had, after all, been making really good stuff.

The chorus of beaming faces had sung out: "Just like poire!"

In went the yeast, and on went the airlocks.

The cider would ferment in the kitchen while we were across the country, hanging around the San Francisco Bay, where I was going to look at some small distilleries. As I packed, I daydreamed about what kind of bottles we should buy for the stuff. Squat, clear-glass wine bottles? Swing tops? Ceramic jugs? Should we age some? I'd had some applejack made by a distiller as an experiment; he put the spirit on oak for two short weeks and it was already toasty and full of vanilla. What kind of oak should we get? Would we have enough to give a few bottles away? Should we have a party?

I gave my brother-in-law keys to the house, and he promised to check on it.

He called me from my house a few days later and said: "Smells weird in here, but I think it's just the sulfur."

Everyone mentions that cider, while fermenting, stinks for a while, and then calms down. I wondered if the carboys had overflown.

"Oh, yeah, there's stuff all burped up into the airlocks, and all down the sides. It's okay though. No big mess. It's really going."

It was fermenting. Did it taste good?

"It smells really weird. It's really boiling and moving around. I think it's fine."

He'd made batches of putrid cider as a brewer. His apple cider had turned bone-dry, astringent, and bitter. He didn't want to taste it. I told him it would be great and let him off the hook, no need to taste it now. With the exception of a few pleasant walks with my son, looking out over the bay at Alcatraz lit up by the morning sun, my time in California was blurry.

I was visiting distillers, and that means tasting . . . constantly.

At Stillwater Distilling the still hands were shoveling cabernet grapes from a square vat into the 550-gallon Vendome still. Don, the distiller and owner, is a happy man with a full beard and a light in his eyes. He's overworked but in love with what he does. He insisted I slurp a handful of the grape must right out of the vat, and we did, spitting the seeds out onto the warehouse floor. It was fruity, vegetal, and delicious.

We drank organic Asian pear eau de vie, with a pear in the bottle. It was subtle and sweet and fruity.

We drank his malt whiskey. We drank some of the cabernet grappa, the finished product that was being made on the floor that day. A man with a plan to sell absinthe accoutrement had stopped by and brought Marilyn Manson's Mansinthe with him, as well as another absinthe. We drank Stillwater's vodka and some of the distillate Don was experimenting with in his stainless-steel vacuum still. Vacuum stills are used in Japan to distill shochu, which is a little stronger than wine. While we were there, they hit the heart of the run on the grappa they were distilling, and they pulled some of that and we drank it. People came and went, and Don pulled beer out of the lowboy behind the tasting bar and gave out excellent, hoppy California microbrews.

The highlight was a Gewürztraminer grappa that tasted of lemon grass, citrus, and pepper. It was one of the best spirits I have ever tasted, a masterful job.

I ate dinner at Noonan's, an unassuming place in a strip mall in Larkspur Landing with a virtual library of booze, the biggest back bar I have ever seen. The owner, Brendan, brought out plates of pheasant and kept a steady stream of delicate grappa glasses with tastes of this and that coming. We drank Steve McCarthy's eau de vie of pine trees. (Beyond interesting, I have no idea why you'd want to drink it, unless you were looking for something to talk about. It's not that it's bad, it's just that there's no getting around the fact that it is an eau de vie made of Douglas fir.) We drank 1992 James MacArthur's Old Masters Irish Whiskey, Cask Strength—by far the best Irish whiskey I've ever had. We drank Del Maguey Mezcal Pechuga, infused with nuts and distilled in a clay and bamboo still with a chicken breast hanging in the boiler.

I scribbled a lot of notes, and about half of them made sense.

It didn't stop. Out in Alameda, in the 65,000-square-foot Hangar One Distillery, I talked to Jorg about the process of eau de vie (learning that there are two ways to do it: one is to distill from fermented fruit, and the other is to distill fruit that has been infused into grain alcohol; you cannot make a mash of raspberries, after all).

They gave me their pear eau de vie, made from Oregon fruit, the distillate full of focus, with lots of great pear skin flavor. I drank a raspberry (the berries from Washington State), and I said it tasted like nori. Apparently, it contains a chemical in common with seaweed. Kirsch made from Michigan sour cherries (less focused, a simple flavor that never went deeper than the surface). They contract with Rosenblum Cellars for zinfandel grapes, and the grappa they make from them would have been the best grappa I'd ever had, had I not had Don's Gewürztraminer.

Then the vodkas.

Hangar One Straight, Buddha's Hand Citron vodka, which had a silky mouth feel and was incredibly sweet; Mandarin Blossoms vodka, which tastes like flowers and makes you crazy just thinking about the fact that you're drinking a vodka that tastes like flowers. Keffir Lime, which was too round for me and tasted like a gimlet made of Rose's lime juice, which is disappointing considering all the work that went into it. Fraser River Raspberry vodka, like an explosion of very big berries. I drank their aged apple eau de vie (and was inspired), and their St. George Single Malt. They gave me chipotle-infused vodka, and Thai Basil eau de vie. We ended our session by rubbing straight grain neutral spirits on our hands and feeling it evaporate.

I sampled the infusions with which they make the Mandarin. They use two: one is left as an infusion of flowers, and the other is distilled after it's been infused with mandarin blossoms. Both are no less than 165 proof. The oils in the infusion make it perfectly drinkable; the distilled one is like fire—I took a mouthful and spit it out onto the street, thinking my head was on fire.

All the while, I was talking to the distillers, learning. The process was demystifying. I was building a good vocabulary of tasting adjectives and was no longer lost when a distiller ran me through his process.

Up at Jepson vineyards, in Ukiah, I talked to Alison, who talks about blending brandy as if the brandy were a living thing. "Sometimes, you think two barrels are going to go together well, you think they'll get along, but they're like bachelors who have lived alone for twenty years, and when you move them in together, they pace circles around one another. They won't blend." We were drinking various stages of their delicious brandies on a barrelhead in a barn that had been converted to a still house. She gave me hope in a roundabout way: their thermometer had broken, so she'd tied a Coke can to a rag and hung it from the lyne arm of the still with a dab of wax. When the run started, the lyne arm got hot, melted the wax, and the Coke can clattered to the floor.

I was getting comfortable. I was learning. One big-picture concept shimmied into focus, and that was this: volume is key. You have to throw away a lot of foreshots, and you have to permit slow, low alcohol fermentations if what you want is good booze. Whiskey and rum you want to drink come from washes that stop at about 10 or 12 percent. My cider wash was low even for that, but what I began to understand was that having 6.5 percent in 12 gallons wasn't a problem; it was a boon. Low alcohol wash meant my stuff was likely to taste less like something you'd strip paint with and more like something you'd drink.

While I was more and more enthusiastic, I wasn't looking forward to the process. Watching distillers shovel 200 gallons of grape must into their pot still made me yearn for a bigger still. How long would it take me to distill my cider? Twelve gallons is over 45 liters. I couldn't really fill up my Erlenmeyer flask past the 3-liter mark without the thing puking into the coil. That's fifteen runs, fifteen batches of wheat paste, fifteen balancing acts on the drum stand, and all just to get the first pass—what distillers call the low wine! By the time I was done with the second run, it'd be spring.

Plus, although I had a deep sentimental affection for my worm, I was tired of how quickly it heated up. I had to manually refresh my water bath, which meant ladling out the hot water and replacing it with ice water.

I was going to need a bigger still.

Maybe something copper.

I wanted to be able to run off 6 gallons at once. In the distilling world, that's still the nano side of things, but I wouldn't be fermenting in greater quantity for the foreseeable future.

Unfortunately, knowing the size I wanted barely narrowed down my options for acquiring a still. Should I buy it? Should I make it? I was compulsively sketching designs in my notebook, looking at the features of the stills I visited, dreaming about still heads of different shapes, and of different features I might build into the thing.

It'd be easy—but expensive—to buy an apparatus. A 10-gallon moonshine still might cost about $1,000 if it were copper. And the stainless-steel ones for sale at places like Mile Hi Distilling were cheaper—around $350 for an 8-gallon still—but they were stainless, and most of them were column stills, which would yield high-proof, low-flavor distillate more suitable for those turbo yeast distilling folks who wanted vodka (or fuel).

There are companies in Portugal that make beautiful copper stills, hand-hammered pieces of sculpture like the onion dome on an Orthodox church. (Hoga, for instance, makes absolutely stunning stills, probably worth buying just as objects, even if you never intend to run anything through them.) They'd ship me a 30-liter still for about $600.

I couldn't shake the feeling that something wasn't right. They were beautiful, and I probably should have bought one, but I wanted to learn, and I wanted it to be, for lack of a better word, moonshiney.

Historically, moonshiners have not made their own stills. There lived in Franklin County, for instance, a coppersmith whose product was so prized that moonshiners would occasionally get caught because they'd try to run while holding their still head. It was a piece of art, and they were unwilling to leave it to suffer the revenuer's axes. Of course, some moonshiners do make their own stills. Brazing copper is relatively low on the learning curve for welding. My mission was one of discovery and investigation. Buying a still seemed like cheating. If I were thinking and writing about hot rods, I wouldn't buy one, I'd build the thing.

I came to a sort of compromise. I found a good-looking antique boiler on eBay and PayPalled my $66 off to the seller. It held 6 gallons with some room to spare, and it had a brass fitting that screwed into a 4-inch opening in the top, which in turn screwed into a brass elbow joint that had some threads.

It was beautiful, it was cheap, and it felt authentic.

I had big crazy plans for added features—thump kegs, gin heads— but to begin with, and to get through this 12 gallons of fermented cider, I'd just solder together an arm to come off the top of the boiler, wind up a coil, and screw the whole thing onto the head.

I returned home from California for Thanksgiving, and while the turkey roasted in my smoker, I coaxed my guests into some "sensory evaluation" of the fermented cider.

It did not go well. Faces were made. I hadn't just turned this wonderful cider into not-so-great hard cider; I'd turned it into something truly strange, something awful. There were wretched, *off* flavors, biting astringency; it was so dry that it seemed to suck all the saliva off the top of the mouth, leaving us working our tongues over our palates like dogs lapping at peanut butter.

Never mind, I crowed. We're distilling it, not bottling it. It'll be fine once it's 140 proof! I not only proclaimed it, I believed it.

No one looked convinced.

I set to work on the still, smug in my belief that, once it was ready, we'd pass the cider through it and end up with something great. The boiler was old, and the pieces were crusted together. With a vice and some steady, gentle knocks from a hammer, I got it all separated. Now, a simple trip to Home Depot for some tubing . . .

The array of tubing and couplings and reducers was dizzying and vast, and I could not find what I needed. I went to a plumbing supply, and they told me they'd never seen a fitting like the one to which I was trying to attach a pipe. They couldn't help me. I went back to Home Depot, each time purchasing a little bit of what I'd need—a propane torch, a heat-resistant cloth—but never any copper. I'd make a new list, draw up a new plan, and when I'd look at the copper available, the things that I'd written down didn't seem to match the things in the little boxes on this interminable shelf.

I felt like Kafka's character in *The Castle* who, despite his efforts, cannot actually get to the castle itself. I opened the cider to check it out. It'd been in the mudroom, keeping cool. I knew I should have racked it, but it was already nasty, so I figured I didn't have anything to lose.

The worst had happened. The cider smelled sharp and acidic.

Vinegar!

Discouraged, I turned my attention to other matters, burying myself in reading and forgetting, for now, the embarrassment of having taken 12 gallons of the best cider I'd ever had my hands on and ruining it. Maybe I'd make pots and pots of apple cider vinegar barbecue sauce—salvage something out of it, anyway.

The building of the still had run aground. I was unable, it seemed, to make a plan that would reflect the materials available to me—or unable to make sense of those materials. There were too many options, and even when I looked at published still plans—in Matt Rowley's book, for instance—and worked from there, I couldn't make all the pieces of the puzzle come together.

Weeks dragged by and the cider stayed where it was, two crusty carboys against the mudroom wall. In the first week of the New Year, I decided to look in on them again. Something would have to be done, and if the cider had turned to vinegar, so be it. I'd get the damned vinegar. I couldn't just leave it there. I pulled a scant half-cup of cider.

It was much clearer than I remembered.

It still smelled vaguely acidic, but not unpleasant. Certainly, vinegar would smell stronger. Wouldn't it? I sipped. I wasn't sure. How could I not be sure? Wouldn't vinegar be, well, *vinegary?*

I resorted to the telephone, asking everyone I could think to ask if vinegar had to be distilled to show up as vinegar, or reduced, or processed in some way. Vinegar was vinegar, it seemed. I would know if that was what I had. This was not vinegar.

I siphoned two carafes full and put them on the kitchen table. They were light and golden. They smelled, surprisingly, even nicer than the cup I'd just evaluated. In fact, this stuff approached *drinkable*. I wouldn't want to slap a label on it and sell it, but I've had worse hard cider come out of a draught tap.

I hadn't hooked up the Erlenmeyer in months—hadn't even thought about it, having focused solidly on the new still—but I ran downstairs to get all the pieces and hurriedly set up my old friend, excited to run these two quarts to see what I got.

Within twenty minutes there was an odd-looking white foam on the top of the wash, like a beer head. Then the steam started to poke through the glass tube that connects the stopper to the beginning of the worm. Condensate surged up the tube and then fell back down into the flask with a drip, leaving a leggy streak of clear alcohol on the glass tube. It was a wonderful sight.

The pipe at the end of the coil makes a wonderful gurgling noise when the liquor is getting ready to flow—moonshiners call this piece of the still the money piece—and I was ecstatic when I heard those first noises of anticipation.

Steam was breaking on the stopper, and alcohol was streaking down the clear glass of the flask. There was alcohol here, and I was about to get it.

Then came my trickle of heads. I was patient. I took the heads off a little at a time, smelling them and throwing them away. When the distillate was pleasant to the nose, I tasted it, and then I started collecting.

Well within an hour, I was done. I sniffed at my catch jar. It certainly wasn't vinegar. I tasted it. It was alcohol. I had about half a pint, and I dropped the hydrometer in it and saw that it was approximately 75 proof—¼ pint per quart, and I had 48 quarts, which meant that I'd get 12 pints, or 6 quarts. That wasn't bad at all. And what's more, it seemed like it was going to be very good. Then I remembered the funky, amoebic masses that had floated in my previous first runs of cider. This was practically applejack already. For a first run, this was the best I'd ever made. How did it happen? What had I done right?

Two tasks lay ahead of me. I was going to have to figure out what had happened in that mudroom to take horrible cider and turn it into something good, and now that I was, in fact, going to distill 12 gallons of hard cider, I was going to have to buckle down and build the still.

The Sugared Sun
Was Shining

I mean it seems he was arrested in Flatbush because he
promised a gentleman that he would bring him some very,
very good scotch and they mistook him for a bootlegger.

—ANITA LOOS, GENTLEMEN PREFER BLONDES

FOR THIRTEEN WEIRD YEARS, THE CONSTITUTION OF THE
United States of America made beverage alcohol illegal.

The population of the United States in 1919 was 104,514,000,
and those folks were serviced by 180,000 licensed saloons and many,
many unlicensed ones. Per capita consumption of alcohol hovered
around 20 gallons a year, and most of that (90 percent, by some
sources) was beer. Whether or not the dries had actually been winning their war against ardent spirits, tastes had been changing with
immigration, transportation, and refrigeration. Whatever we drank,
however, we drank quite a bit. We were, just as we had always been,
tipsy.

David Wondrich wrote about the Eighteenth Amendment and

the Volstead Act in "Prohibition, Repeal, and Beyond" and suggested that "from this distance, banning the sale, manufacture and importation of a commodity without which a very large part of the world had, since time immemorial, concluded that life could not flourish, seems like a rash and vindictive act."

Especially for a nation of drinkers.

There's always the possibility that the sumptuary law was representative of the desires of the constituency. Perhaps the public, or at least the voting majority of it, was really desirous of a more sober nation. When I set out on my research, I assumed I'd find that Jazz Age Prohibition was more isolated than it is made out to be, that lurking behind all those bangled beauties and cigarette holders was a nation like the one that elected Nixon, a silent majority of drab and sober folks who supported the legislation and did not carry flasks or dance the Charleston. I was sure that the colorful front put on by Zelda and Scott was just the shiniest object in the room, and most of America did not spend their time gleefully crashing cars, going to psychiatrists, and drinking martinis.

While vast segments of our society had nothing in common with Robert Benchley and no money for silver hip flasks, it would be foolish to think that they were sober. The scofflaw spirit was not limited to the flashy classes.

Fred George Russ Gordon wrote a rantish pamphlet titled *Prohibition: Its Failure* (or at least he wrote some of it: he seems to have cobbled together a great deal of stuff from newspapers and civic documents and letters and farmer's almanacs and greeting cards).

He included the story of a Prohibition enforcement sweep in downtown New York City. On an unspecified date, 240 agents raided south of 14th and east of the Bowery. "The descent was made simultaneously on the hundred places which had been selected beforehand and for which search warrants had been issued upon the sworn statements of prohibition agents that they had purchased liquor in the various establishments."

The little stores were of all sorts and conditions, but most of them were places where food and beverages are sold regularly, such as restaurants, ice cream and soda parlors and lunch rooms. Frank L. Boyd, supervising agent for the district, his force of 121 men augmented by an equal number of operatives drawn from Boston, Philadelphia, and Baltimore.[sic] They found liquor in 56 places, and arrested fewer than 70 people. Agents who took part in the raids said last night that the law lost out in most of the cases where no arrests were made through the manual dexterity of the store-keepers and their staffs. On the East Side hootch is usually dispensed from coffee pots, well stained with coffee, to make them look natural, and manipulated near sinks or drains so that they can be spilled instantly in case of alarm. It is the general rule on the East Side for him who is selling booze on the sly not to keep more than a coffee pot full on his premises at a time.

These were not the fabled saloons, that den of bad manners and loose morals that was the touchstone of the temperance movement, nor were they fancy speakeasies like the '21' Club with their secret wine caves. These were coffee shops!

When it came to drinking, there was no silent majority of reform-happy teetotalers. Americans of every stripe disregarded the law.

Many folks made their own, and hardware stores stocked copper tubing and mash tuns to help them along. Traveling salesmen drove trucks stocked with 1-to-5-gallon stills. A woman sent a letter to Fred Gordon—he copied the letter into the book—and wrote that she'd seen a man in Vermont selling such stills for $25, and they were going as fast as he could make change.

Other folks turned to prescription drink. Whiskey was still available if prescribed by a doctor. Washington State had gone dry in 1916, and one month later, in Spokane, there were issued 34,000 prescriptions for medicinal liquor—the town had 44,000 registered voters. In Chicago, just after the Volstead Act was signed into law, there were 15,000 applications from doctors desiring to sell medicinal liquor, and 57,000 applications from retail "pharmacies."

The Eighteenth Amendment put many California wineries out of business, although overall grape production increased tenfold in the thirteen years of Prohibition.

Beringer Vineyards made a fortune, and much of that business was due to the very sharp thinking of Bertha Beringer, who had recently married into the family, and owned the vineyard with her husband, Charles. It was Bertha who thought of producing "raisin cakes," which were legal for the production of fruit juices in the home. It was very easy to turn juice made of raisin cakes into wine, and wholesalers worked hard at making everyone understand just how easy it was. Edward Behr, in his excellent book *Prohibition*, wrote that wholesalers would send attractive, well-spoken young women to stores as demonstrators, where they would "draw attention to the wine-making possibilities of their cakes (or 'bricks') while ostensibly warning against fermentation—their straight-faced cautionary patter urging buyers 'not to place the liquid in a jug and put it aside for twenty-one days because it would turn into wine . . . and not to stop the bottle with a cork because this is only necessary if fermentation occurs.' The bricks were sold with a label that read, 'Caution: Will Ferment and Turn into Wine.' "

The well-to-do did not bother with home production, unless out of enthusiasm. The Yale Club is a private club across the street from Grand Central Terminal for alumni of the institution. It was designed by James Gamble Rogers and built on the spot where Nathan Hale, a Yale man and America's first spy, was hanged for espionage against the British. With Prohibition imminent the club laid fourteen years' worth of bottles down in their cellars. It would be leisure as usual there.

Newspapers helped to make sure that the population understood the new laws. The *Daily News* published the following guidelines on January 16:

You may drink intoxicating liquor in your own home or in the home of a friend when you are a bona fide guest.

You may buy intoxicating liquor on a bona fide medical prescription of a doctor. A pint can be bought every ten days.

You may consider any place you live permanently as your home.

If you have more than one home, you may keep a stock of liquor in each.

You may keep liquor in any storage room or club locker, provided the storage space is for the exclusive use of yourself, family, or bona fide friends.

You may get a permit to move liquor when you change your address.

You may manufacture, sell or transport liquor for non-beverage or sacramental purposes provided you obtain a Government permit.

You cannot carry a hip flask.

You cannot give away or receive a bottle of liquor as a gift.

You cannot take liquor to hotels or restaurants and drink it in the public dining rooms.

You cannot buy or sell formulas or recipes for homemade liquors.

You cannot ship liquor for beverage use.

You cannot manufacture anything above one half of one percent (liquor strength) in your home.

You cannot store liquor in any place except your own home.

You cannot display liquor signs or advertisements on your premises.

You cannot remove reserve stocks from storage.

That is not a list aimed at a readership on the wagon.

In 1929, Francis Redfern visited the United States as a representative of John Walker & Sons, and he wrote of his experiences for the *D.C.L. Gazette,* which was published by the Scotch whisky conglomerate Distillers Company Limited. He took the title of his piece from the response given to him by a bookseller when he asked for all the titles in the shop dealing with Prohibition: "Prohibition! why there ain't no sech thing."

Redfern spends much of the article belittling and condescending to Americans and complaining that he has traveled "thousands of miles in the dullest and least inspiring country my eyes have yet beheld." I can't imagine how cranky he would have been had we not managed to keep him in booze, but we more than managed. It seems he almost drowned in the stuff.

Immediately upon disembarking, a friend gave him the name and number of a "thoroughly reliable and respectable" bootlegger. He needn't have bothered. Relaxing before dinner in the lobby of the hotel, Redfern inquired after a parade of "sad-looking individuals arriving and departing, all carrying suitcases." He was informed that they were liquor delivery men. At dinner he befriended the headwaiter. "My needs were modest and promptly supplied. He charged a dollar for each 'Scotch' consumed in the restaurant." (No doubt Redfern would have distrusted the provenance of his "Scotch," and therefore put it in scare quotes, even if the stuff had been smuggled directly from his own employers, which, after all, it probably was— why else would he have made the trip?)

He visited many speakeasies, "from mere drinking dens to palatially appointed private houses where you find whole families, including children, dining together with the utmost decorum, the elders taking wine." Everyone he met sang the praises of the bootlegger, and many of the restaurants at which he dined openly served whiskey. At dinner parties he was amazed by the numbers of cocktails consumed before the meal. In the drugstore of his hotel, he found a "glittering array of hip-pocket flasks and drinkers' sundries of all kinds. What struck me forcibly was the size of the American hip." The bell captains at his hotels delivered to him pints of rye and Scotch. Every chauffeur he engaged claimed to have run liquor, and got some for him. He recounted the story of a friend of his who was stopped by Prohibition officers and had his liquor seized. In court the next morning when called upon to produce the evidence, the officers could not comply. They'd drunk it. He met a surveyor who complained that he'd had to install a new drainage system in the town to handle the refuse of the citizens engaged in home brewing. On the transatlantic crossing homeward, he conversed with an American Catholic priest who said, "My country is just mad on this subject of drink and I have felt it my bounden duty as a priest to teach my flock how to make good honest liquor."

Yes, even the priests.

Elaine Davis wrote in *Minnesota 13,* her book about the booming prohibition era moonshine industry in Stearns County, Minnesota, that many of the clergy there had come from countries "where distilling and brewing was a source of great monastic pride and tradition." These priests made sure that their congregations understood that while it was illegal to make alcohol, it was not morally wrong. They preached that those caught should pay their fines but know that moonshiners had no trouble with God.

Davis, in her research, had the National Archives at Kansas City compile a list of Minnesotans who got locked up at Leavenworth. There were 479 of them.

George Kennan, the explorer, in a letter dated November 2, 1923, wrote:

There is more drunkenness here in Medina [Minn.] now than there was when we had 12 or 15 open saloons. Four families out of five make alcoholic drinks, of one sort or another, in their homes, and an immense amount of liquor is smuggled across the lake from Canada. There are so many intoxicated automobile drivers that I don't feel safe even in going from here to Albion, a distance of 12 miles.

The Jazz Age should not be denied—flappers danced with hip flasks tucked into their garters, there is no doubt—but neither is it the whole story. Our nation's noble experiment in sumptuary law was met with national disregard.

Henry Cabot Lodge, speaking on the floor of the U.S. Senate said: "Where large masses of the people would consider it even meritorious—at least quite menial—to evade and break the law, the law would inevitably be broken constantly and in a large and effective way." What's more, once a single law is disregarded, the law in general is called into question. The instant creation of a huge class of criminals is not without consequence, and the national nullification of Prohibition led to a reckless season of general lawlessness.

Herbert Asbury wrote the cornerstone book on Prohibition, titled *The Great Illusion*, and in the biographical note, he included a remarkable hedge: "It must be remembered," he wrote, "that the fourteen years from 1920 to 1934 were not only the era of unparalleled crime and corruption; they were also the era of the Big Lie." The capitalization is Asbury's. He continued: "The drys lied to make prohibition look good; the wets lied to make it look bad; the government officials lied to make themselves look good and to frighten Congress into giving them more money to spend; and the politicians lied through force of habit."

Sometimes it seems as if every bit of information one receives about Prohibition is tainted, slanted, biased, and organized toward a goal. There is, however, at least one underexplored source, honest about Prohibition because alcohol was not the focus.

In 1896, New York State passed the Raines Law, which restricted the sale of alcohol on Sundays, with a crucial loophole: hotels could serve drinks. Every saloonkeeper in town must have scratched his head, rocked back on his heels, and wondered how much the apartment upstairs might cost. Raines Law "hotels" were soon common, but saloons had little legitimate use for the rooms. Like butterflies to a sweet-smelling bloom, the Raines beds were soon filled with prostitutes.

In 1905, a group of mostly well-to-do and right-living citizens founded the Committee of Fourteen with the purpose of cleaning up these establishments. The Committee sent investigators to the hotels, and lobbied in Albany.

They entered into a complicated system of allegiance with the Brewers Association. On the face of it, the interests of these two groups would seem to conflict, but the brewers feared that if the hotels were not cleaned up, public opinion would shift and New York would go dry. Brewers had an enormous amount of influence over the saloons. Mara L. Keire, in her essay about the Committee ("The Committee of Fourteen and Saloon Reform in New York City, 1905–1920," *Business and Economic History*, Volume 26), wrote that "New York was a high license state which meant that the economics of alcohol distribution gave brewers tremendous power over saloon proprietors." The licenses and bond cost $3,000, and because most saloons couldn't make that cost themselves, they became "tied shops." Not only did they buy all their beer from one brewery, but the brewery often owned the building. The saloon put all of its fixtures into hock with the brewery, and the brewery would often front the money for all the fees and license costs, for which the saloonkeeper would also sign over power of attorney.

Together the Brewers Association and the Fourteen set about deciding who got licenses and who didn't. They compiled blacklists and put saloons on probation. In 1907 they further expanded their influence by arguing in the Supreme Court of New York that the Excise Department "was not primarily a revenue gathering department, but also had police powers."*

By 1911 most of the "hotels" were closed.

The Fourteen, however, continued to monitor and suppress prostitution and vice in the city. The Committee's investigators worked hard. They roamed the streets at all hours of the night, visiting speakeasies and bars and saloons and hotels and apartments and having adventures. They also wrote good reports.

One investigator, S.T.† makes the narrators of Dashiell Hammett's stories seem mousy. His style was tough and telegraphic. Hemingway would have loved it.

---

* A precedent that was useful a little over a decade later, when the lines between the revenue men and the police would blur.

† All the names and initials have been changed or redacted from the following transcripts, save one.

N.E. Cor. 53rd St. & Park Avenue

S.T., March 21st 1923

About 11.10 P.M. I covered above said house and visited at
same time Kinvara's Cafe located at 381 Park Avenue. Found in
there only five men in a bar room and two men in a rear room.
All appeared to be from neighborhood. Nothing disorderly was
observed, all behaved. Left this place about 1.00 A.M.

Although it is 1923, S.T. doesn't seem to have a problem with
drinking—or with settling into a place to really make sure it was on
the up and up. He will throw liquor violations into the mix as color,
and to further discredit an establishment, but he will just as frequently mention that drinks were served in his rundown of a place he
is describing favorably. Such as this report:

MCGINLEYS SALOON

1115 Lexington Avenue

S.E. Corner 78th Str. & Lex. Ave.

From 8.30–10.30 P.M. I covered above said saloon. In bar room I
found about fifteen men, among them chauffeurs and taxi drivers.
All behaved. In rear room were two couples, both appeared to be
intoxicated and at same time none of them acted rough.

Nothing disorderly was observed. Liquor was served only
to people who were known. No unaccompanied men were
permitted in back room or served there. No hang out of
suspicious characters was observed.

According I was told this place was known before as Kirks Cafe
and conducted by a man name _____ ___.

Neighborhood is very clean and quiet. No prostitutes were seen
hustling or soliciting men. According my observation this saloon
is conducted better than any other in the vicinity. Some men

who were here are old timers in the neighborhood and like to sit down for a few hours and kill time by drinking, smoking or chewing tobacco, or talk about various things. I got in touch with a few men who are well acquainted in here, among them a shoemaker from Third Avenue and tried to obtain information regarding conditions in this place and whether they couldn't give me any leads. But they knew less than I knew and acted as if they were not interested in women or anything that concerned prostitution.

S.T.

The insights he gains are remarkable, for S.T. has a way with people, it is clear.

While dining at the St. Regis restaurant, he managed to coax a confession from his waiter: "While I was talking to him, he told me, that he was making his own whiskey at his house, but it isn't as perfect as the real. He claimed, that he and his friends drank of it some time ago and they got sick." So S. T. tells him to be sure to "use white copper inside."

His reports are not written for the public; he's a detective recording the real life of the city. At times, his prejudices offend (or at least surprise) the modern reader: "We went to pick up prostitutes in vicinity, but it started to rain and we gave it up and followed fairies in Central Park, the result was that [Officer] Ryan made two arrests." Or from another report: "We tried to pick up a few Chinamen in here who shall lead us to white girls. But they wouldn't fall for us. We also got in conversation in here with a sailor from U.S.S. *Oklahoma*, who just arrived from San Diago [*sic*]. He told us about wild life here and liquor, that anybody could get. He had with him four quarts of whiskey and was willing to drink it with us providing we'll show him the town and take him along to every place we'll go tonight. We adviced him to go home and rest."

He visits a saloon on Sixth Avenue:

First I asked bartender (short, Italian) who was behind bar at that time to give me whiskey, he refused claiming that only beer I could get or soft drinks. At same time I noticed, that other men got liquor at the bar and asked him why other do get and I cannot get any. He said, that he don't know me and must be very careful now days. I told him, that I arrived only a few days ago from Montreal and was surprised to see New York "dead." After I convinced him with my membership card of the Canadian Oriental Club, I gained his confidence and obtained liquor. I really don't know what he gaved me, by according taste it appeared to be a very strong liquor and could burn easy somebodys throat if not used to drink. In fact my throat was affected and felt bad when came home. Bartender told me, that it is Rum. It was filled in bottles from ginger ale. Price for a drink 50 cents.

He investigates every type of place, and although his grammar is often strange, he is capable of flights of poetry that would make Hubert Selby proud: "The greater majority of these women and girls appeared to be of immoral character and the unaccompanied men were sports, men of good appearance, cheap sports, rounders, and track gamblers."

S.T. understood the value of deep cover, and often went very far in his pursuit of vice. He visited hotels, restaurants, speakeasies, dance halls, dives uptown and down. Some of them sound fantastic: "Duke Ellington and his colored orchestra furnished the dance music and the Cotton Club Revue entertained at 10 o'clock. The place was crowded, mostly by a cheap young element. . . . Most of the men appeared to be Spanish or Italian. Some of them had liquor in their possession which they drank in the Gents room, or at tables while in company of hostesses. Some of the hostesses were dancing indecently."

The Committee compiled a document titled "A Report of Speakeasies on Numbered Streets." Some of the entries stretch out to two or three paragraphs (if there are lots of whores), but most are short and to the point. On 56th Street, "Investigator was brought here early in the evening by a prostitute-hostess employed at the Back Stage Club, 110 West 56th Street, prior to going to her own club. The place is located one flight up, over a garage, with entrance through a hallway, the door of which is guarded by a lookout. On the second floor there is a peep-hole in the door where visitors are again carefully scrutinized before being admitted. Inside is a 40 foot bar, made entirely of glass, containing water filled with gold fish. All types of drink are sold and the place was very elaborately furnished."

What's most surprising about the "Speakeasies on Numbered Streets" document is its size. It's 120 pages long. Some of those pages list a dozen joints.

The drys, having achieved the reform for which they'd fought so mightily, expected the 1920s to be the dawn of a new age, a tranquil era of hopeful sobriety in which all would find God, wealth, and happiness. They had looked out on the multitudes and imagined them transformed—urchins into freshly scrubbed, fat-cheeked, well-meaning boys; violent drunks into trustworthy, clear-eyed, and industrious men; women who had been widowed by the saloon would find themselves at the helm of a pacific domesticity, with chickens in their pots and clean, good clothes for everyone. The trumpets of the angels would blow a fanfare, the Pearly Gates would swing open, and light would fill the air.

What they got was something else entirely. Bootleggers and rumrunners took to the seas, and the beaches were awash with foreign spirits. The police, the politicians, and jurists were corrupted seemingly overnight, transformed into a venal network of crooked scoundrels. Restaurateurs drew the blinds, invented a password, and asked that everyone speak easy, so as not to draw the attention of the one or two cops in town who had not been paid off.

Robert Lacey, in his biography of Meyer Lansky titled *Little Man*, wrote that Prohibition was the real turning point for Lansky. It turned him into a full-time gangster, "and it offered the same career to hundreds of others." With all the legal breweries, distilleries, and importers criminalized and shut down, the industry was handed over to the lawless. The business of liquor continued, and now that it was illegal, there was suddenly a "vast and lively pool of wealth to tempt police, magistrates, and public officials."

Meyer Lansky gave an interview to Uri Dan in 1971 in which he discussed the liquor business: "To cut costs and increase efficiency, we chartered our own ships to bring the Scotch across the Atlantic . . . I must say in all modesty that we ran things well . . . By the middle twenties we were running the most efficient international shipping business in the world."

Al Capone, Dutch Schultz—the big gangster names—all of them started in Prohibition, and as Al Capone famously said, they were like public servants. Capone told the papers: "All I do is satisfy a public demand."

Herbert Asbury wrote that industrial alcohol plants produced about a hundred million gallons of alcohol every year during Prohibition to make paint, varnish, and antifreeze. This alcohol was denatured—a nice, bureaucratic, word for poisoned—and was undrinkable. Folks drank it anyway, and they went blind or died.

The Coast Guard estimated that close to four hundred ships were running rum. There were areas of the sea that operated like wholesale markets. You drove your boat out, and there they were, the rum ships, ready to fill you up and send you back to the coast.

Beer posed a special series of problems and opportunities. Permits were issued to make "near beer" by the government, beer that would have an insignificant alcohol content. To make near beer you had to make real beer first, and then remove the alcohol and ship it to the government, where it would be poisoned and stored in warehouses. Naturally, bootleggers would pay you more for the excess alcohol than the government would, just as they would pay you still more for a keg of beer that hadn't had the alcohol removed from it. So real beer went out in near beer kegs, and near beer went out with surreptitious shipments of supplementary alcohol that could be added to the brew in the barroom to create "needle beer."

Rounding out the picture: the moonshiners. The government seized 696,993 stills during the years between 1921 and 1925. When General Lincoln C. Andrews appeared to present at a congressional committee in 1926, he estimated that 500,000 people were engaged in moonshining, and that for every one of the 696,993 stills they'd found, nine were not located.

In May of 1929, President Hoover appointed George W. Wickersham to head the National Committee on Law Observation and Enforcement. It was the first reflexive national study of policing. The Wickersham committee produced a strange, gigantic report, summed up rather neatly as follows: "The Eighteenth Amendment represents the first effort in our history to extend directly by Constitutional provision the police control of the federal government to the personal habits and conduct of the individual. It was an experiment, the extent and difficulty of which was probably not appreciated."

Booze was everywhere, they said. Prohibition was a failure. They did not, however, call for its repeal, but rather for heavier enforcement.

In the fourth volume of addendums to the report, there is a section titled "Survey of Prohibition Enforcement in Virginia." Frederick C. Dezendorf had come to Virginia for a couple of weeks and interviewed various officials. He surmised that "in one County (Franklin) it is claimed 99 people out of 100 are making, or have some connection with, illicit liquor." He'd interviewed, among others, N. C. Alexander, who remembered the conversation as follows:

DEZENDORF: What about Franklin County?
ALEXANDER: Mr. Dezendorf, there are 30,000 people in
    Franklin County, and 29,999 of them are mixed up directly or
    indirectly in the whiskey business.

He later claimed that he'd been exaggerating.

Thomas Keister Greer authored a doorstopper of a book titled *The Great Moonshine Conspiracy Trial of 1935* (and so many of my facts about this trial and the conspiracy come from this book that it is best assumed that they *all* did, unless otherwise noted), and he wrote, in regard to what happened next, that "it was not to be supposed that the Government, being now on notice that a county was depriving it of revenues, would take no action."

Took action they did, and they soon discovered not only that Franklin County was cranking out the booze, but that the folks making it were under the protection, if not downright organized by, those charged with policing the illegal hooch. A grand jury was convened, and on February 9, 1935, the *Richmond Times-Dispatch* reported its return.

> Findings of a Federal Grand Jury at Harrisonburg give color to rumors which have been circulated for several years with respect to large liquor operations in Franklin County. The report constitutes one of the most sensational developments in the recent history of Virginia. Official action now has placed the county before the world in light of a community in which the liquor laws might be violated with impunity and under the protection of those who were sworn to uphold these laws.

It was, indeed, a sensational indictment. Thirty-four individuals were charged, along with one corporation. Fifty-five coconspirators were named, and not charged. Greer wrote that the indictment was twenty-two pages long "and included the political and bootlegging elite of Franklin County. The first was Charles Carter Lee, Commonwealth's attorney, grandson of General Robert E. Lee's brother and great-grandson of Light-Horse Harry Lee." The indictment named a former sheriff, four deputies, a former state prohibition officer, and an agent of the Alcohol Tax Unit. Eleven of the indicted pleaded guilty or nolo contendere (which amounts, basically, to saying that you are very, very sorry, and although you are not exactly willing to say that you did it, you don't want to argue about it and you promise it will never happen again).

The indictment spawned the longest jury trial in the history of Virginia.

The government's opening argument encapsulated the conspiracy elegantly.

This conspiracy began in the fall of 1928, when Sherriff Hodges and his deputies, along with State Prohibition Officer Beckett, agreed to divide Franklin County into districts. D. Wilson Hodges succeeded his father in this conspiracy, and Carter Lee directed activities from the sheriff's office. There was an elaborate "tip off" system, using telephones and other means to warn distillers before raids. The moonshiners were able to know Government agents' activities through the contacts made by Samuel O. White, the defendant who was himself a federal agent.

All the defendants—all of them except Carter Lee, that is—were found guilty. Reading through the trial, what struck me was the familiarity of so many of the names. People in Franklin County tend to stay put. Throughout, the family names of the area are rife: the Bondurants, the Shivelys. On the defense there was a Davis and, on the witness stand, an unindicted coconspirator named Gray Stanley—just as if it were 1969 or 1996. I thought of Jimmy Beheler. When Bobby Joe had bribed him, or attempted to, in the liquor store, Beheler told me that what struck him most was the ease with which it was done, the familiarity.

"You don't do a thing like that because you've never done it before."

The moonshiners of Franklin County had been doing it forever.

Greer wrote that "the corruption, the bending of laws, the unholy combinations of officers and bootleggers, point to the endless proclivity of the human animal for mischief." He goes on to make a case that the poverty of the South in the first decades of the twentieth century exacerbated the will to mischief, but I think it's clear that the years of Prohibition brought out the reprobate in everyone across the nation.

Wondrich wrote that, by way of trying to explain the root cause of prohibition, that "it's safe to say that, to a large degree, it wasn't about the alcohol; it was about the 'sporting life'; that rowdy, anti-domestic lifestyle that centered in the saloon."

I suspect he got very close to the truth, but I don't think he's hit the nail. The first section of the amendment read: "After one year from the ratification of this article the *manufacture, sale,* or *transportation* of intoxicating liquors within, the importation thereof into, or the exportation thereof from the United States and all territory subject to the jurisdiction thereof for beverage purposes is hereby prohibited." (The italics are mine.)

It is assumed that Prohibition was first and foremost enacted to reform people. The amendment itself criminalizes not individuals, but rather an industry.

There was no silent majority. Volstead's constituency felt betrayed by him and couldn't believe that their own senator could have authored the bill.

It should come as no surprise that governments attempt to enact social change by litigation—that's been the plan since the first city on the hill. Less obvious, however, is that the desired change and the stated change don't necessarily marry. Examining the plain facts of the history, rather than the advertised goals, it seems to me that there is something disingenuous about Prohibition.

The business of alcohol had given the government nothing but trouble. It had dogged all attempts at reform, tempted officials into corruption, and cheated the government out of huge amounts of money. It was run by a hodgepodge collection of farmers and foreigners. How can you force some German who bought a beaten copper kettle, hung a shingle, and started making beer to pay up? How can you regulate the gooseneck stills steaming away behind the barns in the middle of nowhere?

In the early 1800s there were about 14,000 distilleries across the nation—2,000 of them were in Kentucky, 3,594 of them were in Pennsylvania, and together those states produced 8.2 million gallons of liquor each year. The business of distilling followed the course of the nation, and naturally consolidated through the nineteenth century. By 1881, Pennsylvania had only 110 distilleries and Kentucky had 140.

By 1909 there were 613 distilleries nationwide. The slip continued and just ten years later, as the Volstead Act was ratified, there were 507.

Twenty years ago there were perhaps a dozen.*

The Volstead Act was the death knell for small-scale distillers. Five hundred distilleries may not sound like a lot, and compared to 14,000, it isn't. Whiskey production had consolidated, but it was still a local product, made by small interests in hundreds of jurisdictions—a difficult industry to track.

The most obvious long-term consequence of Prohibition was that most of the distilleries (breweries and a huge chunk of wineries, too) were criminalized and shut down. The second, less obvious consequence was that when it was over the federal government had seized control of the production of alcohol, and has regulated that production ever since.

Consider this extract from a press release issued by the ATF on July 1, 2002:

> The Twenty-first Amendment to the Constitution, repealing Prohibition, achieved ratification with unanticipated speed by 5 December 1933, catching Congress in recess. As an interim measure to manage a burgeoning legitimate alcohol industry, by executive order under the National Industrial Recovery Act, President Franklin Roosevelt established the Federal Alcohol Control Administration (FACA). The FACA, in cooperation with the Departments of Agriculture and Treasury, endeavored to guide wineries and distilleries under a system based on brewers' voluntary codes of fair competition. The FACA was relieved of its burden—and effectively vanished from history—after just twenty months, when President Roosevelt in August 1935 signed the Federal Alcohol Administration (FAA) Act. The new FAA received a

---

* Most of the bottles on the shelves at the liquor store are distilled by a handful of companies, each with many labels. In the last two decades changes in licensing have begun to allow microdistilling and the number of small distilleries is on the rise.

firm departmental assignment: Treasury once more found itself regulating the alcohol industry.

Although Prohibition was officially over, the era's side effects continued for decades to mold the shape of ATF. On 10 March 1934 Justice's Prohibition enforcement duties folded into the infant Alcohol Tax Unit (ATU), Bureau of Internal Revenue, Department of the Treasury. At the same time, the FAA, functioning independently within Treasury, was carrying forward its mandate to collect data, to establish license and permit requirements, and define the regulations that ensure an open, fair marketplace for the alcohol industry and the consumer. In 1940 the FAA as an Administration merged with the ATU. The FAA Act continues today as one foundation of ATF's enabling legislation.

It's a great trick, of course, throwing us the gift of drink. The feds had been the enforcers, and now they were the regulating body assuring an open and fair market for beverages.

Is it possible that the true intent of a system of reform would be so far from its stated goal? It was certainly true in the South, where early prohibition was supported not because of a sense of moral purpose, but because the revenue men who collected the taxes and controlled the industry were federal, and the South didn't want to give money to the Union. Therefore, the southern politicians and their constituency supported dry laws. As Will Rogers said: "The South is dry and will vote dry. That is, everybody sober enough to stagger to the polls will."

With only the historical progression of what actually happened, what legislation was ratified and what agencies created, without the rhetoric of the reformers clouding around us, it seems that the main result of Prohibition—whether that result was gained willfully or accidentally—was to destroy a liquor trade that could not be controlled and replace it with one that could be. Since that result is so in line with the historical goals of the federal government, it seems barely a stretch at all to suggest that perhaps that was the real ambition of Prohibition.

Skillet's Place

If you drink much from a bottle marked "poison," it is almost
certain to disagree with you, sooner or later.

—LEWIS CARROLL, ALICE IN WONDERLAND

BLUESMAN JOHNNY SHINES USED TO PLAY JUKE JOINTS IN
the thirties, before he moved to Chicago. In an interview quoted in
the biography of Howlin' Wolf titled *Moanin' at Midnight,* Shines
relates that whiskey distiller Will Weillers ran a joint in his house.
He would "take his beds and things down and they'd dance in one
room and shoot dice in the other one. He didn't charge admission to
them; this was free. The thing was to get the womens there to get the
mens there so they'd gamble. And he'd cut the game, get his money
that way. Sell whiskey, too. Because he had to pay the men for playing [music], he charged a nickel more on a half-pint of whiskey; he
charged 35 cents for a half-pint of whiskey. This was 'first-made' whiskey, that's what I call it: tom-cat whiskey. It wasn't bonded liquor."

Is this where I thought I was headed? It's a short trip from juke
joint to nip joint, after all: black folks drinking bootleg in a converted
house.

In the written history of moonshine, the focus is squarely on the production side of things: The lore of the mountain still, the ever-present bib overalls, the fast cars, and the double-barreled shotgun. In *Thunder Road* we see them make it, and we see them work on the cars. Mitchum drives it to Memphis, and we see it unloaded. We never see anything about anybody drinking it. We never see the retail customer.

There's a client at the end of the run, always, and his story is underexplored. People make liquor because people buy liquor—a simple equation.

Who buys it and why? Where do they drink it? What's the matter with all the cheap vodka and bottom-shelf bourbon at the liquor store? Moonshine costs about $30 a gallon, retail, so does Old Crow, a more than passable bourbon.

Most moonshine is drunk by African-Americans in unlicensed bars called nip joints or shot houses. There is moonshine at stock car races, and bluegrass jams, and all the cliché places you'd think it would turn up, but those people consume a drop in the bucket. Shot houses and nip joints, famously prevalent in Philadelphia, hit the newswires in stories about being busted from New Jersey to Texas and from the East Coast into Tennessee and Kentucky, and these illicit watering holes conduct the bulk of the moonshine trade.

In some small cities, like Danville, Virginia, you could bar-hop nip joints as recently as the eighties. In some neighborhoods there was one on every block; there were entire blocks that were *nothing but* nip joints. Although not as prevalent as they once were, unlicensed watering holes remain a big part of life in Danville, and elsewhere.

I traveled to the Virginia town, right on the North Carolina border, about half a dozen times. I interviewed lots of people, followed leads, talked to strangers, ate barbecue, and drove around looking for something. The town is a dot in the middle of moonshine country, a poor city surrounded by farmland and whiskey stills.

In my cinematic imagination I pictured a dusty room out in a field of sugarcane and sunflowers and tall, proud women in flowing, colorful fabrics, their skirts brushing up against the wooden paneling as they spun and twirled through the night. Lots of smoke but also the smells of fried fish, bay rum, and shoe leather. Everyone sipping out of flasks, glass jugs, pint Mason jars. Folks would be dancing half bent over, joyous, immersed in rhythm. Others would be throwing dice and wearing their hats indoors.

God yes, I was ready. Give me a room full of all the things that make Saturday night a good reason for Sunday morning and put me in the corner with a notebook. I'd be just like an old-time musicologist, one of the famed field collectors haunting the wrong side of the tracks with a recording machine in the Studebaker. It'd be a great adventure. I'd watch and tap my feet, sipping slowly on a half-pint of my own. My notes getting less and less legible, less and less coherent, until I'd volley one last blast of free-associative bebop scribblings and pocket my Moleskine notebook, straighten up, start buying people drinks and listening between songs for the first chirps of the birds.

That Max, they'd all say, he's alright.

Something about the nip joint had me in its clutches. Some ridiculous combination of nostalgia for the South—and especially Southern Black culture—and my obsession with corn squeezings had me duped. In my head, it was 1935.

It's not that I thought they'd be safe. I knew this was rough territory and that it always had been. People die in joints like this. No one stops the fight in a bar that doesn't legally exist—the cops don't rush in seven seconds after the first barstool is overturned. If there's a bouncer, he's there to protect the place, not you. But that just means you have to stay out of trouble.

Albert King once told of a place he saw Howlin' Wolf play: "One night I walked in there. Wolf was howlin'. Guys were gamblin'. Some guy was on the floor and they had their feet on top of him. I said, 'What you got your feet on top of that man for?' They said, 'Oh, he dead.' "

I figured that maybe, late, a razor fight would break out. It would be something that would happen in the other corner of the room, no concern of mine at all.

They're rough places, but rough places don't bother me.

I used to work in a bar in Richmond, Virginia, that had a friendly patina—lots of professors ate lunch there, many youngsters wasted their time with coffee and cigarettes—and a darker truth. The aluminum transom above the front door was pocked with bullet holes. The place was bristling with knives and guns, and a substantial portion of the clientele was made up of weird hustlers (like the rough-trade queen who drove a tow truck around town lifting up people's cars and waiting for them to rush out and bribe him to lower the wheels back to the asphalt) and crackheads. I'd seen fights escalate so fast no one had even noticed them until someone was covered in blood. I'd seen undercover cops come out of the woodwork with their guns drawn, and I'd been thankful they were there to save a friend from the business end of a broken bottle. One night a Hispanic man in a silky black shirt passed out in the bathroom while he was taking a shit and fell to the floor with his pants around his ankles. He was fast asleep, with his pomaded mullet resting calmly against the wall on the urine-spattered and butt-littered bathroom floor. I grabbed the dishwasher and tore a friend away from his bourbon and ginger because I knew that friend always had a gun tucked into his pants. Together we walked to the john and I poked the guy on the floor with a broomstick. He ignored me. A waiter got a pitcher of water and threw it at the man on the ground. He leapt to his feet, pulled up his trousers with one hand and pulled a knife with the other. It was a hunting knife with a shiny, slightly curved blade, and he slashed it through the air, wild-eyed, screaming in Spanish. We took a step back and he dashed out the back door.

I can handle the shit. Mind the rules: Leave early. Keep smiling. Don't gamble (and if you do, by god, don't win).

This is all baloney and I know it. Rules are the lies the lucky tell themselves after the dust clears. I'm writing it here to illustrate not the height of my savvy street sense, but the depth of delusion to which I'd sunk.

I'm not stupid. I do, however, have a vivid imagination, and I had a hard time stopping the movie reel in my head.

"Oh, the White Boy is here! Go get that old guitar and I'll set everybody up with some drinks."

. People would filter in. The joint would get to jumping . . . my reverie was, of course, interrupted by reality.

These aren't public places. These aren't parties. These aren't bars, as we think of them, or clubs. They are decrepit, falling-apart shacks in troubled neighborhoods, peopled with patrons who have known one another their whole lives, and who have sat next to one another on these sagging couches for good portions of those lives. There's no blues in these places. There's no dancing. There's $5 a game on checkers, side bets welcome. There's women: a fine mix of old drunks and young crack whores.

There would be no welcoming smile. No quick explanation offered awkwardly by my tour guide ("That's just Max, he's cool; he's writing a book") after which we would shake hands and I'd buy everybody drinks and we'd be off to the races. No.

They didn't want me. It wouldn't matter if I could make a joke or hold my liquor. The more I learned about nip joints, the more I saw that the gap was unbridgeable.

The best-case scenario, I realized, was that I would walk in and everything would stop. All would be denied. They'd just sit and stare at me until I left. There were plenty of worse scenarios—a laundry list of misadventures.

For while a decade of prosperity and rising property values burred the rough edges off of much of the nation (and softened my old mean streets in places like Richmond), one cannot assume that gentrification is universal. The major markets for moonshine are those pockets of the nation that live in what seems to be a permanent decline—a slump without a peak. The good times are so distant they might as well be fiction.

The recently built neighborhoods of Danville are pale imitations of what happened in the rest of the country during the turn-of-the-century real estate boom. They are a vast improvement on the shanty-town housing stock that dominates the worst blocks of the city, but while the rest of the nation built five-bedroom houses with media rooms and granite countertops, the people of Danville built grids of small, single-story ranchers on square lots.

Danville is shackled by limited opportunity, isolation, and bad luck.

Markets for cheap intoxicants flourish in places like this.

Liquor wasn't legally sold by the glass in Danville until 1982;* a classic sumptuary law that attempts to keep poor people from spending their money on booze. People with $7 in their pocket, it is thought, will spend some of it on a cheap drink if they can get one, and they'll buy food for their family if they can't.

Top-down regulation of our inebriate ways doesn't work, and the fact of the matter is that people with just a little bit of money will find a drink. If licenses are not available, the places they go to drink will be unlicensed.

If licenses are available, the types of places that have them aren't necessarily the types of places people with just a little bit of pocket money would go for lubrication.

I'm fond of the bar at the Danville outlet of the Texas Steakhouse & Saloon chain of restaurants; there's a frosty tray that runs along the inside of the horseshoe, and you set your mug upon it to keep your beer fantastically cold. Brilliant stuff. As I wedged my tall Yuengling back into the hoary surface, I wondered what percentage of my tab covered the cost of running a refrigerator coil down the entire length of the bar.

It's hard to run a dive bar in Virginia. To have a liquor license in the state, the establishment must serve food, and while there are some bars in the cities where the priorities are clear and the chicken wings are cheap, in Danville, as I drove around town, it seemed that if you wanted a cold glass of beer you were going to pay three or four dollars for it at a family restaurant like Applebee's.

---

* In some of the communities nearby, drinks might as well not be legal, for no one bothers to sell them legally.

For a large segment of the local drinking population, drinking at Applebee's is not a legitimate option, and that's not only because you cannot gamble or light a joint while you nibble on your mozzarella sticks.

Family restaurants close early, last call can come as soon as 10 P.M. You cannot get drunk. Applebee's will cut you off; in fact, they seem downright eager to end your beverage service.

More subtly, family restaurants employ the same autodiscriminatory policy as their distant cousins at the high end of the food chain. Just as you're expected to wear suitable clothes to the '21' Club, at Applebee's you're expected to be dressed like everyone else. Surely blue jeans are passable in every mall and every chain restaurant in America, but there is an agreed-upon level of sartorial cleanliness. You wouldn't feel right sidling up to the bar in a torn t-shirt that you bought at a thrift store and your working day shoes any more than the man in an ill-fitting blazer and cheap khakis feels at home among the swells in the Palm Court at the Plaza Hotel.

A drinker in an old t-shirt with seven bucks in his pocket can go to a nip joint and buy a baby-food jar full of bootleg corn for a dollar. Someone there will have recently mown a lawn, or won a lottery scratcher, and have another dollar to buy him a drink. He can sit with folks he knows, and they can cuss and laugh and he'll buy another jar and now he's got 9 ounces of 100-proof sugar jack in him. He's spent $2.

I'd learned that the house at 327 Westridge Street* in Danville, Virginia, had been a nip joint. It may be still, although it didn't look very lively.

Nestled between rotting houses with plywood over their windows, 327 had grimy white clapboard and a red, corrugated metal roof that had bucked, exposing rotting beams underneath. The door was blue, and a red bedsheet functioned as a blind across the grimy window.

---

* This is a fake address.

The porch was an extension of the concrete slab of the foundation, and went 4 or 5 feet beyond the threshold. A random collection of posts held the roof up—one of them a pressure-treated four-by-four, one a turned and lathed column; another was a formerly straight whitewashed post with chipping paint. A length of heavy, rusty chain was strung along the porch beneath the two-by-four railing, like the side of a tugboat. Up against the porch railing, a barbell rested on a homemade weight bench skirted with plywood that had been painted in swirling red and green pseudo-African patterns; next to the bench were three chairs. The one in the middle was covered with the sort of floral wallpaper found inside a cupboard, and was cocked and leaning against its neighbor as if a drunk had fallen asleep on it, leaned out for support, and vanished into thin air. A roll of chain-link fencing was wound loosely around a fence post in the yard (what purpose it ever could have served was not at all clear), and the weedy grass grew in tufts of scrub around a couple of cinder blocks and a wrecked Honda scooter, leaning on its kickstand. The proprietor used to deliver moonshine on the Honda, before it broke.

I'm not sure I'd have entered 327 even if you could have guaranteed me it was empty.

This neighborhood was serious. One night I'd seen three crack deals go down on the same block in the amount of time it took me to drive from one end to the other. Desperate women walked the streets, looking hopefully at the car or pretending they didn't see it.

I went on a drive-along with Jesse Tate, ABC agent, and Randall Toney, from the Illegal Whiskey Task Force. Jesse nosed the car into a driveway at the end of a cul-de-sac. The house had bars on the windows and the door had a heavy gate. In the large yard was a lighted sign, the kind that would advertise cheap soda in the parking lot of a gas station. It read DIRTY SOUTH HORSESHOE CENTER AND SOCIAL CLUB. We blasted our headlights onto the small stoop where three or four thuggish-looking black men slouched and smoked.

Jesse thought the place had been closed for good when he busted it in 2006. Randall laughed from the back seat: "Damn, guess you better come back around to this one, huh?"

Back in 2006, Jesse had brought a camera with him, and he sent me the photos, which showed a slapped-together series of rooms. One room had been painted bright green, with a tropical motif stencil at the height of the chair rail. Another room was painted black. There were strips of mirrors as decorations, and a Radio Shack disco light nailed to the ceiling. Many of the photos document the fact that the place was running as a business: a cash drawer (three crumpled bills in it), a sign on a door that says EMPLOYEES ONLY, a few of the cards that Roger Coleman gave to members. The cards are decorated with two horseshoes, and the text reads: "Danville Horse Shoe Club, Members and Private Guest Only." At the bottom is the address and the owner's name.

In the kitchen the refrigerator was full of beer (mostly Miller), mixers, and a jar of mayonnaise. There were bottles of Seagram's gin, bottles of brandy, and coolers full of still more beer. The kitchen counter was crowded with cups and receipts (some of which seemed to indicate the sale of cigarettes, which can't have endeared Roger to the licensing agents).

There are PA speakers throughout the place, and black lights, and barstools. There was a room off to the side with a couple of café tables—the chill party room, lit less dramatically.

All of the furniture looked like it was bought at the Salvation Army store, and all of the painting and carpentry (the bar, the brackets that held the speakers to the wall) looked as if it had been done in a hurry by drunk people.

The cops found rocks of crack hidden in the trash can.

It wasn't anywhere I wanted to go. Still, I circled the flame, trying.

●　●　●

I was introduced to a fifty-year-old black man I'll call Skillet.

Skillet grew up in the country and has been a paratrooper, a numbers runner, a crackhead, and a marijuana dealer. Somewhere along the line (after losing his good brick house, his wife, and the company of his two children) he got himself together. He's got a job.

He says his rough times are behind him. I believe him. He agreed to navigate a tour of the town if I drove (he doesn't have a license). That first night, when he asked me to pull into a deserted lot so he could take a piss, I thought I was done. I figured the whole thing was a setup, and I was about to get my car stolen. I was wrong. Skillet, it turned out, was a good guy. During the course of my visits to Danville, he and I became friends. He'd show me around the town, we'd go out to dinner, we'd drink beer together. All the while he'd be narrating the local history of insurance scams, arson, drug dealers, and numbers runners. We talked a lot about moonshine. As a resource, he was invaluable—if you want to know who drinks moonshine, where they do it, and why, he's your man.

I kept asking him if nip joints were a good time. Do people play cards or something? Are people having fun? Finally, he shook his head, sighed, and said: "Lemme tell you something, Max, I'm gonna tell you how it is, this is the for-real for real. Black people can't have fun. Eventually, somebody gets fucked up, somebody gets uptight, and somebody fucks up."

His parents ran a nip joint in the house where he was born.

"There was always people there. We had a record player. It was fun. People dancing." His stories of growing up are from another era, as if he'd come of age in the 1910s. He fed my silly technicolor dreams, but he made it clear that those times were long gone.

"That's just how we got things done, for real, you buy a couple a gallons of bootleg and get everbody together and you get what you need done, done. Fix your roof. Pig slaughterin'—line them pigs up and we'd have them big tubs, you know." He made grasping motions with his hands, pulling imaginary hair out of an imaginary pig carcass. "Throw 'em in there. Cookin' them chitlins."

As a kid, he'd work tobacco for $6 a day and plow his parents' four or five acres with a mule.

"Can't make no fucking money on four or five acres."

He's fond of the good old days, his house full of people, and the more peaceful times.

"People'd fight and shit, cut each other, hell." He told me the story of a man called Tuba. "Tuba cut someone every single goddamn weekend. I mean, if it was Saturday night old Tuba was cutting somebody. Drunk as hell. One night, he come out of the bathroom," and Skillet wobbles back and forth, acting drunk, "sees hisself in the mirror and startles. 'What the fuck! Motherfucker!' And he got his razor out, then he says, 'Shit, Tuba, that's you.' "

Skillet smacked the table and laughed. "Shit, Tuba! That's you!"

I glanced around the Applebee's, couldn't help it. What a spectacle were we? I flagged the waiter down for more drinks.

"Nobody shot nobody until crack came along. Shit was bad, you know, but not like this here."

On the phone with Skillet one evening I asked how he was: "Shit, Max, it's Danville. I woke up this morning, walked out on my porch, and I ain't been shot. So it's alright."

We came to like each other. In a sad, honest moment over a couple of steaks with frosty beers, he said, wistfully, "You know what, man? I think you're one of the best friends I have."

He had called up a joint for me, out in the country, where he grew up. He'd been describing a little road with three houses in a row and they are all three nip joints. He knew I wanted to go, but he was offering to buy me some bootleg as a sort of offering, a consolation prize. He had called from the car and turned the speakerphone on so I could hear the conversation: someone answered the phone with a grunt.

Skillet said, with the thick, quick accent of the black South: "Jay up in there?"

"Wha?" came the voice on the other end.

"Jay up in there?"

"Huh?"

"I say Jay up in there?"

"Jay?"

"Yeah."

"Yeah."

Skillet asked if he was asleep, even though it was 7 P.M., and having been assured that Jay was awake, asked to talk to him.

Introductions began again—a repeat of the monosyllabic call and response I'd just heard.

Then Skillet got down to business: "You got anything to drink up in there?"

"Naw."

"Ain't got nothing?"

"Not tonight"—there was a strange pause—"well, I might have something. I don't know."

"When you gonna know? I want to buy a quart."

"I might know by tomorrow morning."

"I want to buy a quart," said Skillet, pushing all the words together so they sounded like one.

"Yeah, ai'ght, I get you some."

"I'll come on up there after work."

They'd hung up just like that.

The next night we drove back roads through the pouring rain, and his stories turned to his childhood: bicycle wrecks and the spooky woods.

The rain was so thick and so heavy that he wondered, for a confused moment, if it had started to hail. I dropped him off at a bend in the road and he walked off into the rain. I would wait for him and he would call me to come back and get him. I backed up, turned the car around, and drove past the small ranchers clustered in front of the hayfields with pickup trucks parked in the yards until I found a farm road that cut through the windbreak and into a field. There was a chain blocking the entrance a dozen feet off the shoulder.

I sat in the dark, watching the rain on the windshield and compulsively checking that I had a signal on my cell phone.

Headlights shone through the rain, the beams glittering on the fat drops.

An old Dodge pickup came slowly down the lane, and I pushed back into the seat and hid my face behind the B-pillar, resting my head against the hinge of my seat belt.

Why were they driving so slow? How long was Skillet going to take? What was I doing here? Why did I drive such an out-of-place car (nothing but a Volkswagen, but still).

Twenty minutes later I began to wonder if I should keep the car running. I had been idling the car the way police park in front of the precinct, battle position, no turns necessary, just gun it and go.

What if Skillet turned on me? Or, with my money in his pocket, what if he decided to simply stay in the nip joint and get drunk? How long would he be in there, and when should I leave?

What if they thought I was a cop?

Would they drive slowly down the road looking for the cops? When they found me, what would they think? What would they do?

Or, in another scenario, what if they threatened Skillet? Criminal histories are complicated; someone has always done someone wrong. Wouldn't he just wave his hands in the air and scream out that he was buying for a white boy? "Shit, he's up the street in the car. Wallet full of money. I saw it. Let's go."

Such are the fantasies one has while waiting in the car like a high school kid for a quarter-bag of pot. You hand a buddy your money, and he tells you to wait while he walks past the vans and motorcycles in the parking lot to the front door to knock furtively, get the nod, and duck in alone. While your buddy sits inside watching television with the sound turned off, listening to King Crimson and doing bong hits out of the bag he just bought for you, you sit in the car and wonder when the cop cars are going to pull up. Or worse. Maybe he's not going to come back at all. It's a bad moment for fantasy, and your imagination can easily run away with you. What if the Mexican cartel everyone inside is involved with had decided that these particular idiots had pissed them off? What if behind that door the heavies had arrived to settle a debt, bringing down the power of real criminals with their huge handguns, their AK-47s, and their chain saws upon the otherwise peaceful lives of some small-time pot dealers who thought they'd gotten ahead. Your friend unwittingly opened the door to a bloodbath. They killed him. You being the only living witness, they are going to come after you.

Unlikely, but how long do you wait to find out if it's true?

Several more cars rolled along the road. Was this nip-joint traffic? Why did they all seem to slow down to see who was parked by the side of the road? Would the phone ever ring? Why do I have New York plates?!

Forty-five minutes or an hour later Skillet collapsed into the passenger seat, damp, laughing, and carrying an unopened beer.

"You mind if I drink this here?"

I said I didn't care.

"I'll get rid of it before we hit the main road."

There were a lot of people in there, Skillet explained, and he'd had to buy them all a drink.

"Folks ain't got nothing to do. They just sit around up in there waiting for somebody buy 'em a drink. What I'm gonna do? I know 'em all. Hell, some of 'em help me before. You got to help people out. Otherwise they figure you ain't their friend."

He put a green plastic 12-ounce soda-pop bottle that had held Sierra Mist in the cupholder between the seats.

He'd bought a few for himself; he was expansive and happy. While the screws in my brain had tightened right up to the edge of a freakout, Skillet had started a party. I'd been feeling as if I were scoring crack; Skillet had been tossing them back with his buddies.

We went out and got some pizza. Skillet looked up from his menu and asked me if he could order a beer. We drank and talked about the nip joint.

"Sitting around in there, just watching the TV, waiting for someone to come around. Waiting for someone to buy them a drink," he said, and he shook his head and shrugged. It was a sad scene and he knew it. "That first place didn't have nothing, anyway. Had to go to the house in the middle. That's the man I tell you sometime he cuts it."

Skillet had said that there was a source who cut their liquor, everyone knew it, and some suspected that he used bleach.

Bleach? Wouldn't you know if it was bleach?

"Well," said Skillet, "it's something." He came down on that last word, hard.

Back at my hotel, alone, I sat at the desk with the bottle in front of me, sipping a beer and staring it down.

I unscrewed the plastic top, wondering if someone had drunk the Sierra Mist that had once been inside. Had they drunk it right out of the bottle? They wouldn't have washed it. They probably would have thought that a skim of leftover soda pop sloshing around in the bottom would enhance the flavor of the bootleg.

I poured a small shot into a glass and breathed the aroma in as if it were any other whiskey, burying my nose as deep into the glass as I could and breathing deeply, thoughtfully.

A mistake.

I had a recorder running and my gasp for air is violent, as if I'd been punched in the throat. I never say a word. It's just me, gasping, catching my breath, and grunting softly as I tried to take a sip. I muttered something like "Awful stuff. Unimaginable." Then I went to bed.

The next night I tried again, determined to understand the tastes.

Again, I started with the nose.

It is difficult to find a metaphor, a way to classify the smell, basically: it smelled like poison.

Steeling myself, I took a sip.

Bile. As if I'd burped up vomit. But stomach acid and puke is thick and viscous; this was sharp and thin. As if you took the stomach acid from acid reflux and strained it through a cheesecloth and blended in a dash of simple syrup to sweeten it.

The only flavor that I can describe as such was that of sour sugar, not like Sour Patch Kids, but like sugar gone sour, sugar gone wrong.

There was no lingering flavor. The drink pushed into my mouth, exploded, and then vanished, leaving me feeling as if I'd swirled with some sort of experimental kerosene-powered mouthwash.

I hadn't had anything like a whole shot. Perhaps I'd drunk half an ounce before my right cheek went numb and I poured my glass back into the bottle.

It is the only liquor I've ever had that made me feel that I was hurting myself. I could feel my liver squirm when it hit. I could feel the drip of the lead salts depositing themselves into a pocket of my brain.

This was complete shit.

In the first of the series of books edited by Eliot Wigginton on Appalachian culture called *Foxfire*, there is a chapter on moonshine titled "Moonshining as a Fine Art." It's a nostalgic thing, but that's par for the *Foxfire* course. Those kids were up in the mountains trying to preserve the "old ways," and they were told stories of a moonshine trade that had been overrun by greed. The art of whiskey making was almost lost, and moonshiners were distilling liquor for profit, not for craft.

Forty years later, the result of that corruption was what sat on my desk at the Marriott.

Jimmy Beheler had said that in sixteen years of busting stills he never found any liquor he would drink. I could see what he meant.

This rotgut really might pose some sort of health risk. Maybe that line the cops feed the press wasn't a fabrication. Maybe they really had the public welfare in mind. If the vile, hazardous stuff inside my Sierra Mist bottle was typical of the bootleg pouring into nip joints, it *should* be kept off the street.

I was troubled.

The Master of Sparks

A good friend and I put our heads together one day and went out of town to his folks' spread where we got the help of the black foreman there to weld a bunch of sucker gauges, which is the kind of pipe they use to build windmills, into a steel cage, a ball of sorts. We put a door on it, a seatbelt on a bucket seat. It even had shock absorbers to cushion the points of impact. Then we'd get drunk and roll this thing out of the back of a pick-up truck at 'bout fifty miles an hour and when it would hit the ground it'd send up a rooster tail of sparks a hundred feet in the air. Man it would tear you up to get in that thing. It was the most amazing spectacle I'd ever laid eyes on.

—BILLY GIBBONS EXPLAINING THE STORY
BEHIND HIS 1973 SONG "MASTER OF SPARKS"
IN SOUND MAGAZINE.

ON TOP OF MY NEWLY PURCHASED ANTIQUE BOILER, THERE was a 3½-inch threaded hole into which screwed a large brass fitting resembling the bell of a rustic, steam-powered trumpet. This cap was topped with a smaller threaded hole. I figured the smaller hole was nominally an inch but it measured more like an inch and an eighth. Perhaps it was therefore nominally an inch and a quarter, since people selling you materials rarely round things down.

The plan was simple enough: attach a column to the threaded 1-inch hole on the top of the brass fixture. Put a 90-degree fitting on top of that column and attach an arm that would, in turn, attach to a coiled length of soft copper tubing—the worm.

The boiler I'd bought was converted from a copper washtub, as were many small moonshine stills, and every one of the dozens I've seen for sale has one of these steam-powered trumpet bell thing-amajigs on the top, reducing the 3½-inch hole to 1 inch. It's unlikely that they were drop-forged for moonshining. They must have a legal application, but no one seemed to know it. I drove around with the thing in the pocket of my jacket and showed it to plumbing suppliers and hardware men—no one had ever seen one.

"What are you trying to do?" asked the man behind the counter at the plumbing supply on the highway.

Um, well, I—ha-ha—yes, um: irrigation. Ha! Found an old, it's like a . . . *rain cistern,* you know, for watering plants? This here is the . . . I'd like to attach something to it.

They'd blink at me, and I'd smile an encouraging smile.

"Never seen one of those before."

When asked if they knew what kind of thing might thread onto it, they shook their heads and shrugged their shoulders. I suspect that the piece must, in fact, be from a cistern, or the coolant cap for an old Massey Ferguson tractor—something, in other words, that is quite common around a farm, but which bewilders plumbers whose livelihood centers on the installation of incredibly expensive shower heads into the relentlessly renovated bathrooms of the Hudson Valley.

I put the fitting back in my coat pocket and drove again to Home Depot to stand before the dizzying, intimidating wall of fittings and flanges and pipes. My first sad realization was that there was not one wall of randomly arranged dusty cartons with bent corners and smudged labels, but two. If there was an organizing principle, it escaped me. One wall of boxes seemed to be filled mostly with copper things, and the other with mostly brass things, but on both walls one out of every dozen boxes would be filled with plastic fittings, or aluminum valves, or steel straps. Something, in other words, that bucked whatever sense of order I was imposing upon the shelving system.

With the fitting in my hand I moved from one box to the next, searching for anything I could thread into the smaller hole. I started at the top left corner, proceeding from left to right and top to bottom, looking in each box. Some of the boxes were easy to skip. T-couplings or tiny pressure valves were useless to me.

On Wikipedia, I'd learned that there are different types of threading: some threads are squared off, some are sharp, some are fine. For instance: "ANSI/ASME standard B1.20.1 covers threads of 60-degree form with flat crests and roots in sizes from $\frac{1}{16}$ inch to 24 inch Nominal Pipe Size." Of course, this meant absolutely nothing to me, but it did imply that I'd need to get not only a fitting of the proper size, but also of the proper *type*.

There I stood, attempting to screw any likely candidate into the small hole of my steam-powered trumpet bell and having no luck. Things that looked like perfect fits would resist the threading, having been intended for some other standard and some other job.

Second row from the floor, far right, almost as far from my beginning as Florida is from Washington State, after I'd dug through more than a hundred boxes, I found a "pipe repair" setup. This was a foot-long length of 1-inch copper pipe with brass fittings at either end.

It screwed into my cap.

Bingo.

My boiler had a column.

Now that column needed to make a 90-degree turn. It was easy enough to find an elbow joint that fit. The elbow, in turn, accepted the advances of a ¾-inch copper pipe. The arm needed to reduce in diameter to ⅜ of an inch. I found a straight coupling that led to a compression coupling, which would reduce my pipe to ½-inch—almost there. I grabbed a length of ½-inch pipe and looked for a fitting that would reduce that to ⅜.

I asked a passing employee if he knew where such a fitting might be—something that would connect a ½-inch length of pipe to a length of ⅜-inch soft copper tubing.

He told me that it couldn't be done.

I stared at him until he left, suspecting silently that his answer did not reflect the reality of plumbing.

I dug through the boxes again, and soon enough I had a brass fitting that slid over the pipe and ended with a ⅜-inch compression fitting. Three and a half hours later, I'd connected the dots—or so I thought.

I tried to slip all the pieces together, just to double-check.

It was not a smooth process. Things that should have slipped together like a couple of mating eels would reject my manipulations.

My antics amused a septuagenarian man working the pipes and plumbing section and he approached, smiling in a condescending way.

"What are you trying to do?"

I said, vaguely, that I was trying to connect these pieces.

"Yes. But what are you doing? What for?"

Here we go again. Laughing my way through, nervous and absurd, I said I was ha-ha-ha building a . . . you know, ha-ha . . . an irrigation thing. I have a rain bucket, a catcher, right? Ha-ha-ha, and I'm trying to . . . I want to fabricate a, um, watering system, ha-ha. *Irrigation.* Connect all these pieces, you see.

I waved my hand over the cart like a priest blessing a child, and hoped that it wouldn't occur to him that I was claiming to be building an irrigation system in the middle of winter.

"You gonna cut that pipe with a *hacksaw*?" gesturing to the hacksaw in my cart as if it were the most repulsive thing he'd ever seen.

That's what I was thinking . . .

"Use a pipe cutter."

Okay.

"Follow me."

He led me to the pipe cutters.

"Follow me."

I scurried along behind him. Was he *laughing* at me?

We rummaged through the fittings and he produced a different fitting.

"Follow me."

And he produced a different length of half-inch pipe.

I noticed that he'd grabbed the most expensive length of pipe, and I tried to switch it out sneakily for a cheaper one.

He was fitting the pieces together, showing me that it was going to work, and he stopped with the cheap pipe in his hand.

"What's this? This won't fit. I thought I had type L."

Oh, right, I had two pipes in my hand, I must have put the wrong one back . . . wondering what the hell a type L pipe was.

I grabbed two of everything I'd gathered, sure that I could never find any of it again.

He left me with a piece of advice: "Make sure the pipes are clean."

I answered with a hearty "Sure thing" but wondered what he meant. "Clean?" Like with soap?

Soft copper is incredibly malleable. (It's the sort of thing that connects the gas line to the back of your stove.) I simply bent it around a jug and dropped it into a 5-gallon bucket fitted with a couple of faucets for taking heated water out and putting cool water in. I'd cut a hole in the side of the bucket for the end of the coil—the money piece—to stick out. It was quick work: twenty minutes with a drill, a penknife, and a tube of caulk, and I had what's known in the world of illicit distilling as a flake stand. I felt the flush of confidence (the one which usually foreshadows my fall).

Now all I had to do was solder some pipes together and make the arm.

Every piece of literature that discusses the soldering of copper pipes begins with a sentence along the lines of "Although many people are intimidated by the idea of soldering copper pipes, sweating copper is a very straightforward job and requires no special skills."

Indeed, the skills I lack are not special; they are basic.

My brother-in-law, Rob, came over to "help," and together we turned what should have been the work of ten minutes into a seven-hour job.

To give a sense of the scale of our incompetence: I've read that ½ of an inch of solder should be enough to solder the joint of a ½-inch pipe. We had five joints to solder, three of which were ¾-inch joints and two of which were ½-inch joints. If done properly our five joints would be sealed by a length of solder equal to their total diameter: 3¼ inches.

We ran through *yards* of the stuff. I am not being hyperbolic. We wasted *spools* of solder trying to get the pipes to join.

We would heat up a piece of the pipe, melt the solder into the joint, and let it cool. Then we'd touch the pipe and the two pieces would slide apart, solderless and slightly discolored.

I read more instructions: "Solder will flow into a joint as if following detailed directions."

Our solder was joint-averse. It had clearly been given the wrong marching orders. The mission of our solder seemed to be to pool up into a ball and fall to the floor, spattering our sneakers with droplets of molten metal.

Rob had a friend who had done this before, and we called him.

"Don't burn the pipe."

Burn the pipe? How could one burn a pipe?

"You've really got to flux the shit out of it."

What qualifies as having the shit fluxed out of something? How much flux is that exactly?

We went back down to the basement and tried to flux the shit out of the pipe. "Like this much, you think?"

We'd put the torch back to it and give it another shot. For no apparent reason—maybe just to keep us on our toes?—the propane torch spurted out a 2-foot roar of flame. Surprisingly, a couple of pieces eventually joined together. The joint was horribly ugly, with wads of excess solder and drip marks, but it was firm.

But we soon lost whatever magic we'd found. After some small success, we were getting *worse* at soldering. We took a break and watched a streaming video of a guy soldering a pipe. (This, I wondered, is what it's come to? Watching DIY videos on the Web on a Saturday afternoon?)

In the video, the guy held the torch *opposite* where he was going to put the solder, and he held the solder right on the joint the whole time. The moment the pipe was hot enough to melt solder, the solder flowed into the joint.

He said something like "this way, you won't overheat the pipes."

That was it. We'd been heating our pipes up too much. "Don't burn the pipes," Rob's buddy had said. We finished the job.

My 24-inch contraption looked like a sloppily constructed cross between a Gatling gun and an opium pipe, but the whole thing fit together, and it bridged the gap between the column and the coil.

I'd built a still.

I had 12 gallons of cider waiting.

As I drifted off to sleep, happy that neither of us had been burned too badly, I thought to myself that I should name the still. I was thinking about all the fire, the solder, the silly madness of the whole adventure. It made me think of the old ZZ Top song, "Master of Sparks."

I'd name my still Billy Gibbons.

Lightning Strikes

Nah, boss, just saying something's your job don't make it right.

—COOL HAND LUKE

THE PEOPLE WHO LIVE ON THE TROBRIAND ISLAND OF KIRIwina speak Kivila, or some of them do, and they've given us the word *mokita*, which means a truth that we all know but agree not to talk about. In the moonshine hills of Virginia, it's a good word to have on hand. The folks at the Blue Ridge Institute put together a sanguine exhibit of folksy moonshine memorabilia while I was researching in the moonshine country, and displayed it first at their Blue Ridge Institute in Ferrum and then at the Virginia Historical Society near where I used to stomp the cobblestone alleys of Richmond. It was fun—who doesn't love to see the polished-up stills and sepia photos of old hillbillies with straw in their teeth? They had a classic old Charles Kuralt video on loop, and a case of wide-mouth quart canning jars artfully angled against a hay bale. They claimed, pridefully, that a larger collection of moonshiniana had never been gathered.

The business of moonshine can't be avoided altogether—there

was a quote from Homer Philpott on the wall: IT AIN'T MADE TO DRINK, IT'S MADE TO SELL. But the curators of the show did their best to shelter viewers from any of the harsh reality of real moonshining and thoroughly cloaked the liquor trade in a romantic scrim of old pickup trucks and prideful coppersmiths.

Further, throughout the show there was a willful insistence that moonshining was a thing of the past. From the wall text:

> Though a large industry, moonshining has clearly been shrinking in the Virginia Blue Ridge. Operation Lightning Strike, a major bust centered in Franklin County in 1999–2001, revealed that the local company selling bootleggers their supplies annually bought more than 500 tons of sugar and 125,000 one-gallon plastic jugs over a four-year span in the 1990s. However, even these amounts show a decline in moonshining; the same company had purchased 2,500 tons of sugar per year in the 1980s. No one knows if large-scale moonshining will ever return to the Blue Ridge.

When I called to speak with the resident moonshine expert at the Blue Ridge Institute, Roddy Moore (who designed that exhibit), he told me that if they were going to help me, they'd have to see a synopsis, some evidence of serious scholarship, and that from what he understood about my project, I was going in a direction of which he did not approve.

I got more of the same at the Franklin County Historical Society, where Linda Stanley also asked to see a synopsis of the work, claiming that journalists had been there before and that it hadn't ended well. She and I would see one another occasionally, and she would smile and tell me that she'd love to help, but she would never return my calls or actually answer any questions.

I'm sure they believed me to be a sort of crank, some weird Yankee pretending to write a book, a hack journalist who had arrived at the party far too late.

Then again, there's always the possibility that I was understood to be a threat. I believe Morris Stephenson felt that way, and that although he liked me, he knew that I was a handler of Klieg lights, that people might just start driving to Franklin County looking for moonshine, wanting to take bus tours . . .

I took the Northeast Regional down to Richmond, where I was picked up by an old friend in a rented Dodge. We drove out Interstate 64, laughing and listening to music, happy to see one another. We were staying at the grand Hotel Roanoke—one of the nation's great and true hotels, a pile of Tudor architecture on a hill with enough rooms to billet an army. We spent the evening drinking with a wedding party in the bar, while the mother of the bride slurred at us about how much she respected our choice, and how proud she was that we were public about being gay and being together. Then she fell to the floor like a plank. She bought us another round on the way out, because she loved us: We'd listened to her story about how happy she was for her daughter and how sad she was that there had been a fistfight at the wedding.

We were finishing our last-call beers on the patio when a college student burst out of the emergency exit, setting off the alarms. He hovered near us, very obviously on exciting drugs, making schizophrenic small talk and trying to blend in as if he hadn't been trying to burglarize the hotel. He wondered if we were heading to Blacksburg tonight.

Lost in the hotel on our way back upstairs, searching for the right elevator and admiring the potted fig trees, we wandered into the convention area, where we came upon a man driving a sort of motorized hydraulic scaffolding system, like an indoor cherry picker. He lowered his basket slowly to the floor and stepped out onto the polished tile. We asked where the "secret elevator" was, and he spoke into the collar of his shirt, as if he were in the Secret Service: "Stand by."

We were on our way to the Franklin County Historical Society's annual "Moonshine Express" bus tour. It was a strange affair, like a school pageant put on by semicostumed grown-ups, all of whom were overcome with nerves and shaking at the prospect of boarding a bus and reciting a romanticized, and canned, monologue on the moon-shining lore of Franklin County. They staged cheerful vignettes: we watched as a couple of locals dressed up like Tom Sawyer tried to fill their Mason jars in the gutter, catching the "liquor" poured out into the street by the revenooer and stealing away for a drink of the old mountain dew.

The bus chugged to a halt across the street from the Helms Farmers' Exchange. Another historical caricature boarded the bus and delivered a shtick. We drove on.

The largest antimoonshine operation ever staged (excluding, I suppose, the suppression of the Whiskey Rebellion) centered on the Helms Farmers' Exchange, and the Moonshine Express passed it by without a mention.

Amid the short stack of moonshine literature, through the memoirs and profiles of the revenue men, the folk and oral histories, the serious and light scholarship, and even through the instructional manuals, runs a common theme of nostalgia for a time when moonshiners were honest men who made a small living doing something well. Universally, it is agreed that this time has passed. Sometimes this sentiment is evident in the very titles of the books: Jack Powell's *A Dying Art*, Jerry Alexander's *Where Have All Our Moonshiners Gone?* More commonly, it's a part of an epilogue, or the roundup of "Modern Times" that one gets before the glossary, the appendices, and the index. Almost without exception we learn that somewhere along the way moonshiners substituted quantity for quality. Rather than making their corn squeezings the right way, they aimed at higher yields and faster fermentation. They began to rush the process.

First, they abandoned grains almost entirely and simply cooked up huge pots full of dissolved white sugar, tossing a token pound of wheat germ or hog feed into the mix, like a drop of vermouth in a pitcher of martinis.

Instead of classic, copper, turnip-shaped pot stills, they devised and built the black pot submarine still, a rough, slapdash job made from a couple of sheets of galvanized metal and some poplar planking.

The still holds 800 gallons, and key to understanding the mindset behind it, and the liquor produced from it, is that the 800-gallon capacity is utterly arbitrary. Eight hundred gallons just happens to be the size you get when you weld together the two off-the-shelf pieces of sheet metal end-to-end and bend them into an oval like a caterpillar track. Moonshiners don't cut the sheets or waste material. The black pot still is a study in rough, rural efficiency.

Modern moonshiners got rid of the fermentation tank and the mash tun and moved to fermenting the mash right in the still itself. No longer would they move hundreds of gallons of mash from point A to point B. They wouldn't have to pump the mess; they'd just wait until it was ready to go, and then they'd turn on the propane flame, which would gush out of the jerry-rigged superburners they'd laid on the dirt.

The burners are nothing more than 1-inch pipes with holes drilled in them, or slices cut halfway across with a thin hacksaw, and the roar they make when afire has more in common with the sound of an Airbus taking off than it does with your backyard grill. The propane empties so quickly that the decompression will freeze the works and crack the tank unless it's heated. The solution is a frightening, hell-bent bit of recklessness. They crank open a second tank with a spout affixed to the valve and fire an open flame directly onto the metal of the primary propane tank. This has led to some spectacular accidents. One unlucky trio of still hands was inside a concrete building when the propane tanks exploded. They ran from the building after the explosion, in shock, unaware that their skin had been melted and charred and that they looked like something that would chase teenagers around in a B-movie. One of them died.

The combination of mash distilled on the yeast, without separating any of the solids, the downgraded content of that mash, and a super-hot open flame heating it up as fast as it can be heated, makes some horrible liquor. You don't have to be an antique corn-likker maker or a single-malt snob to find the stuff repulsive. The old-timers complaining about the degradation of a craft are right to grouse.

The folks interested in moonshining in a scholarly way (as opposed to those who make it or chase it) want very much to preserve the idea that moonshining is a folk tradition, part of our culture and national heritage, a harmless thing done on a small scale in the Southern Highlands, like an inebriating version of summer sausage.

Big-money criminal enterprise is a hard thing to cherish. It's much more comfortable to take the easy way out, to rumble right past the Helms' store and get on with the discussion of the glamorous Willie Carter Sharp, who drove as if she were being chased by the devil and wore a diamond in her teeth.

But the hole left there, the lack of data, is at best a poor representation of the facts. Some people desire to ameliorate or maintain the reputations of southern highlanders and protect their own siloed bit of the scholarly map, and are willfully distorting the truth. Other folks are simply overcome by nostalgia.

At lunch with a handful of retired liquor chasers, I was regaled with endless comparisons to the good old days. Time was, they'd say, you could simply tell a man to see you in court on Monday, didn't have to cuff him and drag him in, didn't have to humiliate him. They was good people—good liquor, too.

Those complaints have continued for decades. The cry seems to have gone up first during Prohibition—"These young'uns don't care for nothin' but money!" *Foxfire*'s famous chapter on "Moonshining as a Fine Art" echoed the complaint:

> The small operators were being forced out of business, and moonshining like most other manufacturing enterprises was quickly taken over by a breed of men bent on making money—and lots of it. Loss of pride in the product, and loss of time taken with product increased in direct proportion to the desire for production; and thus moonshining as a fine art was buried in a quiet little ceremony attended only by those mourners who had once been the proud

artists, known far and wide across the hills for the excellence of their product. Too old to continue making it themselves, and with no one following behind them, they were reduced to reminiscing about "the good old days when the whiskey that was made was *really* whiskey, and no questions asked."

This trope has become de rigueur for moonshine books, but no one ever follows it up. After announcing the end of the age, the author will hunt down some last vestige of the old ways, some fellow with a corncob pipe, and record their conversation with as many of the local vernacular tics as he can jam in. "Ain't seen nothing like that round here for a coon's age, course, but when I was a young'un, we'd keep a jar right there on that there table. Give them babies sips out of it to cure the colic, we did." We'll read a couple of stories about hauling liquor down the mountain, and how he'd build him a good copper still right by the branch where the water weeds grow, etc. etc.

Of course, there is a grain of salt to be taken with all this. If moonshiners and revenue men were caviling about a decline of the product in the 1920s, and the 1960s, and the 1980s, and in 2008—well, it's impossible for an industry to deteriorate continually for eight decades, isn't it? Old men loathe the young ones, each generation is lazier than the last; it's cliché.

Then again, the old-time moonshiner might know what he's talking about. He probably has a friend, a cousin, a son, who went from producing a bit of corn liquor to a few hundred thousand gallons of sugar liquor. He doesn't tell the folklorist, the anthropologist, or the journalist where that friend is at or what he's up to, of course. And as a result, the people studying the traditions tend to have an overly Panglossian view of the moonshine trade. They have no idea of the scale of what's being discussed, and if they did, they'd hide it anyway on the grounds that the revelation of the sugar jack trade would degrade the folk tradition and cast doubts on the honor of all those dear old mountain men.

We can give the benefit of the doubt: *no one* seemed to have put it all together. It wasn't until the 1990s that anyone understood what the term "greedy moonshiner" actually meant.

In 1992 a sign went up in the window of a mobile home on Route 40, just outside of Rocky Mount, announcing that the trailer was for rent. Jimmy Beheler and a couple of his colleagues in the local arm of the ABC board saw an opportunity. The trailer was right across the road from the warehouse of the Helms Farmers' Exchange, which was a notorious supply depot, a barely kept secret link in the moonshine trade where bootleggers could buy 100-pound bags of sugar and heavy-duty plastic jugs. Beheler had always hung around watching, following the trucks, and getting leads. One of the Helms brothers, Ramsey or Billy, would typically roll up on him and ask what he was doing.

"We'd get caught watching them. We'd be set up on the side there, trying to see."

Having a base across the street would help; they'd no longer have to haunt the parking lot.

"We had a female deputy from Pittsylvania County come up, she rented the trailer." She was to pose as a college student.

They put a camera in the window and trained it on the warehouse. A typical time-elapse surveillance model, the camera could run for about forty-eight hours before they had to change the tape. They would steer clear of the place during the day. No one ever caught on.

"We taped for four or five months, I guess, all of the trucks that were coming in and out of the warehouse."

Moonshine has always been a business, and with each opportunity the business grew. Some combination of elements—low sugar prices, lack of funding in the ABC Board, an ATF more concerned (rightfully) with the smuggling of truckloads of cigarettes from one state to another and the trade in firearms—led to the recent boom in bootlegging. Well after most of the country was wet, even after by-the-drink restrictions were lifted, moonshiners kept on pumping the sugar jack. The greedy moonshiners, these heathen bootleggers, dismissive of tradition, compelled not by craft but by avarice, flourished in almost unimaginable ways.

When the ABC Board rented that trailer and turned on the camera, it was as if they'd flipped on the lights in a roach-infested apartment.

Shelves lined the walls of the United States attorney's office on the fourth floor of the federal building in Roanoke, Virginia—industrial, cream-colored shelves, architectural in scale, floor-to-ceiling edifices that suggested an army of modern scriveners tracking an unthinkable assemblage of documents. Every inch was evidence. Boxes of evidence stacked like ammunition for the prosecution.

This was not the woody, bookish law office so familiar from televised courtroom dramas.

I sat in a small windowless conference room lit by a harsh array of overhead fluorescents, feeling as if I was about to be audited. Simple, straightforward table, simple straightforward chairs, and more shelves of the ubiquitous evidence boxes—the labels read: "Documents Seized by the Police," "J & S Automotive Specialties," "Battery Harness Power Diode Evidence Dockets."

The United States of America v. Helms et al. was mammoth, even by federal standards. The case was the product of years of investigation and made it to trial, barely, in 2001. Twenty-one named defendants had been accused of seventy-eight charges, including Money Laundering, Conspiracy to Violate the Travel Act, Perjury, Possession of an Unregistered Still, Production of Untaxed Liquor, Removal of Untaxed Liquor, Receipt of Untaxed Liquor.

Sharon Burnham, the prosecuting attorney, sat next to me in a gray pants suit, pecking at her ThinkPad and trying to remember where she'd filed the photographs she used in her opening statement. She'd arrayed file folders on the conference table in front of us, no doubt plucked from a box she'd stored on one of these shelves.

Burnham is a svelte woman with sunlight in her wispy hair. She grew up in California and studied at the University of Redlands and at the University of Hawaii. She carries those sun-drenched days with her like a stash of happiness hidden in a nest of palm fronds. She's quick to laugh, clever in conversation, and pretty, and she's not to be underestimated. Before she went to law school, she was a marine chemist. She's cautious and intensely focused.

I could see that she was accustomed to taking careful steps toward an end and that methodical procedure is something at which she excels. She radiated due diligence.

The United State v. Helms et al. was keyed on William Helms, who, with his brother Ramsey, ran the worst-kept secret in the world of moonshine. Their shop in Rocky Mount, the Farmers' Exchange, sold a little bit of chicken feed, a few sacks of lawn fertilizer, and warehouse after warehouse full of moonshine supplies. Sharon showed me pictures of the Farmers' Exchange from 1988, when the ATF stopped by and looked around. On the floor at the time were 58,000 heavy-duty plastic 1-gallon jugs and 80,000 pounds of sugar.

The Helms brothers had a warehouse out on Route 40, where all the sugar was, and offices and a retail shop on Main Street in town. I walked into a Rocky Mount beauty shop to ask the three ladies standing around the reception desk where the Exchange was—I knew it was half a block away, but I wanted to see what they knew about it—and they had never heard of the place. It seems that if you weren't in the market for pallets of sugar, bundles of heavy-duty plastic jugs, and 1-pound cakes of yeast, the Exchange didn't show up on your radar.

The Exchange was empty when I visited, closed down, a flat façade of dark brick with plate-glass windows and a garage bay, the trim painted a fresh white, and the roof stepping up in sections like an Old West warehouse, the sort of shape that would have inspired the Prairie Style of Frank Lloyd Wright. The former hub of the sugar jack trade was but an empty shell at a stoplight. Inside, I saw the detritus of a deserted business—a beautiful old table with red wrought-iron legs, marks on the floor, a box of trash. I circled the building, wondering at the random patches of paint and repairs that suggested something once vibrant. In the small gravel patch before the loading docks, I kicked my feet, reached down and grabbed a pebble. Curious, I halfheartedly chucked it at a nearby building and watched it clack against the back door. A stone's throw to the Franklin County Courthouse.

Moonshine was the overwhelming business of the Farmers' Exchange. They moved sugar like a child psychologist moves Ritalin. A chart Sharon drew up of the total costs of goods purchased and the total cost of sugar and jugs purchased shows that the moonshine supplies comprised about seven-eighths of the store's business.

The agents and the Helms brothers both assumed, with frustration and glee, respectively, that there was nothing illegal about selling sugar. William and Ramsey Helms simply sold lots of it. That makes them successful, and you cannot be indicted for success.*

"We found out that the Farmers' Exchange was the second-largest consumer of a certain brand of sugar . . . second only to Hershey's candy," said Sharon.

Pursuing white liquor, Jimmy Beheler and his crew would stake out the Exchange. They'd see a blue superduty Ford with a wide bed and planks built up tall like fencing for the side walls, an old cattle truck, pull into the warehouse and leave with pallets of sugar. The agents could establish production patterns; they could keep tabs on the regular operators.

The Helms boys would try to run them off or hide the business from the agents—strange sales were made in the predawn, loads of jugs and sugar were received at two in the morning. Harold Poindexter worked at the exchange for twenty years and lived in a trailer next door, so that he'd be available twenty-four hours a day to load sugar, jugs, and supplies.

Although the agents knew what was going on and had a good idea of who the players were, the law failed to fully understand the magnitude of the business.

Then they installed the camera in the trailer across the street.

---

* The ravages of crystal meth have, however, caused pseudoephidrine, an ingredient in the production of the drug, to be semicriminalized through an act of Congress, the Combat Methamphetamine Epidemic Act of 2005.

Jimmy Beheler said: "We put a camera in and taped for four or five months, I guess, all of the trucks that were coming in and out of the warehouse. There was such an unbelievable amount of activity there. [We] were aware of it prior to that. But not at the scale it turned out to be."

The scale was astonishing.

It had been a long time since someone upped the stakes in Franklin County. Although his action would spell excommunication from the community, although he would disrupt a pattern of lawlessness and careless enforcement that was virtually taken for granted, Beheler decided to make a real case. He wanted to deal with the moonshiners as if they were drug dealers. They were big-time liquor criminals, and they should be met with appropriate retaliation. He took the tapes to the feds, and Operation Lightning Strike was born.

Over the course of seven and a half years, Beheler, the ABC Board, and the ATF recorded what happened at the Exchange and slowly built real cases against the vast ad hoc network of liquor producers in Virginia and North Carolina. Between 1992 and May of 1999, when the place was raided, the Exchange sold 12,096,800 pounds of sugar. The government equated that to 1,451,616 gallons of liquor. They were being conservative. The real number probably edges up on 2,000,000.

It's difficult to build a case against a shop that sells sugar, just as it would be very rough to indict a boatwright for building the boats used to smuggle cocaine, but the federal prosecutor has in her arsenal an almost magical bullet: conspiracy. If the sugar dealer *conspires* with the moonshiners, that's another story. The Helms boys weren't just selling boats, in other words, they were designing special cocaine-hiding compartments, building different types of boats more suitable for cocaine trafficking. Once accused of a conspiracy, any overt act you make toward the continuance of the goals of that conspiracy makes a case against you and you are liable for the whole array of crimes.

It's important to understand that to be guilty of a conspiracy you don't actually have to participate in what we would typically think of as "the crime." If a couple of friends talk about robbing a bank, and one of them buys the other some stockings to put on his head but doesn't go along for the ride, he's potentially just as guilty as if he'd been in the lobby waving a pistol around.

At the same time, to be guilty of a conspiracy, you must conspire with someone.

The business that was revealed at the Helms store was a tangly, multifaceted thing, and although the Helms brothers would sell supplies to each of the moonshining groups that showed up at the store, it would be impossible to prove that those moonshiners were all involved in a conspiracy together. It'd be a dizzying case, and most likely it would fall far short of the threshold of reasonable doubt that is the bedrock of our system of prosecution. The jury, after all, is instructed to assume innocence, and with each twisting path, each overcomplicated connection, they would find themselves wondering if, in fact, too much was being made of the direct involvement that these brothers had in the continuing criminal enterprise of moonshine production.

Sharon's stroke of genius, and I believe it exactly that, was to assert that the Helms brothers conspired with one another, and that the Helms conspiracy was a continuing criminal enterprise to supply each set of moonshiners with supplies.

It was a beautiful plan, and I saw a spark in her eye as she moved a pencil around a chart, indicating to me how she could click the web of conspiracy together, how it would crystallize and have at its center the Farmers' Exchange.

Key to the case was a series of desk calendars that recorded, in code, five years' worth of sales. Written into a calendar square, in that perfect country cursive: *Hat Man 96 S.* Hat Man was a code name for Ralph Hale, and he'd bought 9,600 pounds of sugar.

Over the course of five years Hat Man paid close to $700,000 for 1,792,500 pounds of sugar. The feds asserted that with the sugar he could have produced 179,250 gallons of illegal liquor.

That math is easy—they simply moved a decimal point and figured that 10 pounds of sugar gives a gallon of hooch. But in a black pot moonshine still, 10 pounds of sugar produces more like 1.6 gallons of liquor.

In the harsh light of the spartan conference room where we met, I asked Sharon why her estimates were so conservative.

"Who would exaggerate these numbers?" she said. "We didn't need to inflate this to make a point."

Inflated numbers will blow the credibility of the case at trial. Rather than appear as if she were stretching to make a point, she had used the lowest conceivable estimate. If given a range, she told me, she'd pluck from the bottom. The amounts were still significant, more than enough to show that this moonshine racket was a serious criminal enterprise and not the work of a couple of lazy hillbillies.

The prosecution must tread lightly around this, for the greatest hurdle in prosecuting a moonshine case is convincing the jury that moonshining is a serious crime and not a folk tradition. The culture of moonshine is such that people tend not to think of it seriously, and the defense will play right into that with what I've come to think of as "the Overalls Card." If they could fill the court room with bluegrass music to accompany their tales of simple farmers trying to put a loaf of bread on the table, they'd leap at the chance.

"These numbers speak for themselves," said Sharon.

The formula entrusted to me by the Illegal Whiskey Task Force is as follows: 750 pounds of sugar into an 800-gallon still to get 120 gallons of liquor. Ralph Hale was only one of the defendants, only one of about eight groups producing moonshine. His production numbers alone, when refigured with the real formula, were more like 276,000 gallons: $2,760,000 worth at the still, $8,380,000 retail.

Moonshiners separate pretty easily into two camps: those who get caught a lot and those who seem to always slip by. Ralph Hale was one of the latter. I asked Randall Toney, of the Illegal Whiskey Task

Force, and Jesse Tate, of the Virginia ABC, how it was that Hale could get away with it. Hale had no arrests, although the agents knew perfectly well what he was up to.

"Seems like every time I'm walking in the front door, he's just walked out the back."

They knew he was there, buying the trucks, funding the stills, organizing the shipments, but they couldn't catch him.

For decades, as moonshine cases were tried on the county and state level, if the accused hadn't actually been caught stirring the mash or filling the jugs, it was almost impossible to pin a conviction. One man, facing liquor charges in Franklin County, went so far as to complain that the agents had used binoculars. "It ain't fair. They didn't see me with the naked eye."

The law used to have to see the deed done, recognize who was doing it, and then, on top of all that, physically apprehend the perpetrator. If they waited until tomorrow, you would just claim it wasn't you, someone borrowed your car, you've never been out that way. Even fingerprints at a still site were unlikely to get a conviction, since moonshiners are well versed in the defense that they handle all sorts of things, and might have touched a pipe or a tank of propane anywhere. Tanks of propane are portable, pipes are just pipes—these don't prove a thing.

As a result, when a moonshiner hears a stick crack in the woods, or when the dog he's got out there to watch the still barks, he runs. Much of the bootlegger mythology, the car chases and the getaways, come out of this. In the days before dispatchers and two-way radios, the bubble lights in the rearview mirror were downright comforting. Gun it and go: the law's state-bought car was no match for a triple carbureted 1950 Ford with a Cadillac 8.

This developed into an unstated agreement, or so the liquor folks thought. Bill Davis was a lawyer in Rocky Mount until his death in 2004. He was a regular defender of moonshiners, knew many of them since childhood, and was a very serious presence on the local social and political scene. He likened the relationship of lawmen and moonshiners to a "gentleman's agreement," and told the papers that if the law hadn't actually caught someone making liquor, that should be the end of the story.

Naturally, in those times, the money men like Ralph Hale had it made. They rarely set foot near a distillery, hauled the liquor, or handled the jars. No one is going to walk up on Ralph Hale in the woods while he's stirring the mash. He's not out there; he's home. To put the cuffs on Hale would require something different. Lightning Strike, with its hours of videotape and its financial records, was just that: different.

Sharon's idea to prosecute not directly as a liquor violation, but rather as a conspiracy to produce liquor and defraud the government of taxes meant that charges could be filed against people who never touched a gallon. Suddenly, Ralph Hale's wife was implicated because she paid the mortgage on a building where there was a still. His daughter was implicated because she had bought an F-350. The man who misrepresented the oil bill (Ralph Hale fired his stills with oil burners) was implicated.

This offended the sensibilities of many townspeople, including the sheriff, who said, "We don't have a moonshine problem in Franklin County. We do have a drug problem in Franklin County. There's no comparison," adding that he'd "never heard of kids drinking moonshine, but we do have kids smoking crack and marijuana."

The Roanoke Times sent a reporter to the Rocky Mount Farmers' Market and got a quote from Jay Lynch, where he was selling produce: "They talk like a man making a drop of liquor is the worst thing in the world. People don't realize moonshine brings money into the county. When you can't get a job, and there's no other way to feed your family, you'll go to the holler and make some liquor and that beats stealing." He continued: "Ralph Hale is one of the finer boys to walk this earth. They went up and took all his farm machinery. I can't believe the law's got that much authority."

The reporter interviewed Mr. Midkiff in the garage of his grocery store on Route 40, and he leaned back on his black pickup truck and said: "It's about taxes. That's the only reason. Most are hardworking people. A real bootlegger is as good as his word."

Bill Davis said in the *Roanoke Times* that the crackdown was "meaner." He accused the ABC Board of being lazy and letting the feds take over. He was quoted in the *New York Times* saying, "To me, it's the hobnail-boot approach. They're riding roughshod over people, calling them liars. They are mean." Absurdly, even at the brink of proof, he charged that while "people have historically made liquor here," he had "never seen" the "hundreds of thousands the government is alleging." (Just like a lawyer: of course he'd never *seen* it.)

With federal involvement also came the federal power of civil seizure, with which the government can expropriate funds and property before the defendant is found guilty, before the case is tried, before, in fact, the grand jury even decides whether or not the charges filed are worthy of a trial. The goods themselves are guilty, since they were involved in the perpetration of a crime.

For anyone who believed the rhetoric of the American Revolution (all that stuff about soldiers not being able to move into your house, those limitations on eminent domain, and the redesigning of due process to allow that the burden of proof was on the accuser), this should send a shiver down your spine.

It's a startling fact, but it is true. One's stuff is not necessarily entitled to due process.

Peter Kilborn wrote an article for the March 23, 2000, issue of the *New York Times* titled "U.S. Cracks Down on Rise in Appalachia Moonshine."

> . . . The investigators' leading targets are 60-year-old Ralph D. Hale and several members of his family. The agents say that from 1990 through 1998, Mr. Hale and his wife, Judy, filed tax returns showing annual joint income ranging from $21,149 to $33,139.
>
> Yet, the government maintained on March 6 in an affidavit related to its request for a search warrant, Mr. Hale is the person code-named Hat Man in the journals of the Farmers' Exchange.

According to the journals, Hat Man bought 17,925 100-pound bags of sugar, paying close to $700,000, and 2,710 bundles of one-gallon containers for which he paid $42,000. With the sugar, the affidavit said, he could have produced 179,250 gallons of illegal liquor, worth $1.8 million at $10 a gallon.

The Hales have also amassed many assets, including land on which illegal stills have been found. Holdings that the government has frozen are mostly in Mrs. Hale's name, with the rest in the names of family members other than Mr. Hale. They include nearly 400 acres worth $681,900, $59,405 in mutual fund accounts and $54,991 in bank accounts.

Ralph Hale began to be referred to as the "kingpin," and frequent references were made to his arrivals at church in a Cadillac.

One never hears about the kingpin of the fried chicken racket, and the patriarch of an old family of brewers is never referred to as a kingpin. "Kingpin" is reserved for the world of crime, and is easy newspaper shorthand, setting off a series of associations in the mind of the reader without requiring much work from the newsman. Ninety percent of the time, the kingpin concept is a fantasy, implying as it does a level of organization and hierarchical rigidity that rarely appears in black market operations outside of comic books.

One of the central problems faced by all law-abiding citizens in their approach to the world of crime is an inability to understand what's happening over on the other side. Reporters think in terms of kingpins because their newspaper has an editor in chief, so they extrapolate that the criminals must have bosses. Everyone loves a cartel or a crime family. It's reassuring to imagine that at the top of the heap there's a ruthless but calculating chief of operations. It's more comfortable than confronting the anarchic truth that most crime happens in disorganized and self-centered isolation. Even lawmen stumble regularly in their enforcement duties because of their inability to release their preconceptions about organization. Perhaps because they, themselves, live in a world defined by rank—and many of them learned it in the army and took it forward into the police force—they assume that such structures and systems are universal.

Buddy Driskill, the special agent in charge of the Illegal Whiskey Task Force, once told me that there was always someone at the still who was trusted: "I call him the lieutenant."

They imagine a sort of Moonshine Inc., with employees, underlings, and clear-cut responsibilities.

The truth is far from that. Like any clandestine, cash-driven marketplace, a series of individuals are trying to make good for themselves, taking advantage of whatever they can, and operating only in their own best interest. There are exceptions to this, and certain moonshine families had some sort of slapdash, doomed design, but what usually happens is that someone simply drives up to the still site, someone the shiners know, takes the liquor, and is in hock to the shiners until he sells it. He'll pick it up on a Thursday, and come Tuesday he'll meet his man and hand over the cash.

I suspect that it is only on television that coke dealers have servants and organizations. The black market is a haphazard place. One guy happens to know another guy, someone has some money, someone wants some drugs, or some moonshine, or some fireworks, or whatever, and the next thing you know they're all hooked up.

Hale certainly sold enough to buy a few Cadillacs. (That he was always driving them to church in the papers was interesting, as well, as if the journalists were preloading the bias in the jury for nullification.)

In the case of Ralph Hale, there would be no jury. He pled guilty.

The Stanley family has been, throughout their moonshining careers, as different from Ralph Hale as peaches from pigs. Where Hale was cool and collected, stealthy and sophisticated, the Stanleys were reckless, wild, and dangerous. They are drinkers and brawlers, and there has never been any mystery about their careers in the liquor trade.

Sheriff Overton was quoted in a newspaper: "I know Mr. Stanley. I know him real well. I know his boys, too. What I don't know is where they make their whiskey."

I don't mean to suggest anything untoward in regard to Mr. Overton when I suggest that he was one of the few lawmen who never tripped over a Stanley still or pulled over a truckload of their sugar jack. The Stanleys weren't subtle, and they got busted a lot. Ralph Hale drove to church, they drove at breakneck speeds up Interstate 81, drinking from a case of beer on the floor of the new Econoline 250, loaded with 400 gallons of liquor, pot smoke rolling out the windows as if the seats were on fire.

Lucky for them, the whole family was Teflon-coated and charges would not stick. They were reckless outlaws, and they got away with it for years.

In 1989, for instance. According to the *Washington Post*:

A squad of Bureau of Alcohol, Tobacco and Firearms agents watched two still-hands jug some fresh moonshine, load it into Dee's truck, drive the truck to Dee's house and park it in Dee's driveway. The still-hands left in another car and were arrested. Dee climbed into the truck and drove off and he was arrested, too. At his trial, he testified that he had lent the truck to some friends and had no idea there were 246 gallons of moonshine in it when they brought it back.

He got off.

Karen Peters, who prosecuted the case, called the proceedings "crazy" and said: "He's a very good liar. He gets on the witness stand and he looks so decent and polite. He's a chubby-cheeked kind of good ol' boy and he doesn't look like a criminal. He looks you straight in the eye and he says he got in trouble with liquor years ago but he wouldn't go near it again."

The very next year, 1990, Jimmy Beheler found two 800-gallon stills in William Gray "Dee" Stanley's garage, 1,600 gallons of mash, 43 gallons of moonshine, and 193 empty jugs. Dee was acquitted.

He didn't always walk; he saw the inside of the jail twice, once in 1992 and once in 1995. It doesn't sound like hard time. It was Dee Stanley who was allowed to go home once a day to feed his cows.

Then came a luckless two weeks in 1996, the beginning of a serious spiral.

ABC agents have told me that bootleggers are the best counter-surveillance drivers in the world. They take roundabout routes, they stop for no reason, they pull over and go back the way they came. They drive slow. The Stanleys, it seems, were an exception to this rule.

On February 21, a Wednesday, Dee Stanley's sons, Jason and Scott, were drunk, they had a bag of marijuana, and they were on the move. They got pulled over on Interstate 81, in Winchester, Virginia, three and a half hours or so north of their house on Scuffling Hill Road in Rocky Mount.

The officers had Jason on driving under the influence and Scott on public intoxication and possession of marijuana.

Then the cops looked in the van. The Stanley boys were loaded. They were hauling 446 one-gallon plastic jugs of moonshine stacked in three neat layers.

Captain Rick Seabright called it the biggest seizure he had seen in a long while.

The van was impounded, and the boys were charged with possession of untaxed liquor. They made their bond and got back to work.

Within days the brothers were again pulled over on Interstate 81. Jimmy Beheler had followed the boys from the still in Boones Mill. Jimmy was building a case—no doubt an ingredient of Operation Lightning Strike—and didn't want to reveal to the Stanleys that he was onto them, so he called in an anonymous tip. The Stanleys were loaded with 453 gallons of white liquor. In court, Bill Davis argued the defense and pressed Jimmy Beheler about the tip, which he'd previously denied. *Why did you lie?*

Beheler said, simply, that he'd lied because he wasn't under oath at the time.

Beheler didn't spend a lot of time trying to make friends. When the court recessed, he told reporters that he was "not obligated to give any details of any investigation to any defense attorney."

Davis filed a petition.

Beheler told a reporter that Dee Stanley had brought it all on himself. "He has yet to be stopped by us in a vehicle that did not contain whiskey, jugs, or sugar—every single time. To suggest that we are randomly stopping him on the road is absurd. We just follow the liquor. If these people don't want to be inconvenienced by us, all they have to do is get out of the liquor business and they won't have to deal with us."

Davis suggested that Beheler wanted to get the case out of Franklin County and into a court system that took moonshine more seriously. Davis was furious, and he wasn't alone. In typical topsy-turvy form, the community believed that Beheler's unchivalrous behavior toward the Stanley boys was more of a problem than the van sagging beneath the weight of 453 gallons of white liquor.

The Stanley boys were not easily discouraged. Again they made their bond, and again they got right back to it. A week later Jason and Scott were pulled over outside of Charlottesville, Virginia, with 421 gallons.

Senior Special Agent Jay Calhoun, now retired, told me the story of that bust. The whole Illegal Whiskey Task Force was following them up the road, making fun of them on the CB. Dee was driving when the Stanleys left Rocky Mount, and Jay was joking around, imitating him.

"I could just see them at the dinner table: 'Y'all bunch of fool boys done cost me two trucks! Two loads a likker! I'm gonna drive this time, I'll show you little pissants how this is done!' "

The ABC boys called it in, trying to get some troopers to stop the van.

"Twenty miles, no troopers. They stopped at a convenience store.

We called it in again—thirty miles, no troopers. We called again; we wanted to stay anonymous. Nothing. Finally, Jimmy [Beheler] called. He said something like 'The Eagle is on the move! We got Dee Stanley driving a truckload of liquor! We need troopers!' Well, we drove another forty miles, I think, and then there they were, three troopers sitting in the median. Alright, boys, it is on! When they pulled them over, Dee wasn't driving. They'd switched at the convenience store. We shoulda checked."

The Stanleys laid off for a while, or managed to better evade the police.

In February 1997, their father Dee Stanley was pulled over in a brand-new Ford van with 643 gallon jugs stacked up on palettes. The officer said he could smell booze when Stanley rolled down the window. (Dee was, of course, acquitted.)

It had been a bad year, but they hadn't seen anything yet. A couple of weeks later, it really hit the fan.

Deputy Tim Woods was dispatched to the house on Scuffling Hill after a 911 call and found Dee waiting outside.

"My son's been shot!"

Woods asked who had shot him. Was it safe to enter the house? Did someone still inside have a weapon?

"Just help him," he remembers Dee saying. "He needs help."

Woods wouldn't budge without confirmation that there was not a very freaked-out person on the other side of the door still holding a hot gun.

According to the court documents, Dee finally said, "I shot him."

Scott was found in his basement bedroom, shot several times in the chest. Woods sat with Dee in the kitchen while the medics stabilized his son.

"I asked Dee what type of gun he shot him with, and he replied, 'I don't know, I threw it away.'"

After a moment of silence, Dee said: "I told you I shot him? I don't remember saying that. I don't think so."

The affidavit notes another silent stretch, suggesting that Dee was sorting things out, getting ready to defend himself. Woods testified: "Out of the blue, he looked up at me and said, 'How'd you like to have the shit beat out of you every night?' " And then showed the deputy a few scratches and bruises on his scalp and back.

Dee laid it on: "I tried to hide it from my family, from y'all, but you can only take so much, you know what I mean?"

Scott spent a long week convalescing in a Roanoke hospital. Dee was charged with malicious wounding. Dee needn't have bothered setting his self-defense plan into motion. After Scott recovered, he took the stand at the pretrial hearing and claimed that he didn't know who had shot him. "I was very heavy on drugs and alcohol that night," he testified.

Dee pled guilty to possessing a firearm while on probation and got six months in the clink.

The family had not yet hit bottom. It was coming.

Daryle Johnson—who was described in the *Washington Post* as "a clean-cut young fellow who also happens to have several moonshining convictions on his record"—was hanging out at the Scuffling Hill Road house with Jason and Scott. Dee was still in jail. There was a keg of beer on ice out back, and everyone was having a good time. They had four black pot stills in outbuildings near the house and 600 gallons of moonshine in the garage, ready to be piled into their two specially modified bootlegging vans. Around the property there was about $9,000 in cash.

Scott was getting meaner as they drank. The brothers started fighting about a Hank Williams Jr. cassette. Daryle decided it was time to go; Scott had pulled a gun on him once. He told the papers later that as he drove away he heard Scott yelling at Jason "in a hateful way." He was convinced that "something bad was going to happen."

When the police arrived, Scott was dead in the bedroom, shot four times in the chest. Jason was lying on the floor, shirtless, still on the phone with the dispatcher. There was a .38 on the nightstand, and a bedpost had been ripped off the bed and smashed into the baby's crib.

Scott Stanley had been engaged to Jackie Dyer, and she would soon testify that Scott had beaten her, threatened her with a knife, and shot a puppy. She told the court that his daily drinking regimen consisted of "plenty of liquor" on top of three or four six-packs of beer.

Jason's wife, Kimberly Stanley, also testified at the hearing. She said that Scott had beaten up Jason. She also recounted that Scott had pointed a pistol at her baby girl's head and threatened to "tear out her guts."

Scott's fiancée said, "He begged me to kill him. He would kill himself but he was afraid he'd go to Hell."

The prosecutor asked the judge not to send the case to the grand jury. Bill Davis argued that Scott had backed Jason into the room, up against a wall, and Jason had no choice but to kill his brother in self-defense.

The judge disagreed. "I've got a homicide before me and there's a missing element," she said. "I have no evidence from the defendant himself." She announced that she would send the case to the grand jury.

Jason's wife burst into tears and bolted from the courtroom with Jason on her heels.

The prosecuting attorney lingered, hangdog, answering questions. He said he would try the case if he was told to, it was his duty, but he didn't think he could convict. "The defense evidence was overwhelming."

Bill Davis had pulled out all the stops, it was true. Jason's mother had cried on the stand, saying that Scott was violent and drunk and that Jason was jolly and quiet.

There was no mention of the moonshine, the stills, or the cash. No charges were filed. The *Washington Post* noted that "three convicted moonshiners had testified in Jason's support, and the wife of a fourth had guaranteed his bail bond."

A reporter asked the prosecution if that indicated that Franklin County's moonshiners were in cahoots.

Dramatically, albeit somewhat nonsensically, he answered: "You've seen *Chinatown*, haven't you?"

Jason was convicted of voluntary manslaughter and spent a year in jail. Dee was allowed out of jail for Scott's funeral.

On May 7, Operation Lightning Strike struck: agents raided the Farmers' Exchange (both the office in town and the warehouse out on Route 40), busted Ralph Hale's 9,600-gallon still site in Craig County, seized 19 vehicles, 6 tractors, and $33,000 cash; they froze several bank accounts, searched houses in North Carolina and Virginia, and broke up four more stills.

It was a vast and violent readjustment of the world.

For Ramsey Helms, who ran the Helms Farmers' Exchange with his brother Bill, the new world would prove overwhelming.

Barbara Bowling worked at the Farmers' Exchange for more than twenty years and talked to Ramsey Helms on the Friday following the raid. She said he seemed "distressed."

"They've taken everything," he told her. "I don't know what's here. I don't know what I have left."

On Sunday morning he talked to his brother.

On Sunday afternoon he put a shotgun to his chest and pulled the trigger.

Bowling later said that an article in the *Roanoke Times* had been the final straw, and she claimed to reporters from that same paper that moonshine was not discussed during all her years working at the store.

"He's not a villain. He's not a Mafia kingpin. He didn't live an extravagant lifestyle."

His nephew, Jim, asked that the media leave them alone and stated that the family blamed, at least in part, the attention.

The paper quoted J. C. Law, a retired mechanic living in Rocky Mount.

> He was frustrated with how the ATF and local news media treated his longtime friend. "Ramsey was never involved in bootlegging. That man was selling a wholesale business," he said. He said the ATF's seizure of supplies sold at Helms Farmers' Exchange and its move to freeze Helms' funds hit him hard financially. "The ATF may not have pulled that trigger, but they might as well have. It was humiliating and embarrassing, and it done him in," he said. "They left him with 15 cents in his pocket. They took fertilizer and potting soil. Does the ATF have that kind of authority?"

> Beheler said the suicide was tragic. "It feels really bad. Objectively, we did what we had to do, but I don't think that you can separate that from what has happened. Nothing was meant to be personal. It was just an investigation, and it evolved. We had to act on it. It was a bad situation to begin with, and now it's worse."

Despite Ramsey Helms's suicide, the case was building. The Stanley boys might have assumed their debt to society was paid, but their various brushes with the law—all their plea bargains and acquittals—had established a pattern of criminality. There exist two key rules of court by which defendants are protected from overzealous prosecution. The first is known as "double jeopardy," which ensures that you cannot be tried for the same crime twice with the same set of facts. The second ensures that the prosecution cannot use past crimes as evidence of your current guilt. (A very good idea—you wouldn't want to stand in a courtroom and hear that it was obvious that you were guilty, because after all, the last time this happened, the perpetrator was you.) Unfortunately for the Stanleys, these protections are not quite as straightforward as they appear. It's true that just because you've been arrested before doesn't mean you did it this time, and it's true that if the court decided you didn't do it, you're permanently innocent, but it's also true that if you are later accused of a continuing criminal enterprise, or a conspiracy, those past crimes can be used as evidence to establish a pattern.

In the grand jury indictment that was the culmination of Operation Lightning Strike, every arrest during the period considered is represented. Every time the Stanleys were pulled over contributed to the establishing of a pattern of criminal activity that proved the existence of a conspiracy. Plea bargains they'd made, sentences that had been suspended, acquittals on charges they no doubt thought were long behind them were suddenly laid out in succession, like a trail of bread crumbs leading to prison.

Count 38 of the indictment states that Dee and others "did knowingly, willfully and unlawfully conspire, confederate and agree with each other and with other persons, and did aid and abet each other in so doing, to commit the following offenses against the United States." No longer is the issue at hand a matter of whether or not the liquor in the truck was owned by Dee. They weren't charged with something as simple as a crime, they were being charged with the "intent to promote, manage, establish, carry on, and to facilitate the promotion, management, establishment and carrying on of an unlawful activity, the unlawful activity being a business enterprise involving liquor on which the Federal excise tax has not been paid."

There in black and white, all the evidence: the sugar purchases: 148,300 pounds of sugar in 1994. Dee was working with a man named Kenny Cobler. Cobler purchased 34,100 pounds of sugar in January of 1999. There were the bank deposits. Overt act number thirteen: "Beginning on an unknown date and continuing until

September 7, 1992 Lonnie Quinn operated an illicit distillery on Rt. 789 in Franklin County, Virginia, to produce untaxed liquor for resale, at which a 1970 Ford truck in the name of DEE STANLEY was seized."

The evidence against Ralph Hale was, of course, more oblique.

"On or about January 19, 1990, RALPH HALE was observed near a still site located near Rt. 781, in the Ferrum section of Franklin County, and later assisted the entry of a 1972 Ford truck . . ."

I asked Sharon Burnham, "What do you mean? Do you guys have cameras nailed to the trees?"

"I'm not going to answer that."

Later, she used the term "supporting surveillance."

Throughout all the charges there was evidenced a systematic re-counting of telephone calls, forged fuel bills, truck purchases, and deposits. The pattern was undeniable.

The feds had an 83-page spreadsheet listing their entries into evidence, 71 witnesses, and 12 further pages of potential evidence for which they sought admission. On Ralph Hale alone they had a 23-page spreadsheet cataloging his pickups at the Farmers' Exchange.

They'd tracked down details. Hale had purchased a horse trailer for cash and registered it to someone else—it was a giant, shining stainless-steel thing, a beauty. He claimed it wasn't his, he hadn't bought it, but the investigators found the dealership, and there, up on the wall, a snapshot of a smiling Ralph Hale, a barrel-chested bear of a man, in front of the purchase.

Sharon has great admiration for investigators: "They just keep gathering things. They don't always know why. But they keep going. It's tedious."

Indeed, the amount of work is incredible. Agents sifted through huge boxes full of slips of paper, and jumped, inspired by a crumpled receipt, to chase wild geese. Sometimes it paid off. Every once in a while they'd earn a prize.

One of the Helms brothers had a torn corner of scrap paper in his pocket. Apparently, he carried with him at all times a sheaf of receipts, phone numbers, and checks. The scrap read:

BLACK HORSE
12345 67890*

This was the code with which all the phone numbers were encrypted, and this was how it was discovered that Hat Man was Ralph Hale, along with the identity of every encoded name on the desk calendar.

The evidence accrued like rocks upon the board that crushed Giles Corey.

Dee Stanley was looking at sixty years in prison and $2 million in fines; Jason was facing forty-five years in prison and up to $1.25 million in fines. Serious time in a real prison.

The Rocky Mount man who evaded conviction despite being caught several times in vehicles loaded with jugs of moonshine was not able to escape his own paper trail. He capitulated Monday to a crackdown on the illegal liquor trade called Operation Lightning Strike after prosecutor Sharon Burnham described some of her evidence—telephone and financial records.

In what could spell the end of an illegal liquor dynasty that has been marked by violence, 55-year-old William Gray "Dee" Stanley, and his son, Jason, both pleaded guilty in federal court to one count of conspiracy to take a criminal enterprise across state lines and two counts of money laundering.

The entire Hale family went to trial, resistant to the end. After Burnham's opening statement there was a meeting in the judge's chambers during which the judge said to the defense: "Your clients must feel like dead men walking. I suggest you work out a deal."

---

* How to Be a Criminal, Item 3: Do not write down the keys to the code. If you can't count to ten, think of another code.

They pled.

William Helms held on, tenaciously. He would go to trial and see how he fared, but it didn't look promising.

The morning they were to begin trying the case, two jet planes flew into the World Trade Center.

Helms said to the judge that he didn't feel that prosecuting him was a good use of taxpayer money; he didn't think that the government should spend its time on him.

"I don't have the heart."

He pled guilty. The *Roanoke Times* reported:

The last defendant in the federal moonshine crackdown known as "Operation Lightning Strike" was ordered to undergo treatment for alcohol abuse, stay under house arrest and pay a fine. A federal judge sentenced William Lewis Helms on Friday to six months of alcohol rehabilitation and six months of house arrest, a fine of $8,500 and three years' probation for his role in two moonshine conspiracies. He pleaded guilty a year ago. Prosecutors said Helms and his brother, the late Ramsey Helms, conspired to sell moonshine-making supplies such as sugar and jugs out of Farmers Exchange, a Rocky Mount store that has since closed. Ramsey Helms committed suicide two years ago after he was named as a key suspect.

A week later the Associated Press carried a story titled "Moonshiners' Property on the Auction Block" that began "Neighbors gathered in front of the Farmers Exchange for one last glimpse of a moonshiner's haven and the end of an era." The article rounded up the convictions, the pleas, and the case, and cited Sharon Burnham's claim that over the course of five years, the goods sold by the Exchange had "led to $20 million in unpaid liquor taxes."

Gary Poulsen called the auction before a crowd of about 75.

Nine properties were sold, some at fire sale prices: Poulsen had to goad the crowd past $25,000 for the Farmers' Exchange itself.

"You know it's worth more than that. Probably drove up here in a pickup that was worth more than that."

The Main Street store went for $55,000. The two warehouses went for $35,000 and $28,000. The highest price of the day was $176,000 for a house and 50 acres "that used to belong to moonshine kingpin Ralph Hale."

When I asked the Illegal Whiskey Task Force if they thought that any of the folks caught in Operation Lightning Strike were still moonshining, they answered, laughing, "They're still breathing, ain't they?"

Colorado Whiskey

The mass of men serve the state thus, not as men mainly, but as machines, with their bodies. They are the standing army, and the militia, jailers, constables, posse comitatus, etc. In most cases there is no free exercise whatever of the judgment or of the moral sense; but they put themselves on a level with wood and earth and stones; and wooden men can perhaps be manufactured that will serve the purpose as well. Such command no more respect than men of straw or a lump of dirt. They have the same sort of worth only as horses and dogs.

—HENRY DAVID THOREAU, "CIVIL DISOBEDIENCE"

FLYING DOG RANCH IN WOODY CREEK, COLORADO, IS AS FAR from Franklin County as can be. With the exception of what I can only assume is a small army of Aspen cocaine dealers, the outlaws in these mountains are mostly in it for the kicks: avocational outlaws. I was in Gonzo territory, tucked up in the mountains with George Stranahan, a man after whom a whiskey is named. I told him I thought that was impressive, and that I'd once known an autistic kid named

John Walker, but he didn't seem to get it. George is an attractive, jaunty man in his early seventies, weathered and thin. A belt held up his Levi's, clasped with a big silver buckle that read GSS. He carried a pen clipped into his shirt pocket, and frequently daubed his chapped lips with balm. We stood in a small gravel lot surrounded by cedar-sided barns and cabins.

"That's the original homestead cabin, right there, 1876, the first structure in Woody Creek, they tell me."

Below us, a herd of wild elk, a hundred-strong, grazed one of his fields. Woody Creek is tucked into the valley of the Roaring Fork River, and the green hills around the valley—they look like hills, but the elevation of the valley is well over 7,000 feet—rise softly in the summer, rounded and gentle before the rough, jagged, snowcapped peaks that loom in the near distance. Nailed into the planking of one of the outbuildings was Hunter S. Thompson's famous Gonzo dagger with the double-thumbed fist clutching a peyote button. Owl Farm is right next door, on land once owned by Stranahan. Thompson used to have pool rights to swim in Stranahan's pool between midnight and 5 A.M.

"Hunter was like the night watchman around Woody Creek," said George, "he was up."

Earlier, over Flying Dog amber ales at the Woody Creek Tavern where we'd met, George had been talking about a recent documentary on Thompson, in which George was quoted as saying that Hunter was a horrible neighbor who never paid his rent, broke up George's marriage, and taught George's kids to smoke pot.

"Well, it's all true," George had said, smiling. He clearly cherished their friendship. Anyway, he seems to deal lightly with the obstacles and catastrophes inherent to a complicated and interesting life.

"That's the one that burned down right there," he said, pointing to a nice-looking, small cedar-sided barn on the other side of a stretch of gravel, across from a building filled with trucks, tractors, and piles of the sort of things that pile up around farms: tarps, hay, wood.

"It needed burning. There were things in there I was glad to get rid of. I told them, the firemen, to let it go. 'Do what you have to with the water, put it over there,' " pointing to a small fenced field. "Anyway, it's like when you wreck a car. You want the fucking thing *totaled*."

One of the firefighters who watched the barn burn and helped to make sure nothing else caught on fire was a downhill-ski-racing, rodeo-riding, honest-to-god rebel cowboy who had moved to Woody Creek from Aspen, back when everyone thought it was the sticks. His name was Jess Graber. The story goes, and this is how they both tell it, that the two talked as the barn burned and discovered that they both liked whiskey.

Jess revealed that he liked it so much he was making corn whiskey in a 13-gallon copper pot still. George had converted the barn that hadn't burned to a finished space. He'd put in tie beams to hold the thing together, insulated and drywalled the walls, and poured a concrete floor. Jess moved his still into a small room by the front door.

Over cheeseburgers and Coors with Jess Graber at the Woody Creek Tavern (people in Woody Creek assume that you can't find their house, and they don't come off as anxious to take you there, so they all use the tavern as a sort of hotel lobby) I asked about being a small-scale moonshiner in a tiny town.

"A lot of people around here knew it. It's a small town," said Jess, gesturing at the street that runs by the Woody Creek Tavern and rocking back in his chair. "Small town" barely cuts it. Woody Creek is a scattered collection of cabins and ranches surrounding the tavern, the Community Center, and a trailer park.

"It never really made me nervous."

Jess looks like a man who has lived his life outside. His cheeks are ruddy and his eyes squint against the sun, even indoors. He's tall and handsome, and fits the maverick role he's carved out for himself perfectly.

He shook his head and cocked it forward, like a man getting ready to tell the punch line, or a bird dog listening to the rustle of the leaves.

"I got nervous once," he said. "Someone accused me and three other guys of possibly being the Unabomber. The FBI came up here and they were asking questions about me. Well, you know, I'm not that kind of guy, and word got to me pretty quick that there were people asking questions about me, so I called them. 'This here's Jess Graber, I hear you're looking for me. What do you need to know?' I was glad the still was up at George's place."

At George's place the barn was spacious and open, with gallery lighting all around and dozens of photographs and prints on the wall, mostly by George, at least one by Ralph Steadman.

"I've done a lot of things," said George, humbly (he started the Aspen Physics Institute, was a professor, has traveled in the Himalayas, founded Flying Dog beer, won an award for a bull he bred, started a couple of magazines—it's a serious list), "but the constant is photography. I've always taken pictures. That's the narrative of my life. I'd like for it to endure."

The business of the barn, these days, is trying to make sure that it does endure, and George and his team spend their days cataloging and databasing his immense collection of images so he can publish books and get prints onto people's walls. That's what he really likes, to get his photos onto people's walls. When I stopped on the stairs and looked at an Edward Weston rip-off of an artichoke cut in half, I told him I'd buy it.

"Take it down off the wall. You bought two beers, that's a good trade."

Originally, the renovated barn was supposed to be a community kitchen. "I wanted to get a good meat grinder in here, for people to make their elk sausage, and a stove." It didn't work out. It did, however, work as a party space. Local bands played, George got kegs of his Flying Dog beer, and they lit the woodstove and they didn't have to clean up.

"You get to just go home drunk. Clean it up next week."

Jess would come to the barn and replenish the house supply of moonshine.

"It was great," said Jess, "I could run the still in the winter. We'd just give it away, you know, for Christmas. But man, soon, we couldn't keep up. People loved it. I was making corn whiskey because that's what you do. You're making moonshine, right? That was what I knew, and I could buy corn at the feed store. The first time I thought of doing all this," by which he meant going commercial, "was 1989. I called the TTB* and they sent me the forms and I looked at them." He made his eyes go wobbly while holding up an imaginary form. "Whew. I put them away."

Jess bottled his hooch at 90 proof in leftover Jack Daniel's bottles, relabeling it "Stranahan's American Whiskey" and calling it "The only whiskey made West of the Missouri River."

One morning after a party in the barn, Jess discovered two kegs of leftover beer.

"What's with the beer?" he asked a ranch hand.

It was flat, ruined. The hand supposed that the next time somebody took a trip into Denver they'd return it to the brewery.

"Can I have it?"

"What are you gonna do with it?"

"There's alcohol in there," said Jess.

The hand didn't get it, and figured he ought to return the kegs, just like George had said.

"Just let me cook it up. Let's see," said Jess.

You can imagine the shrug. Crazy guy wants to screw around with leftover beer, let him do it. Whatever. I've got work to do.

Jess charged his still (distillery talk for filling it up) with the spent beer, and soon discovered that distilling from beer made a much better product. "It was *such* a dramatic difference from what I had been doing. Dramatic. The lightbulb just went off. I think it's very difficult to make it consistent with corn."

The beer run was a revelation.

---

* The agency wouldn't have been called the TTB at the time. The Alcohol and Tobacco Tax and Trade Bureau, almost always referred to as the TTB, was created in 2003 when the Homeland Security Act split the Bureau of Alcohol, Tobacco, and Firearms into two distinct agencies. The TTB became part of the Department of the Treasury, the ATF became part of the Justice Department and changed its name to the Bureau of Alcohol, Tobacco, Firearms, and Explosives.

"It was just amazingly clean and pure. From my experience I knew that this was distinctly different. It was distinctly *better*. It was two kinds of beer, and I don't even remember what they were, but the dramatic smoothness, and the aroma, and the softness of the palate, it was just . . . yeah."

He repeated himself, snapping his fingers next to his forehead: "The lightbulb just went off. I could get somebody to do this part, and I could do what I need to do."

Although the federal forms had been intimidating, the idea of going legitimate had never left Jess. He'd looked at dairy farms out in western Colorado, where they grow Olathe sweet corn, looking for a place with running water and concrete floors.

"I never had the wherewithal to get it together," said Jess, but with a newly predictable fermentation process (thanks to the careful techniques of the Flying Dog brewmaster) and a consistently excellent product, his dreams of legitimate distilling were reinvigorated. After the initial discovery, he worked in the barn for three years.

Stranahan pointed to the wall of the foyer, "The beer would just line up right here, all the short fills and all the leftovers, we'd just line them up on the wall."

Jess tried just about every kind of beer they made. Some beer didn't work; other beer did.

"That was the extent of my education, you know, you take apart the car engine when you're a kid, and you put it back together, and if it doesn't run, you've got to take it apart again."

By discovering what kind of beer he liked to extract whiskey from, he discovered what kind of grains he wanted to use.

Jess kept tinkering in the barn, and he and George kept giving the hooch away for Christmas until demand outpaced supply and a spot on the Christmas list became prized, something worth begging for and bragging about. They weren't making any money, but they were still breaking the law. Jess's still was unlicensed and tax is owed on distilled alcohol even if it's given away. The popularity of the product was putting them at risk.

I asked George if he was afraid of being busted, and at first he brushed off the question. "Who would come up here? How would we get busted? And anyway, I weighed the consequences. You take the probability of getting caught and you measure it against the penalty and your ability to afford that penalty. So, I get caught and I get a fine, I can afford that. It's all about balance and probabilities."

Then something in him clicked and he turned to face me: "But it's like Hunter said about civil disobedience and being an outlaw. If the law is stupid, then you've got to break it."

I managed to get a bottle of their legit whiskey well before I met any of these guys, well before it was distributed in New York. People were talking about their whiskey and bootlegging it around, just like they'd used to do with Coors.

I was impressed with my smuggled bottle: There was a metal enclosure keeping the cork on, shaped like a cross between a shot glass and a piece of ordnance. The label was pasted at an angle across the thick glass of the bottle, and in black script over a tan field it read "Stranahan's Colorado Whiskey." It looked Western, maverick. The label said, "Batch 10, Distilled by Jake Norris, Listening to Tom Waits."

The grain flavors came through fully with each sip. It was multi-layered, with the lightness of a whiskey like Jameson underscored by a toasty, darker depth with distinct campfire notes and a substantial layer of chocolate. This was something new. It tasted like top-shelf cowboy whiskey.

To say a whiskey is the best I've ever had is impossible—an absurd exercise. I've had twenty-five-year-old Macallan, George T. Stagg, Ardbeg 10, twenty-year-old Pappy Van Winkle, Corner Creek, an Early Times mint julep as the gates clanged open at the Kentucky Derby, and Elijah Craig eighteen-year-old Reserve while skinning and butchering a deer with a Swiss Army knife in the headlights of a pickup on a dark, cold December night. I drank whiskey on my wedding day, and on the side of a Virginia mountain when the clock ticked midnight in 1999.

I've never sat in a lab to taste whiskey; my whiskey history is all tied up with my life. The best whiskey I've ever had is like the best horse race ever run: the next one.

There are drams, however, that arrest you and grab your attention. Whiskeys that make you stop talking. When a serious whiskey passes my lips, I find myself chewing on it, moving my tongue around, slapping against my palate and exploring the flavors. When I find in my hand a real, deep, layered whiskey, I am always tempted, for the moment that my head is lost in the drink, to close my eyes, let go, and declare that *this* is the best whiskey I've ever had.

Stranahan's grabbed me that way.

While Jess was out in Woody Creek making moonshine for his friends and neighbors, Jake Norris was home-distilling in Denver. As he says of himself: he hobbies hard. His plot in the community garden, of which he's immensely proud, is 450 square feet, and he starts prepping it months before it's time to plant his fourteen varieties of heirloom tomatoes. When we met, he'd just put in seedlings for white peppers and white tomatoes: "Just think of the plating possibilities!" He built a 1974 Honda CB360T motorcycle from scratch and customized it as a café racer with clipped handlebars and a huge 9-inch bucket headlight. One day there was music on while we spoke, his iTunes on shuffle, and he pointed out a trippy bit of drum loops and sampled Vivaldi and said that he'd made it. He makes his own mustard, hot sauce, and pickles. He's been making moonshine since he was fifteen.

His history with whiskey goes back farther than that. He was born on a farm in West Virginia, which his parents had rented from a man named Almon Lewis. Lewis had been a moonshiner, and a pretty successful one. The revenuers came looking around one day, and he and his partner took off in different directions. Almon got away; his partner did not. His partner suspected Almon had set him up, and the suspicion ended both the business and the friendship. Almon was wistful about it, and when he gave Jake's dad a tour of the farm, he pointed out a creek.

"That there is the whiskey creek," he said. "All the best whiskey I ever made came from the water out of that creek."

When Jake was an infant, his dad took him up on a horse and rode him around the land, showing him the apple trees and the meadows and explaining where they lived. He stopped at the whiskey creek, and gave baby Jake a sip of water.

"That was the first water I ever drank, it was the first water to pass my lips. My father said he considered it a baptism of sorts."

For years he tended bar, and people called him "Whiskey Jake" because he could push you through an impromptu class on whiskey. To this day people call him and ask him to teach classes on whiskey. While I was with him, he was negotiating a gig to teach a roomful of dentists.

He worked hard as a hobby distiller, attacking the pastime with devotion and enthusiasm. There was no homedistiller.org at the time, just an old (famous) article in the *Whole Earth News* about how to make fuel. As he refined his technique, he came to two conclusions.

The first was that he wanted a short column on top of his pot still, so he paid a machinist to build him a small, packed column he could clamp onto the top of a keg. He inserted a water-heater coil in the tank. The still he built cost him close to $4,000 by the time he was finished.

His next discovery was that he didn't want to mash his own grain. He approached a manager at Flying Dog brewery (he'd dated the sister of the bass player in the guy's band, years ago, and they'd known each other ever since) and started by asking if he could buy 50-pound bags of grain from the brewery. Better yet, could he buy some beer wash before they'd hopped it.

The brewer, just like George's ranch hand, was surprised to learn there was whiskey inside beer. Jake explained it to him.

Jess and George Stranahan were moving forward, setting up their whiskey company, which would locate next to the Flying Dog brewery in Denver. Jess visited Flying Dog to explain to them that there was whiskey inside their beer and talk about how they were going to make that whiskey right next door. He was surprised to learn they were already hip to the idea, not because they'd heard about the Woody Creek experiments, but because Jake had laid the groundwork.

Jess tracked Jake down at the Celtic Tavern, where he was tending bar.

"I heard you are the guy to talk to about making whiskey."

"Whiskey Jake" heard the question as "I heard you are the guy to talk to about whiskey."

"It was not uncommon for someone to send a friend in for a tutorial," Jake told me. "I did not advertise that I was a hobby distiller."

Jess ordered a Jameson on the rocks.

"I started in with 'That is Jameson, it is an Irish whiskey, made from a mix of malted and unmalted barley. It is going to have lighter characteristics than an all-malt like a Bushmills and so on. The diatribe goes for a bit. Jess is nodding and listening, and he reached into his wallet and pulled out a card and handed it to me."

Jake was floored. "I glanced at it and it stopped me in my tracks. I asked if he was opening a liquor store specializing in whiskey or starting some sort of import company."

"I'm going to make the first whiskey in Colorado," said Jess. "I am going to make whiskey right here."

Flustered, excited, Jake began to yammer: "I just designed a still and I want to make whiskey!"

Jess knew that—that was why he was there.

Jake bought Jess another Jameson, took a break, and they squirreled away to a corner of the bar to talk. Jake drew a sketch of the beer keg pot/column still he'd just designed, and when he showed it to Jess, he remembers feeling very uncomfortable. Jess looked at him cockeyed, and Jake figured that he'd come across as a nutjob and ruined the relationship before it got out of the gate. They left it at that, and Jake was surprised when Jess called a couple of days later and asked that he come in and interview for the job of distiller.

They met and Jake turned in a "pathetic résumé and about three hundred photographs of all the distilleries I visited in Ireland and Scotland."

Then he learned that the still he had drawn on the bar napkin was the same basic design that Jess had just designed over the course of a year's consultations with the engineers at the classic whiskey-still manufacturer Vendome. Jake's was a beer keg, and Jess's 165 gallons. Jake's was fabricated and rigged, and Jess's was solid copper with beautiful brass fittings and portals and adjustable plates in the column. Regardless, the two stills were based upon the same idea.

Jake and Jess were made for one another.

The first thing that hits you when you walk into Stranahan's distillery is how good it smells. The air is warm and humid, and the steamy atmosphere is rich with sweet, bready fragrance. It sends you into an olfactory reverie, out of which you snap as you try not to trip over one of the hoses that run across the floor like a cat's cradle. This is not a showcase; it's a job site. The desk is covered with logs and memos (and for one unfortunate afternoon, a roll of toilet paper). The wall is a puzzle-piece mosaic of business cards and Post-it notes. You don't focus on the clutter for long, thankfully, because of the two beautiful copper stills in the room.

A good still looks like some sort of antique submarine—portals and welds and access doors held closed with wingnuts the size of a child's fist. Tubing shoots off in every direction, delivering steam to heat the wash and taking it back to the heater, delivering cool water to the condenser and removing it, collecting the vapors and measuring the temperatures, handling overflow and sending reflux back down the column for further enrichment.

Stranahan's has two Vendomes, both custom-made. The newer of the two is a squat 750-gallon masterpiece in dull copper. The fat tank is supported on red metal legs. The top is a gentle dome with an odd seam running across on the left, separating the first fifth or so of the tank and suggesting not only that the thing is seriously bespoke, but also that it might have gone under the knife in Frankenstein's lab. The boiler is crowned by a short column with three stainless-steel portals and one at the top of glass. The bottom three are where the bubble plates are, fluelike obstructions in the column of the still where the alcohol is discouraged from rising and therefore gets stronger and cleaner. These bubble plates are adjustable. One can open them up all the way and catch more of the water and the oils and the other alcohols, or close them up tight and get closer to pure ethanol.

The last portal is simply a window into the column. At this point in Stranahan's development, watching this window is about 35 percent of the distiller's job. When the wash is cooking too hot, or when the barometric pressure changes, the suds rise up the column, and if the liquid rises too high, you'll "puke" the still and send boiling hot mash out the back escape valve. You try to keep that from happening.

Stranahan's is a single-product shop. Every run they make is the same. They discovered and decided upon the details long ago. The mash bill is permanent. The settings on the bubble caps are permanent. The length of fermentation is constant (and not their problem anyway, since they contract out the production of the wash to microbrewers—it used to be Flying Dog, but Flying Dog moved to Maryland and now it's Oskar Blues). The cuts separating heads and tails from the heart happen at the same temperature and the same percentage of alcohol by volume every time.

Watching the still is like driving on a straight lonely highway. There isn't much to do, but you have to pay attention. You watch the portal, and if the mash starts to boil up the column, you turn the heat down. After the still has been running for hours, you start monitoring the strength of the distillate that's coming out, and when it gets down to 60 proof, you cut it off—that's the tails cut.

I don't mean to undersell the job, but it's a misunderstood vocation. The artful subtlety in Jake's day comes not, as one might think, as he strolls the malting floor in a hacking jacket running grain through his fingers, but rather from his expert piloting of the Toyota forklift. Having driven forklifts for a living in my past, I can tell you that it is a satisfying skill, but it is not the mossy, pipesmoke scene that one might imagine a head distiller's life to be. It's not all snifters and tasting notes.

Someone in Kansas needed some Stranahan's, it was a new account, and we locked the front door (bums tend to wander in and steal whiskey if there's no one around) and went back into the warehouse where the barrels are stored and the cases of bottles are stacked up in a bay, ready to roll. We ripped the heavy-duty plastic wrap that enclosed a tall pallet of whiskey and moved eighty cases of whiskey onto another pallet, stacking the six-packs in neat, alternating rows. We topped the pallet off with some samples and a box of promotional materials and wrapped the whole thing up in a new layer of heavy-duty plastic. A few hours later, a tractor trailer showed up and Jake loaded the pallet onto the truck.

We sat at the cluttered desk by the front door, answering the phone. "Stranahan's Colorado Whiskey, this is Jake."

Then: "Yep, you can e-mail tours@stranahans.com and we'll schedule one for you," or "No, Jess isn't here . . . You can call back and I'll let it ring through and you can leave a message."

He'd hang up the phone and look at me: "Salesmen."

I monitored the proof of the distillate, looking for the cutoff point by twirling a hydrometer in a graduated cylinder. It bobs like a frail buoy and slows, and you squint and try to read the level of the liquid from the actual level and not from the meniscus clinging to the walls. When the alcohol hit 60 proof, I closed the cock valve on the pipe that led from the condenser to the rectangular stainless-steel holding tank next to the still.

We clamped a 3-inch hose onto the bottom of the still to empty the spent mash into the drain in the floor.

"I like to crank up the heat, it helps to push the mash out," said Jake. We ran the hose to the drain, opened it up, and turned on the heat. The wash smelled cooked, and as the dark liquid swirled into Denver's sewers, it suggested flat beer.

The boiler was hot, and the steam lapped at our faces as we used a flashlight to look for sediment and hose it off of the walls. Every once in a while someone has to actually crawl into the thing and clean it out.

To fill the still again, we wrestled more of the heavy 3-inch red food-grade hoses around the room and ran a line between a tanker-truck—sized dairy storage tank full of Oskar Blues wash and the empty still. Jake hooked up the in-line pump, checked all the valves, and turned it on while I held the hose over my shoulder like a fireman. The dark, beery wash gushed out, pushing the bready, malt scent to a new height. Stranahan's uses four barleys, and amylase makes sure that further sugars are converted and made available to the yeasts. Before it has been cooked off, the wash is malty and grainy. It has been fermented to about 10 percent, and the vapors that rise from the portal are heady and rich.

We also emptied and refilled the spirit still, the original 165-gallon Vendome. The process is the same, only quicker. The second run starts at 100 proof, so it's very clean inside the still. We dumped the waste, filled the boiler back up with 100-proof rough spirit, and turned it on.

We went back into the warehouse to work on the barrels. Barrels, especially at high altitudes, tend to need tuning, and Jake flips them around casually, each 100-pound cask like a can of beer in his hands. He smacked the rings down to tighten them with a hammer and a rod, pushing the staves together. He stood the barrels on end, and I poured water over the top, filling the ¾ of an inch where the staves jut up over the cap. This would help hydrate the barrels, and it would show us if they leaked.

That done, we drove off to get the gold medal they'd won in Kentucky framed and have an early afternoon beer.

Jake and I did a lot of tasting while we were at the distillery. I tasted the specialty runs that they're storing. They're experimenting with wine casks, and the flavors of the whiskey are serious and interesting. The wine barrels give the whiskey new flavors, one is herbaceous; another is rich with stone fruit. Squashed-berry flavors and deep ruby colors abound.* I tasted some Stranahan's which had been in the barrel for seven years, the oldest they've got, and while I liked it, I can't say that it tasted like Stranahan's anymore. It tasted like heavily oaked American whiskey, but it had lost that grainy chocolate porter taste that defines their whiskey. Playing around in microdistilleries makes one realize that while the whiskey world has come to think that old is better (perhaps because it's more expensive), the truth is that old is just old—sometimes young is better.

I gave Jake some of my oaked applejack. It was the first time I'd given my product to a professional distiller, and I was nervous. I played it off like it didn't matter, pouring us a couple of samples into tumblers and sitting down at the desk. He nosed it, raised his eyebrows, and took a sip.

"Wow," he said. "For applejack, you've got some really developed flavors here, real depth."

He thought my still was too efficient, and that I wasn't throwing away enough heads, but he liked it. I was ecstatic.

Our time moseyed on. I shadowed tours. Tours are supposed to be by appointment, but folks walk in off the street all day. If they live in town, Jake might brush them off, but it's hard to tell a guy who has driven three hours to come back later. The public ranges from creepy know-it-alls with chips on their shoulders (why did they stop? who spends time that way?) to enthusiastic families with broad grins. Jake once gave a tour to what he supposes was a military family: they stood in order of height, with the father heading up the five-person stack. Everything Jake said, the family seemed to fact-check. Jake would say, for instance, "We sell the used casks to microbrewers, who use them to condition their beer," and four heads would turn to the father, silently asking for confirmation: is it true what he says?

---

* This became their limited release "Snowflake" expressions.

When the barrels in the back room were ready (we'd tuned and moistened them), we rolled them to the front to fill them with whiskey. Jake spun the casks across the floor and up a ramp on their end while holding one hand flat on the butt of the barrel, the 100-plus-pound container moving along the concrete floor on its edge as if it were on a track. I struggled and heaved and overcompensated and threatened my toes and every extension cord or hose within 30 feet of me.

Jake stirred 400 gallons of raw whiskey with a canoe paddle, to make sure the clear distillate was properly mixed with the water with which he'd cut it down from about 140 proof to something more like 110.

We weighed each barrel, wrote a number on its end, stuck a gas-pump-style handle into the bunghole and filled it up. Then we hammered a disk of poplar (the bung) into the hole and weighed the barrel again, recording the weights in a log as the basis of the tax Stranahan's would owe on the distillate. In the log he wrote my name next to the batch, and after those barrels have rested for a couple of years, he's promised I'll have an opportunity to get some of the whiskey.

After we'd filled, sealed, and weighed the barrel, Jake plucked it up with the forklift, balancing the barrel itself between the forks, and drove it back into the warehouse.

At harvesttime, we stacked two- and three-year-old barrels by the scale and weighed them again before opening them to see what they'd lost. Whiskey evaporates as it's stored, and what's lost is called the Angel's Share.*

I cracked the bung on barrel number 246 with a chisel and a hammer and put my nose down near the barrel to smell the whiskey as it touched the open air for the first time. It's as if the two atmospheres, inside and outside the barrel, struggle for an instant to create an equilibrium. The air from inside the barrel sort of poofs up into a little

---

* In Scotland, whiskey is weaker coming out of the barrel than it was going in, but in Kentucky, it's stronger.

cloud and then sucks back into the barrel. For one beautiful moment you are surrounded by the luscious, humid vapor of freshly harvested whiskey, rich and fruity.

Three of us worked on the harvesting, and my job was to pull samples out of the pump line. I'd pull 750 milliliters into a graduated cylinder by cocking a valve—the whiskey would rush and froth into the cylinder, foaming. I'd discover the proof with a hydrometer, then I'd pour the sample in a bottle and write a label with the batch and barrel number and the proof. Stranahan's keeps a record of every barrel they've opened. I took a lot of sips. When we cracked the older barrels—every batch is made up of some whiskey that's about two and some that's older—I poured myself a small glass.

This was whiskey without oxidation, without any water, it hadn't taken a tractor-trailer trip in a bottle. Stranahan's is an excellent whiskey no matter when you're drinking it. Sipping it at cask strength straight out of the barrel you just cracked open is sublime.

This was the heart of the matter.

It's enough to make you want to start a distillery of your own.

Quality Products

Everywhere,
giant finned cars nose forward like fish;
a savage servility
slides by on grease.

—ROBERT LOWELL

"LET ME SHOW YOU SOMETHING," SAID JUNIOR JOHNSON, winner of the 1960 Daytona 500 and International Motorsports Hall of Fame Inductee.

We left the breakfast table, and I followed him outside to a run-in shed. Junior's a big man, well over 6 feet tall, with thick white hair and a quick smile. He's relaxed and graceful, like a man who has proved everything that needed proving. Next to a tractor and amid stacks of hay was a moonshine still he'd just built for the new NAS-CAR Hall of Fame at Charlotte. There were two wood-fired boilers, each consisting of two sooty oil drums welded together to make a steam chamber and a firebox. A length of stovepipe acted as the chimney. The steam would heat the mash in a large, straight-sided barrel of planking held together with hoops, and the vapor would travel into a second straight-sided barrel, a large thump keg. From there it went to the worm coil, which twisted through a square flake stand made of planking. He'd built a mash box and laid some sort of sandy material over the top to make it look like bubbling corn mash.

Junior never got caught hauling liquor. He was, the story goes, uncatchable. He invented the bootleg turn, by which you yank the wheel and slide the car 180 degrees while downshifting and take off in the opposite direction. Once, approaching a roadblock, he turned on the police lights he'd outfitted his car with. The revenuers figured one of their own was approaching, and they moved the roadblock. He sailed right through.

He did not, however, sail right through his career as a moonshiner. He was caught in 1956 working at his father's still and turned eleven months of a two-year sentence at the federal prison in Chillicothe, Ohio. He turned most of his attention to racing after that.

Junior Johnson embodies one of the great, historical combinations, two elements that got on like a gasoline fire and produced a third. Bootleggers worked on, overhauled, enhanced, and souped their vehicles. They were cobbled together from other cars, and they were learned inside and out. Hot-rod cars were necessary—in the trunk was 250 gallons of white lightning. Moonshine met fast cars, and together they made stock car racing.

Raymond Parks was a moonshiner, and his team, funded by hooch money, won NASCAR's first Strictly Stock Championship in 1949. Lloyd Seay, who was described by Big Bill France, the founder of NASCAR, as "the best pure race driver I ever saw," drove cars owned by Parks until he was shot to death by his cousin in a dispute over a supply of sugar. Roy Hall drove for Parks on the track and drove bootleg on the Georgia ridges. Their cars were tuned by a mechanic named Red Vogt, who not only was the first superstar mechanic of stock car racing, but was also the man who came up with the name NASCAR.

The story goes that bootleggers were a naturally competitive bunch who loved their cars, and one gets the idea, perhaps fanciful, that these guys would have raced no matter what, with or without prize money. Before there was a track, the liquor haulers would hang around a garage, waiting for a load, listening for the roar of the V-8 off in the distance that would alert them to the return of the last of their number who had gone out on a run. To kill time, they'd draw the local cops to the other side of town with a prank call so they could race up and down Main Street.

Early racing stories usually include a scene in a cow pasture, with the hell-bent drivers tearing up the mud and a small crowd standing behind a barbed-wire fence. Famously, Junior Johnson was plowing his family's garden, barefoot behind a mule, when he was invited to race for the first time. He simply put the reins down and hitched a ride to the dirt track. He came in second. Junior was a teenager, but he was already running liquor. There's a wonderful interview out there where the journalist asks Junior if he had a license at that time, and Junior says, "H'it didn't matter, I wuhdn't gonna stop."

Junior described the moonshine cars in an interview with *Hot Rod* magazine and said that while some of his race cars were fast, he'd "never run anything as fast as the fastest cars I had on the highway." They could modify them as much as they wanted to, do anything they wanted to, supercharge them, turbocharge them, "bore and stroke 'em all we wanted. We'd run five hundred cubic inches a lot of the time." The cars were limitless.

"You didn't have no top end on 'em with a supercharger. That thing would just keep gettin' up. It had the power to take it where the road was so narrow, you couldn't imagine how fast that thing was a-runnin'."

The core of the original popularity of stock car racing is a connection to these wild-riding southern ridge runners. They were rock stars. Cars had liberated everyone, and out there on the edge of that liberation were these daring outlaws. Tom Wolfe, in his fantastic profile of Junior Johnson, wrote that the automobile extricated "millions of good old boys, and girls" from "what was still pretty much a land-bound form of social organization." In cars, you could get to work. In cars, you could cover the distance. You were no longer tied to the family spread, or indeed, to the family. The automobile was freedom in powerful, beautiful form. It was soon fetishized. Stock car drivers became explosive magnifications of their fans' reality. Mick Jagger was to the sexual revolution what Junior Johnson was to the feeling of freedom and independence in the breast of the newly vehicular Southland.

There aren't many hot-rodding good old boys remaining with genius in their wrenches and all the guts in the world, but Junior is still farming in North Carolina. Tom Wolfe called him the Last American Hero, and even over biscuits and gravy in his shop I couldn't really shake the feeling that he was, in fact, heroic. Junior Johnson is like a magnet. Even in Pointer Brand overalls and eating a plate of scrambled eggs smothered in sausage gravy, he's got star quality.

Of course, he was eating these eggs under a big green highway sign that read JUNIOR JOHNSON HIGHWAY.

Junior has teamed with Joe Michalek, owner of Piedmont Distillers, to make Junior Johnson's Midnight Moon, a very good white dog. "Better than Vodka, Smoother than Whiskey," they say on the label. It's good stuff, but what's more, it has tapped into something real in the breast of NASCAR fans. Junior and Joe are mobbed at the tracks where they go to promote their hooch.

Junior feels and understands the connection he represents. Joe bemoans having to walk from point A to point B with him, from, for instance, the lounge to the television studio, because Junior will not blow people off. He'll stop, shake hands, and sign autographs. If you try to hustle him along, he'll dead-eye you and ignore your exhortations.*

---

* Joe once had to call Junior to remind him about a radio interview. "I just had a feeling," Joe told me. Junior was out on the farm, riding a tractor. He stopped the tractor, sat there in the field, and talked on the radio. Then he hung up and went back to his hay.

Junior had been approached by liquor companies a couple of times. Someone wanted to make Junior Johnson bourbon.

"I didn't have nothing to do with that," he said; there's no history of Junior and brown liquor.

Joe Michalek, however, had the right idea. Junior joined up, bought a share in the company, and Midnight Moon is flying off of the shelf. Even that, for a microdistiller, can be a frustrating scenario. Shops will simply allow it to run out, and then order the same amount the next month, so for half of the month there is no Midnight Moon on the shelf.

"It drives me crazy," said Joe. "If it runs out, order two cases next time, you know?"

Piedmont Distillers moved about 15,000 cases in 2007. Those numbers are growing fast. Joe—into this for a few years—is almost ready to pay himself for the first time.

Joe moved to North Carolina from New York to work in the marketing department of Reynolds Tobacco, and had a good run there.

"It's not a good time to work in tobacco," he said. One Christmas he heard a member of his extended family muttering about "the tobacco guy." Ultimately, he figured that perhaps they were right. "The golden age of the golden leaf was over."

Utilizing a kind of bent logic for which I admire him, he switched vices and opened a distillery.

The inspiration had come at a party, back when he was new to the South. Someone offered him a pull of a Mason jar full of hooch. He was wary.

"I didn't know what it would do to you. So I let other people go first, and I watched them. Nobody fell over, so I took a pull." He smiled. "It was pretty good."

Enlightened, he noticed moonshine everywhere. For although the nip joint moves far more product than other retail outlets, there are a few that simply cannot be ignored. There is white lightning at University of Virginia fraternity parties, at Christmas parties, and at Ole Miss football games.* It shows up in substantial quantities at NASCAR events and plays a special role there, linking NAS-CAR to its past and reminding everyone that bootlegging was once upon a time the farm league for race-car driving. White lightning is a link to the straightforward, small-money, Southern roots of the sport.

This link has been tenuous, and for some time it seemed as if NASCAR didn't want anything to do with the history of the sport or the core historic audience. There were dreams of a Latte NASCAR, a track on Staten Island, another in Los Angeles. How could they not dream? Look what had happened.

The growth of NASCAR was explosive. The turning point was the 1979 Daytona 500, which was broadcast live from flag to flag for the first time. NASCAR could not have asked for more. Like Unitas and the Colts playing the Giants in 1958, the Daytona 500 had it all. The weather was on their side as well: a huge snowstorm kept millions of Americans inside to watch it. On the last lap, Cale Yarborough (who was racing for Junior Johnson's team) and Donnie Allison got crazy and loose. Allison was in the lead, and Yarborough tried to pass him but connected with Allison's rear quarter-panel. Yarborough's tires dragged into the infield mud, and Yarborough, trying not to wreck, came back onto the track hard and hit Allison again. The cars were hovering and shimmying and smacking together. They drifted sideways like dancers across polished tiles, hit the wall, and bounced off, spinning into the infield. With those two out of the way, Richard Petty won the race and had just gotten the flag when the announcer cried, "It looks like we've got a fistfight!" Bobby Allison, Donnie's brother, had pulled into the infield and attacked Yarborough.

---

* Every year for decades the *Franklin News-Post* would run a big headline sometime in early December that read along the lines of AGENTS CRACK DOWN ON HOLIDAY SPIRITS. The Christmas party hooch industry is an industry in itself, I suspect: smaller scale, higher quality. In the Shenandoah Valley, the hooch on the board would always be apple brandy from the recent harvest. ABC agents will contradict me, and say that the big sugar jack producers are just faking it and saying it's pure apple brandy. We're both right.

It was a perfect race for television. NASCAR began its ascendancy. This was a sport you could talk about. This was fun.*

The snowball kept on rolling. In the 1990s attendance doubled. At the turn of the twentieth century a race day in the NASCAR Sprint Cup Series attracted about 150,000 people, which is about the population of Dayton, Ohio.

At the core of this group, however, are the same fans who went to the races decades ago.

"The bedrock fans," says Joe Michalek, "still come. There are some tracks where I feel completely out of place—Talladega is like that. Some places, I fit in, I look around and I see a lot of people who look like me, people dressed like me"—he was dressed entirely in black, with a nice watch and good shoes and a Pelican case for his laptop—"but other times . . . there are families who go, and who have been going, since the beginning. There's this one family, I see them every year." People get the same spots, he explains to me, year after year, so you develop relationships with people. They're your racetrack friends. "They always set up these tables, wooden tables, and they've got food there, and there's always a couple of jars of moonshine. The first time I saw that, we were standing maybe five yards from a state trooper. They offered me the jar. What's that? I mean, is it illegal or isn't it? How would they react if someone lit a joint?"

It becomes clear, while hanging around the Old School bootleggers of North Carolina and southern Virginia, that the law is not in line with what they believe. With an attitude reminiscent of Elvis insisting that his sandwich bag stuffed with pills contained only medi-

---

* It is worth noting that Yarborough was passing Allison using a technique with which Junior Johnson had revolutionized racing. In 1960, Johnson qualified for the second Daytona 500 in a small Chevrolet that ran much slower than the big Pontiacs dominating the year. He didn't have the corporate backing to put himself in a big car, and he was outmatched. Coming out of the pit during the practice runs, he tucked in behind Cotton Owens and found that he could stick with him. The wind was whipping around the Pontiac, and not only could Junior run without the wind resistance, the wind was actually helping him by creating a little vortex that would push the Chevy along as if it were a tailwind. He was running at three-fourths throttle (saving gas, saving his engine), but he was faster than he had been all day. Junior is a quick study. He waited for the fastest car and hitched a ride. He'd invented drafting. He won the race.

cation prescribed by a doctor, they would insist that marijuana is illegal, but that moonshine's legal status is more along the lines of an inconvenience. Falsely, they promote the idea that it's not the liquor that's illegal, after all, it's the taxes. Obviously, many otherwise law-abiding citizens agree. Morris Stephenson had gotten himself on the fighting side of Jaybird Philpott by printing that Jaybird had claimed that he wasn't making liquor for "fast money, but rather for some of his 'friends,' big wheels and lawyers." The city fathers, in other words, like their moonshine.

The sport's hardest fans, the true believers, bring moonshine to the track because they are still relating to the real history of stock car racing. They still feel in their breast the wild freedom that the car brought to the South, even though they are now tethered to their cars rather than freed by them (you can't buy a quart of milk without driving for it, after all). Still, they relate the drivers of today to the drivers of yore, regardless of the fact that there is almost no similarity between NASCAR today and the NASCAR of the 1970s. That sport no longer exists. The sport they are relating to—the hard drivers, the moonshine cars, the country boys—is gone.*

"It started to change in the late 1970s, early '80s," said Junior. NASCAR introduced more and more rules, trying to equalize the sport. It became expensive, and that's why the big-money sponsorships became important. You couldn't afford to race on your own dime anymore; you needed Budweiser money to put a car on the track.

The sport outgrew the core reason for its initial popularity. For what had originally drawn fans to the races was that the cars were stock. They were (mostly) the same cars on the lot—race them on Sunday, sell them on Monday.

That's nowhere near the case today. The drivers aren't as hard, either.

---

* Something tells me that the hard-drinking, hard-driving country boys are still tearing it up on the dirt tracks that pepper the southern countryside.

Junior calls today's drivers "ice-cream drivers."

NASCAR has tried, as it grew, to distance itself from its origins. Sponsorships from liquor companies were banned until 2004, despite the fact that without liquor there would be no NASCAR.

NASCAR can try to push them away, but everywhere I went to chase the white dog, every white person I met was car-crazy.

Jesse Tate and I would tool around Danville in his state-issued Pontiac Grand Prix. One night we went out to grab a couple of beers and talk over a case he was investigating. The agents were working their way upstream on what Jesse suspected would turn out to be a big bust. They'd busted one guy, and he'd agreed to cooperate.

"He's getting the stuff for eighty dollars a case, so I figure we're pretty close to the source."

But the trail seemed to lead across the border, into North Carolina, where there are two competing enforcement agencies, a mile of red tape, and a fair bit of corruption.*

We parked, and Jesse Tate grabbed his pistol, tucked it into his jeans, and said: "I tell you what, we're not gonna be a character in this story, we're gonna write it."

It was a loud bar, with a DJ spinning hip-hop radio hits and an enthusiastic crowd of mostly middle-aged white folks dancing in near unison on a small dance floor with disco lights spinning all around. Jesse is a young, accomplished agent of the Virginia ABC. If there was such a thing as a "rising star" in that world, he'd fit the description. Unfortunately, the agency is so backward and, at least from my vantage point, disorganized, he may never get the status he deserves. It doesn't bother him. When he was passed over for a promotion, he told me that it didn't matter to him, because so many agents had come out to support him: "knowing that I have my fellow co-workers' support means just as much."

Jesse cares. His job includes licensing, and I've seen him talk to

---

* When the Illegal Whiskey Task Force helped raid a still in North Carolina years ago, the sheriff showed up. The moonshiner turned to him: "What the hell is this?" The sheriff protested: "I didn't know!"

people who wanted to get liquor licenses. He wants to help them stay in business. He wants them to succeed. He also shares his time with vice, and finds himself working to bust hookers in Danville, a job he finds entertaining but grim.

"You've got to play the part," he'll say with a snicker. Most of the girls who get into the car aren't exactly lookers.

I went out to his house one day and stood around in his garage with some of his family and some agents who had gathered for a fish fry. There were cars everywhere. Trucks being renovated. Rolling bodies ready for their engines.

At the bar that night, Jesse and I were talking about a particularly successful branch of North Carolina law enforcement when a Danville sheriff sidled up to our table with his young wife.

"Oh, man!" he exclaimed, "those guys get anything they want!" I saw him drift off into a private reverie, no doubt imagining the Camaros the cops in North Carolina must be tooling around in.

Later he said to Jesse, "What do they have you driving now?"

Everybody is car crazy. And they love NASCAR.

Jesse put together a luncheon for me, and invited a group of retired police and a former bootlegger for chili dogs and burgers. The talk quickly devolved into who was restoring what, who was driving what. Reviewing the tape, you'd think we were at a car club. The bootlegger (I'll keep his name to myself, as I promised I would, although I'm pretty sure he made up the name he gave me in the first place) would stray from the topic of cars only to talk about the Boss Hoss motorcycle he'd just sold. (For the uninitiated, a Boss Hoss is a motorcycle powered by a full-sized V-8 engine, and a horrible idea.) Regarding liquor, his lips were sealed. We met the following day at a Ryan's for lunch, and he opened up.

He'd brought a sheet of paper with him, notes to which he'd refer occasionally, and his stories seemed well rehearsed, if not, perhaps, enhanced.

"He bumped me, and my car went sideways. I went off the side of the road, over a hill, and I heard the pines brushing the bottom of the car." Then it exploded and he ran through the woods for hours with no shoes until he found a farmhouse, and the whole time he's telling you this, you sit and wonder if it is actually a scene from a movie, or just a lot like one.

Some of the cops had professed that the man had hauled white lightning and teased him about it, and I believed him when he told me that he'd married into a clan of bootleggers. I also believed him when he recounted, with detail, every car he'd ever hauled liquor in, and every story began with "Musta been 1956, I was driving a Chevy with an Oldsmobile engine in it, whew, that thing could haul . . ."

A few years ago, on a vacation in Florida, he saw the sign advertising rides around the Daytona track and he walked in.

"In the pit they asked me if I'd ever been in a race car before, and I told them I used to race around a half-mile dirt track. Well, he came flying off of the apron, put that car six inches from the wall. We must have been going 190. I didn't want to seem scared, you know, but I was reaching for the roll cage. Going at that turn, he wasn't slowing down, didn't take his foot off the pedal *at all*. I thought we were done. But those turns are banked, and we just settled right into it. *Woooosh*." He shook his head. He went back and did it again the next day.

It hadn't occurred to me until that moment, but clearly, if I was going to write about race cars at all, I was going to drive one.

I suspect that I am not alone in imagining myself possessed of secret talents, hidden bits of wondrous facility that will reveal themselves when the opportunity arises or at some crucial moment: *There we were, low on food and the blizzard was coming on strong. We couldn't see, and in another hour we'd be stuck on that rock. Of course, I'd never rappelled down anything before in my life* . . . As a youngster receiving my first bow and arrow, I foresaw that upon the first thrum of the cat gut I would reveal myself as an archer of epic proportion, a Zen master. I was surprised that my shaft did not bury itself in the bulls-eye, to be split down the middle by the second dart from my quiver. Robin Hood I was not.

Disappointments pile up. That's the nature of life.

Most of this fanciful self-inflation dissipates naturally as fewer people ask you what you're going to be when you grow up. Brushing up on middle age, settled into whatever mess you've made for yourself, there is little room to imagine that your real skills lie undiscovered like snapping turtles at the bottom of the pond. But me? I am resilient. I know there are still things hidden in the depths, waiting, ready to churn up the water and bite off a toe.

I wouldn't want to go so far as to say that I was *sure* that I was going to be very good at driving race cars, but there played in my mind a scene that I couldn't resist. To save face, I pretended it was fanciful.

The Vision: Talladega under a blistering sun, heat waves rising off the tarmac and country boys drinking Coca-Cola from those waxy paper cups with the white swoosh on the side. A car pulls back into pit row and stops at the feet of the guys with wrenches in their back pockets and radios in their ears. I slide out of the window (I'm much more graceful—and about 30 pounds thinner—in my fantasy life than I am in reality) and take off the gloves, vaguely brushing off my racing suit and perhaps reaching into a pocket for a kerchief to mop my brow or a stick of Wrigley's.

Robert Duvall would approach the car, resetting his bill cap on his head and working his jaw the way he does. He'd hook a finger in his belt loop—maybe he'd spit.

"Damn, boy."

And he'd wait—Robert Duvall is coy, he knows how to string you along, looking at you with that grin in the corner of his mouth. "You just qualified for Bristol."

And they'd start laughing and the scene would fade to black and come back in on me and Duvall and a couple mechanics laughing over watery mugs of beer in some roadhouse.

Bibliophilic, bespectacled Jewish boys have amazing powers of autodysmorphia.

• • •

Fifteen students were arrayed on light folding chairs in the white shed otherwise used as the infield lounge for crew members of the Automobile Racing Club of America at Pocono Raceway. Our instructor, Joel, faced us with lighthearted intensity. We were an odd collection of folks. There were a couple of lithe, deer-hunting types in thick, outdoorsy jackets who looked as if they might consciously model their appearance and attitudes after Richard Petty. They had close-cropped, sharp beards and wore those aerodynamic sunglasses with the lenses that appear to be coated with an oil slick. When Joel asked if anyone had driven race cars before, they calmly raised their hands. Next to me a thin, older man talked more or less incessantly about his sailboat and complained that he might fall asleep before he got his turn to drive. There was a thick Mediterranean with Peter Lorre eyes who would later tell me that he'd never thought of doing this and didn't much like racing. We had a couple of beer-bellied good-old-boys in lined flannel shirts. I hit it off with one fellow, Anthony, because he was ironical and without bluster. He was nervous, and we shared a few raised-eyebrow moments in the class.

"If you go into a spin," said Joel—Anthony and I both chuckled— "it doesn't happen often, but it does happen, it's happened twice this year so far." *Twice?* "If you go into a spin, just let the car do its thing."

What?

"If you try to correct it the way you've been taught," continued Joel, "if you try to steer into the spin, these cars are so tight, you'll bring the back end around and those wheels will catch on the pavement and you'll drive headfirst into the wall."

Oh. My. God.

"You see it every Sunday, right?"

Many of the guys seemed reassured to be reminded that professional drivers, guys who did nothing else but drive these cars, wrecked them all the time. Not so me and Anthony.

"If there's a fire . . ." continued Joel.

The class takes about an hour and a half. There are two videos, which go over the basic rules of the road, what certain flags mean, and what we're supposed to do. The whole thing is delivered in a tone that made me imagine a peculiarly masculine meeting of a self-help group.

"We're here to help you get up to speed."

"All our cars are real, six-hundred-horsepower stock cars, the same cars the big boys drive on Sunday."

"We want you to realize your potential out there."

Replace "six-hundred-horsepower" with "finding undervalued real estate to sell at a profit," or replace the potential to drive really fast with "realizing your full potential as a husband and as a man," and you see what I mean.

What makes it all acceptable, of course, is that we are not here to save ourselves. We are here to have fun, and each of us has decided that doing something terrifying, loud, and dangerous was exactly the kind of fun he was after. So we are excited and scared, like a roomful of fourteen-year-old football players before a game. Joel's tone suits us perfectly. We need to be told that they're going to keep us safe, and we need to be told that we're going to do a good job.

Jesse Roverana owns the Stock Car Racing Experience. He worked at a nearby Indy car-racing school in high school, then he went off to college and studied electrical engineering.

"I got a job fixing copiers . . ." and he looked away, shaking his head and chuckling to himself as another small-block 358 race engine roared into a turn on the track. People around a racetrack don't tend to leave. Joel said, of our instructors: "They have the best job in the world, they drive race cars all day long." Roverana began the Stock Car Racing Experience in 1997. For him, the racetrack is a lifestyle. He drives all the time, but he's not a racer.

"I figured out how to stay in this, and be on the side that actually makes money."

His chief instructor, Steve Fox, said, "I'll never get away from racing. I'm addicted." He's raced most of his life. "And if I owed the power company some money, and I also needed tires, I'd buy the tires and go race."

I went along as a passenger, first, thinking I'd get a feel for it.

I clambered in through the window, wedged myself into the tiny seat, and was strapped in, tight.

I thought I had a handle on what to expect. I heard about the ride along from my bootlegger, and I'd talked to Morris, too.

Morris had given me a nickname, and he'd always answer the phone having already begun to laugh: "Maxwell Smart! How you doin,' dude?"

I told him I was headed out to Pocono.

"You are going to love it, man." He worked for NASCAR for seventeen years after he'd sold his newspaper, and one afternoon, a driver offered him a ride across the infield. Morris got in: "Didn't have a helmet, didn't put my seat belt on, nothing. He was just giving me a ride, you know. Well, he gets to going . . ." Once Morris was in the car, the driver decided to have a little redneck fun with him, blew through the gate on the other side of the grass, and hit the track. "I've never been so goddamn scared in my life. I don't know how fast we were going, but it was *fast*." He paused. "Damn, that was fun. Lemme know how it goes!"

The shoulder harnesses push down on you, the head restraints keep you from moving side to side. Joel had asked if there was anyone with claustrophobia issues in the group, and it's easy to see why. Everything is limited. The windshield is small, the helmet restricts your vision even further. As a passenger, your feet are funneled into a space on the floor that would perhaps fit half of a reasonable man's foot. You stop thinking about this very quickly, because someone slaps the top of the car and the driver—aren't we even going to introduce ourselves? shouldn't we have a little foreplay?—hits the gas and you shoot out of the pit.

It is an immense understatement to write that everything happens quickly. Passenger jets takeoff quickly, and shooting out of the pit road and onto the track makes takeoff feel like a lazy summer afternoon.

My driver shifted through the gearbox, and we were flying by the time we saw the sign that reminds drivers to be in fourth gear as they enter the track. There is no warm-up, and there is nothing on earth to prepare a person for what a race car feels like.

The car shimmied and jumped. It rattled. Every single foot of the track felt like a weather-beaten patch of ruined asphalt. The engine was roaring. The turns came up fast, and the car moved sideways through them, pulled out toward the wall.

Joel had said: "If you feel yourself moving towards the wall coming out of the turn, roll off the throttle. It's natural, believe me, if you see that wall coming, you *will* take your foot off the gas." Then he explained to us that the cars were so powerful that they actually lifted the front wheels off of the ground a little when you gave it gas, and you no longer had 100 percent of the steering.

I was grabbing on to the roll cage as we shot into Turn One. Crying out against my will: "Oh, *shit*."

During the first lap I knew I couldn't do it, I'd never drive one of these things. This was madness. We were traveling 190 miles per hour, and the car felt like a beat-up Honda Civic on a rutted road.

Two turns into the ride, I realized that the car was not going to simply shatter into a thousand pieces, and it seemed that my driver was pretty good at not hitting anything. By the second lap I was watching his rpms and trying to get a handle on what the car could take (seemingly anything). He was massaging the accelerator with the tip of his worn-out sneaker, as if he were trying to squish it down through the floor and open up some last unknown bit of fuel delivery. We were heading into turns at 9,000 rpm and higher.

I was getting it. I was seeing how this worked. It's not what you expect, but it is, after all, a car. By the third lap I was enjoying it, and when we pulled into the pit, I was smiling.

That's what everyone looked like when they got out of the ride-along. Ear-to-ear grins. Crazy. Dazed.

Then they strap you in. I went over the pedals. Gas, brake, clutch. Gas, brake, clutch. I shifted through the gears. I got used to the environment. The driver's seat was bigger than the passenger seat, but still very tight. The dashboard, if one can even call it that, was silver sheet metal. The rest of the car was also sheet metal, mostly gray. There were red switches, and a big tachometer next to smaller gauges for your fuel level, oil pressure, water, and something else that I took to be temperature. The shifter was a tall four-on-the-floor with a white billiard ball for a knob. The steering column was a steel rod. You're sitting in a welded cage, and there is no insulation, and the windows are just netting, and I assume that if I weren't completely preoccupied I'd have noticed that it was loud and cold.

Driving a race car for the first time is a recipe for embarrassment. Guys were stalling out in the pits. For a second, I couldn't even get the car to start. It caught and I pushed the gas. It roared.

Then it was time to go.

We meandered out of the pit, waiting for a group to pass, and then we were off. Wham, I shifted through the gears—I'd accomplished my first goal: get onto the racetrack and be in fourth gear.

There isn't that much to think about. Our duties were as follows:

1. Maintain a distance of four car lengths between the cars.
2. Hold the line. You're not driving the track, you're driving an imaginary line around the track. There are cones that tell you where to roll off the throttle, and where to begin the turn. In the turn, you aim at squares like bases on a diamond and drive over them. There's another cone that tells you you're in the apex of the turn.
3. Remember which turn you're in.
4. Look at the flagman and see if he's got a message for you. He might tell you to close up. He might tell you to back off. He might tell you to let the car behind you pass. He might have a caution flag up. There was a black flag, too, which basically meant that something had gone horribly wrong, and your car,

or someone's car, was probably on fire. Basically, just drop
everything and pull over.

That's all there is to it. (The whole time I was recalling what Jess of
Stranahan's had told me by way of assurance: "Just remember: Shiny
side up, greasy side down.")

The car I drove to the track is padded with foams and wrapped
in soft cloth and supple leather. Whatever connection to the road I
felt had been created by the engineers who built it. A race car is just
the opposite. The cars are not as heavy on the ground as I'd thought
they would be (it feels like a Honda Civic because it weighs about
the same, but it has 600 horsepower and excellent spoilers), and the
power steering is soft. There's a fair bit of corrective steering needed
to keep the car up the track near the wall, where I was supposed to
be. Our first laps were run at about 4,800 rpm, which is about 110
mph, and I was having no problem staying with Anthony, who was
behind the instructor, second in our line of three.

There's the cone. There's the second cone: Turn! And the bases
would slide under my seat like pills into Pac-Man's mouth. Perfect.

We went faster.

At about 6,500 rpms, I was too far off the wall going into a turn.
Instinctually, I overcompensated for my bad position on the track and
slowed down. Anthony opened up on me.

At these speeds there is no room for error.

I pushed to catch up.

Then things got interesting.

I was gaining on them. Coming out of Turn Three onto the longest straightaway, the flag man waved me to close up my gap, so I
gunned it.

One of the key reassurances they give you in the class is that you
are following an instructor. So if the instructor is doing it, you can do
it, too. If he is going into the turn, and you've held the correct distance from him, then you are matching his speed and you'll make it
through the turn, because he knows what he is doing. But now, I was

playing catch-up. I was trying to close the gap. I was shooting through the straights faster than the guys in front of me. I looked down at my rpms going into a turn and I was turning 8.

Holy shit.

I rolled off again.

They opened up again.

Every turn, now, I'd push it coming out. It felt amazing, the g's pulling the car over to the wall and the engine roaring and you know you are really moving, but each daring exit onto a straightaway would set me up badly for the next turn. I was losing them.

It didn't matter. The drive was incredible.

By the end of my eight laps I was exhausted. I could barely remember where the pit entrance was.

Doing this for hundreds of laps? I can't imagine.

Doing this for hundreds of laps with a car touching my bumper? Are you kidding?

The result of my mistakes, ironically, was that I'd driven a much faster top speed than many of the other students. They click the rpm gauge before you get out and it shows you your highest mark: 8300—according to their chart that's just over 170 mph.

Although the car I drove is a distant heir to the original stock cars—almost nothing like the cars that Junior Johnson drove—there are some constants. The Ford 9-inch rear end has been unchanged since 1957, and housed the rear axle in the car I drove. The engine in my race car, while certainly jammed full of contemporary improvements, was a carbureted small-block Chevrolet V-8, which was first built in 1955.

Vestigial hallmarks remain. Sitting around in Junior Johnson's shop after breakfast while a bunch of old guys chewed toothpicks and talked trash, the past was palpable. Throughout his career, Junior was one of the good old boys, one of the guys who had been there. To this day he's like the Ford rear end in those cars, one of the connections between racing's past and NASCAR's present.

In the shop there are subtle clues pointing to a life that has been a great success: just something about the way the television is mounted to the wall on an arm, and the humming True refrigerator with the glass doors that is shoved full of soda and Budweiser and a big box of apples. The whole place feels like wealth combined perfectly with humility. There are mementos: dented stock car hoods hanging on the walls. There's a display of Midnight Moon.

I asked him if the still he'd built for the Hall of Fame was like the one's he'd used, and he said that it was almost identical to the one he'd been caught working.

Then he asked: "You want to take a field trip?"

Of course, yes.

Joe Michalek got in the back of Junior's Chevy crew cab truck, and Junior's dog Princess hopped in as well. She loves going for a ride and won't let Junior drive off without her.

An assortment of wrenches and tools were scattered along the dash and the center console. I climbed in next to Junior.

"You're in a farm truck, now," he said, easing it into gear.

We laughed. It smelled like cows.

We drove out into the country, down twisting roads at surprisingly respectable speeds. Could Junior put a truck through a bootleg turn? Should I ask him to? Junior was pointing out where moonshiners and bootleggers had lived (seemingly in every third house). We talked moonshine and racing and history, and I think he must have driven me in a very roundabout way.

He pulled the truck off of the asphalt onto a long dirt driveway and stopped to open a farm gate.

A piece of the electric fence had come off the post and was hanging down onto the lock. Junior walked back to the truck, said something like "Damn fence is hanging on that lock" and grabbed a pair of chrome pliers with cracked Bakelite handles. I was sure that he was about to electrocute himself, but there must have been enough insulation to protect him.

Back in the truck he chuckled and said, "Extra security. Look out for them wasps, too."

Up the driveway a few hundred feet we hit a clearing and drove up a hill, where we took down a piece of electric fencing wire hung to its post on a hook, with a plastic handle so you could grip it. We crested the hill and were surrounded by Black Angus cattle.

We came to a barn so new it smelled like wood glue. There was a four-wheeler parked in front. Everything was suspiciously clean, it didn't look as if much farming had happened here.

I still didn't know exactly what we were doing. Joe had mentioned that Junior had some friends and might be able to show me something pretty cool, but I could not have imagined that I was about to set foot inside a very big, very illicit moonshine operation.

Inside were rows of wooden barrels and four half-ton field bins (square plastic tubs used in fruit harvesting and wine production), all full of whiskey mash bubbling away—3,000 gallons of mash. All of it getting ready to go into the 800-gallon stainless-steel still built out of a dairy tank. The place was neat and clean.

There were empty bags of malted barley flour folded neatly in a stack, and there were swollen whole grains floating and clinging to the edges of the barrels.

In a boiler room there was an oil furnace that would steam-heat the dairy tank. The mash boiled into what was to my Virginian eye a disproportionately large thump keg, which Junior told me the maker filled with the tails of the run. Then through a coil condenser, and into jugs. (This is how Joe and Junior both said it was done, but it strikes me as impossible, because the alcohol by volume changes over the course of the still run, and the first gallons would be incredibly strong, while the last would be 50 or 60 proof. They must proof the batch in the plastic tank below the money piece, which was full of the tails of the last run.)

We leaned against the barrels and looked the place over. Junior dipped a finger in the mash.

"H'it's still sweet; ain't finished yet. When h'its finished, it'll taste sour, like beer," he said. "These boys make a quality product."

"In fact," Joe said, "when we had to expand and build a second still, we modeled it on this one."

We drove home on the Junior Johnson Highway and stopped for a second to look at the old North Wilkesboro Speedway, fallen into disuse. Weeds as big as trees grew up through the bleachers behind the faded sign that read JUNIOR JOHNSON GRANDSTAND.

The Red Mountain Pass

The cowards never start and the weak die along the way.

—KIT CARSON

THE VERY FIRST CONFERENCE HELD AT THE SEELBACH Hotel in Louisville, Kentucky, had been a conference of distillers in 1905, and the staff there seemed to feel that they were headed toward a homecoming.

They were greeting us at check-in with the usual "Welcome to the Seelbach, Mr. Watman," but they were adding "we're very happy to have you—and the Distilling Conference—with us."

The honeymoon didn't last. Complaints starting rolling in immediately: drunks were wandering the halls; there were suites where the doors never seemed to close and the parties went on until dawn; the bar was clogged with rambling roughnecks, many of whom seemed to have brought their own bottles of liquor. The wide welcoming smiles began to narrow.

I sat in the Oakroom one evening with my friend Jay Erisman, who produced from his blazer not one, but *five* pints of full-strength barrel samples from a top Lawrenceburg distillery. We gathered our glasses into a row, and Jay looked furtively about the dimly lit room, watching for the waistcoated cocktail waitress who would be our undoing. I begged him to relax. Act like everything is as it should be, I suggested. Stop ducking and peering around and making a spectacle of the thing.

"Well," he said. "I think you're more accustomed to breaking the law than I am."

The hotel should have given us a floor of our own, isolated us like the criminally insane, with a hospitality suite of our own stocked with liquor, coffee, and bottles of Gatorade. They could have locked the doors to the floor and kept the blue-blooded hard boots happy. They must have assumed we were going to act like grand distilling families of Kentucky, that we'd drink and chat like we were at the club with the Beams and the Browns. Instead, they got a cross-section of America: cowboys and hippies and hipsters and football fans, brawlers and hustlers and businessmen. Recent college graduates and semiretired PR men who had decided to change their lives. There was a kid from Montana who lived on a farm and made fuel out of trash he Dumpster-dived from behind the Dunkin' Donuts. ("Sugar *and* starch! You see?") He was convinced that the government didn't want him making fuel—you could almost see the black helicopters circling around his head. We had hundreds of distillers at every stage of the business. Some were expanding, some were still writing their business plans, some were on the verge of releasing their product.

We even had an honest-to-god bootlegger. Her name was Charlie, and she was in the dawn of her twenties. She was a woman of arresting beauty, so drop-dead ridiculously gorgeous that she stopped everyone in their tracks. She had brought a friend with her to the conference, and I never could get a real handle on why they were there. One day they were passing out samples of liqueur, but even that seemed improvised.

I sat across from her and her friend at lunch one afternoon.

"Do I have anything in my teeth?" said the friend, baring her teeth at Charlie.

"Nope, me?"

"Oh, yeah, you do."

"Get it for me?"

Charlie opened her blossomy lips and her friend stuck a dainty finger inside to pry out the particulate.

I almost fainted.

Charlie's mother had started making moonshine while she was pregnant because, as Charlie tells it, "she was curious about the tradition." Mom turned out to be pretty good at it and hooked up with a friend of the family to bootleg it in small amounts. Charlie still works with the guy, though her mother doesn't know it, and together they make about 6 gallons a week. Charlie lives in a shadow network of young, pot-smoking bluegrass fans who have parties and stage contests where they judge each other's liquor. The network is concentrated in the Middle South but stretches all the way from New York to Miami.

In charge, trying to wrangle this herd of cats, stood Bill Owens, the president of the American Distilling Institute.

He's a hilarious man with a white crew cut and a raunchy sense of humor (a raunchy sense in general). He wears steel-framed glasses and has a lot of energy if he gets to bed before nine and doesn't eat too much. (He has a love-hate relationship with food, He claims it makes him sluggish and heavy-feeling, but he'll rhapsodize over the chickens he cooks in his ceramic Kamado-style smoker-griller. He'll stop your fork in a restaurant so he can take a picture of your plate.) He lives in a tiny, funky house in Hayward, California, across town from his second wife. They're still married, still love each other, still sleep together. I asked him if she ever wanted him to move back in with her.

"Jesus. No fucking way."

Bill was born in San Jose in 1938 and grew up on a farm. He traveled and spent a year at California State University, Chico, before joining the third wave of Peace Corps volunteers with his first wife, Janet. Together they taught English in India and Jamaica for two years. Back in San Francisco, Bill hacked a cab to pay his way through San Francisco State, then left college to work as a photographer and a photo editor. He photographed the Rolling Stones at Altamont (most of the film was stolen), and the scene in San Francisco, and somewhere along the line he found his niche.

Bill turned his camera on the suburban neighborhoods in which he lived and photographed the people around him. The result is something like the photography of William Eggleston and Stephen Shore, but even less is manipulated, even less is arranged. What's more, Eggleston and Shore took lots of landscapes and still lifes, and few portraits. Bill's world is populated.

His shots of Hayward, California, became a book called *Suburbia*. Originally published in 1973 (signed copies of that edition sell for hundreds of dollars), it was rereleased in 1999 with a foreword by David Halberstam. It's a classic.

After the success of *Suburbia*, Bill published a couple more books, which were equally good but didn't do nearly as well. In 1983 he opened Buffalo Bill's in Hayward, one of America's first brew pubs. He started the magazine *American Brewer* and published it into the 1990s.

When the microdistilling scene began to rumble, Bill saw an opportunity. He sent out the American Distilling Institute's first newsletter in January of 2002, and ever since he's been answering the phone, hooking industry people up, and throwing conferences in Kentucky and San Francisco.

The conferences are run on the goodwill of those around Bill, whom he has lured and bribed into organizing lunches and giving people rides and running to the grocery to buy sixty cases of bottled water. Often, the event seems as if it is about to dissolve into chaos, but it doesn't.

The highpoint of the conference proved to be a tasting with the eminent whiskey writer Jim Murray, a rumpled, tweedy man, full of sparkle and bitterness. He paced around the front of the room, telling funny stories and rolling through material, his hair flying, his nose perched above a glass. He was self-deprecating and honest to a fault. He led us through five whiskies, and it was like playing guitar with someone much better than you are: you rise to it, find yourself doing things you didn't know you could. Jim would be up there saying, "What do you taste? Fruit? Yes? What kind of fruit? Citrus? Yes?"

He makes very good and surprising choices, and lays some sort of mindfuck hypnotism on you. We, a room full of distillers and whiskey writers, not a civilian in the house, were convinced, for instance, that a two-year-old peated malt from India was a sixteen-year-old Oban. We weren't ashamed or insulted to learn its true provenance, just happy for the surprise, and happy to learn about another excellent whiskey in the world.

It was at this tasting that Rory Donovan first came to my attention.

He sat at the table next to mine, leaning back in his chair with an arm flopped toward the ground, looking too cool for school.

Jim was asking if people drank their whiskey with ice. Much of the time I do, and I was sheepishly raising my hand. Rory said what I was thinking.

"Listen, man, sometimes I'm drinking."

I knew exactly what he meant. There's a difference between tasting and drinking. You can still taste what you drink, of course, but many is the night that I prefer, above all else, three and a half ounces of Early Times with lots of ice. I wouldn't mow my lawn with a double IPA, either.

But this was Jim Murray, and that was fearless.

Rory was sitting with the cool kids, too, with Jess and Jake from Stranahan's and James Whelan from Edgefield, the hippest and best distillers in the room.

We tasted Sazerac rye, a drink with which I'm very familiar. Jim was coaxing flavors out of it I had never found. He leads your palette, refines your understanding. Sazerac is always a good whiskey; at this tasting it was amazing.

We all thought so. The room was nodding and chomping their clackers and chewing on the drink, mouthing every bit of taste out of it.

Jim asked: "Who's thinking of becoming a rye distiller?"

"I am now," said Rory. "I'm thinking of it because of what happened at this table just now."

Later that night I was standing on the sidewalk outside the Seelbach bar, talking on the phone. I hadn't settled my tab, because I had every intention of going back inside and continuing the festivities with the good folks gathered at a long table in the back.

Jake and Jess and James Whelan and Rory and a few others came rolling around the corner filled with mischief and momentum. There's magic in the way that groups of happy, tipsy guys hit a city sidewalk, telling jokes and punching one another in the arm. It can be all innocence, all swinging from the lampposts and girl watching, or it can escalate into a riot. It's the binding fabric of street gangs and bachelor parties. You never know where it's going to end, and if you're included in the charming mojo of fraternal energy, it is almost impossible to resist.

"Max Watman!"

"Come on, boy."

And I fell into step with them, bouyed by their momentum, caught up in the laughter. It felt as if my motorcycle gang had driven by my house to pick me up, and I'd gunned it out of the driveway and melded with them. We were gonna make a run. We were gonna have a party. I was where I belonged.

Suffice to say that a series of very questionable decisions ended with our somewhat deflated group standing on the street in front of a very questionable bar, having been urged to leave by the bouncer (not before one of us, who shall remain nameless here, said, with a disbelieving laugh, *"That's* your fucking bouncer?").

We walked back to Fourth Street, where it was more like spring break, and the music blared, and the Heinekens cost five bucks. Somewhere along the way I talked Rory Donovan into putting me to work pitting apricots at his distillery.

I never actually pitted any, but I did visit.

Peach Street Distillers operates out of a small building painted the color of the pale red Colorado mesa that rises in the near distance behind it. They are 37¾ miles from Utah, in Palisade. The building is simple, and fronted by a large parking lot that is hard up on some train tracks. There's a trellis, some outdoor seating, and barrels stacked against the wall. In the back of the building are a couple of offices, and there's a storage and work area off to the right, but the big room in the middle is where almost everything happens. The room is split in half, and in the back they've got all their filtration equipment, the still, storage tanks, mash tuns, and fermenters. The front of the room has a beautiful copper bar with a few stools. Board-plank shelving displays Peach Street t-shirts, stickers, vodka, gin, grappa, eau de vie, peach brandy, and most recently, bourbon.

Rory founded Peach Street Distillers in 2005, and he cut himself his first paycheck in 2008.

"Turns out people know this. Turns out I should have studied a little more about running a small business. Apparently, it's pretty typical to not make any money for the first three years. It takes three years to turn any business around." We were in the side room. Rory was leaning against a stainless-steel table amid half empty boxes of glass and cases of booze. Next to me there was a full-size model of R2-D2.

Palisade sits in the river gorge of the Colorado, and from the proper vantage point looks like a gigantic, fruity oasis. Mesas and desert surround it, but along the riverbanks the land is lush and verdant. Incredible peaches grow there, and Rory and head distiller Davy Lindig use those to make their aged peach brandy.

It is a light brown spirit with a very crisp and clean nose. It tastes like an August day, like the wet ripe juice just under the skin of a perfectly ripe peach. It has picked up a little vanilla from the oak that rounds it out, and as it evaporates off the tongue, it leaves a stripe of peach candy that lingers on the palate.

Peach Street's Jackalope gin is another of my favorites. The hang tag reads:

Rarely seen and often misspelled the Jackelope isn't Colorado's answer to the minotaur, nor is it some bogus animal like the snipe or the antelabbit. It's a real creature. They say a flask of whiskey set out at night will work for bait when hunting Jackelope, but it doesn't (we've tried . . . many times), and why would it? It doesn't make any sense. The Jackelopes live among Colorado's junipers— Gin is the obvious answer. But we're not wasting this on Jackelopes, even if they do taste like lobster.

"This has got to be the best gin I've ever had," said a gin-drinking friend of mine one evening. It's a soft spirit that luxuriates on the tongue and kicks in with a second wave of spice and pepper. They got lucky. It takes most folks dozens, if not hundreds, of recipes to hit their gin. This was their first recipe.

There are two business models in microdistilling. One is to raise capital, make whiskey, and wait while it ages until you can release it. This means that you are running a plant, with employees and insurance and telephone lines, and making product and buying ingredients and storing barrels for at least two years before you have a product you can take to market. The other is to make a lot of white spirits and sell them to get cash flow into the business. Stranahan's is a model of the first method; Peach Street is a model of the second. Many distillers, upon embarking on the second path, find themselves trapped. They can't stop making vodka or gin, because it's floating their business, but they don't have the capacity to make whiskey. Peach Street has managed to balance it, but I'm sure it's difficult.

In fact, everything is difficult.

Rory has spent the last three years on the phone, selling. What he sold, he delivered himself out of the back of his Dodge pickup (he puts over 40,000 miles a year on his truck). One of Peach Street's pear eau de vie comes with a whole pear in the bottle, and if it's time to put the bottles on the trees out at the pear orchard, he does that, too. He's living on his credit card and hoping that his own company can afford to put fuel in his truck.

I went with him to Silverton, Colorado, to pour drinks at the Silverton Jamboree. (The Jamboree is "The Highest Music Festival in America"—you can take that however you like.) We spent the night before the show in the raucous bars of Silverton. It's a tiny town, but it rocks hard. Rory kept introducing me as "Max Watman, he's from the *New York Times*, he's going to make us all famous."

In no way was I from the *New York Times*.

"Dude, did you pay for that beer?"

I hadn't; he had a point.

"Exactly."

Late that night, we were standing in the middle of a field. It was very late, and we were very cold. Some of the guys were camping, and we'd come out there to build a fire and close out the night, but nothing like that was happening. Someone had locked his keys inside his car and was lamenting that his date (a piñata named Penny) was stuck inside the car while someone else tried to break into it. (This involved a surprising amount of climbing onto the roof of the car.) Rory Donovan reached into the back of his truck and pulled a bottle of Stranahan's out of a case. One thing about hanging around with distillers: high-quality liquor is ubiquitous.

Rory and I were talking about the Red Mountain Pass.

The Red Mountain Pass is traversed by a tiny, switchback two-lane road that twists through the Red Mountain, separating Ouray and San Juan counties. The summit is just over 11,000 feet. The road is treacherous: there is no guardrail; often there is no shoulder; sometimes there is no white line. The passenger side wheels, if you're driving south, are inches from a precipitous drop of over a thousand feet.

Every fifteen minutes or so I came to a pull-off, and nosed into it. The road was too twisty and narrow to allow for much sightseeing, and there was a steady stream of insane Colorado cowboys on my bumper, revving their diesel engines and dying to whip the horse trailer around me and get up the road. I'd get out of my Jeep and wonder at the mountains. The scale is staggering. This is bighorn country.

"I told you it would change your life," Rory said. "Coolest thing you've done all year."

I suggested, hopefully, that people probably don't go over the edge that much.

"Are you kidding me? People go over the edge all the time."

Well, it's no surprise, considering how they drive.

"You people, flatlanders, you piss me off. That's a thoroughfare. I've got to drive over that mountain to get to work, you know? Get out of the way!"

I did, I protested, I pulled into every overlook I could!

"Good," he said with a shake of his head, clearly remembering being stuck behind some tourist ogling the sights and white-knuckling on the turns. "Fucking beautiful though, isn't it?"

This is the dichotomy at the soul of Rory Donovan. He is at once a roughneck and an artisan. A remarkably blustery, loud-mouthed, hard-drinking, good-timing man, with a soft streak a mile wide and a delicate aesthetic sensibility. One side of Rory wants to share the stunning majestic beauty of the Colorado mountain; the other wants you to get out of the way so he can step on the gas and get on. He's a superb fly fisherman—he's worked as an outfitter and a guide. At the same time, he seems to live in closer proximity to a bar fight than any man I've ever known.

Going to parties and driving around with a pickup bed full of booze is one thing. Waking up to stir 26 gallons of Clamato with a dozen bottles of Worcestershire is another thing entirely. We were a bleary bunch, but the drinks got poured. At some point I tired of listening to what seemed like an endless set of badly DJ'd dub reggae, and tired of watching a very self-absorbed girl in a belly-dancing costume hula-hoop, and went back to my room, where I promptly fell asleep in my shoes. I woke up hours later, startled, the television still on. I'd missed most of the headline act, Reverend Horton Heat.

Back in Palisade, Rory tallied up the case sales from the Jamboree.

They'd sold 19 cases of their Goat vodka, 6 cases of Jackelope gin (and they'd used 52 bottles of Clamato, 7 bottles of Tabasco, 12 bottles of Worcestershire, 9 bottles of pepperoncini, 17 bottles of pickled okra, 3 jars of celery salt, 6 bottles of pickles, half a case of black pepper, 19 packs of celery, and 21 jars of cherry peppers). You couldn't expect much more. It added up to some money.

We tasted some bourbon out of the barrel. It was still young, but it was complicated, layered, and it reminded me of the polenta taste I'd gotten out of the first mash I'd ever made. It was what I'd hoped my whiskey might taste like—young, grainy, and chewy. At the finish, the bourbon coalesced into solid honey flavors.

After dinner, we went over to head distiller Davy's place for beers. He's built a walk-in cooler and a production-quality microbrew setup in his backyard. He's the only person I've ever met who does decoction brewing, and he's the only person I've ever met who might brush up against that 300-gallon-a-year limit set by the government.

I suggested, amazed, that coming home from a job as a distiller to brew beer seemed a little focused. Like maybe he should pick up golf or something, mix it up a bit. He laughed at the idea and walked me through his highly developed brewing system, showing me the equipment and talking about the beers he was looking forward to making.

For every American who dreams of pension plans, benefits, and a steady rise through the ranks, there is another who wants nothing more than to hang out a shingle and become his or her own boss. They want to open restaurants and shops; they want to sell steaks or ATVs, books or blouses. Some of these lone-wolf types are motivated by a desire to surround themselves with something they love (clocks or yarn or cheeses), others are motivated by a pure entrepreneurial urge, and some are driven craftsmen, artisans. Ideally, the three things blur. I'm sure that Rory would rather be distilling than driving the product around, but he's got to make the business work.

Before I left for San Francisco to take Bill Owens's class on distilling, I called Rory. He said, "You don't need a class on distilling."

Well, thanks. I'd still like to watch one.

"Anyway," he said. "Distilling is the easy part. They should be taking a class on selling."

I walked into Don Payne's Stillwater Spirits in Petaluma (site of the brilliant Gewürztraminer grappa) to find about a dozen students and an indeterminate number of hangers-on and contributors.

Don had spent the year working on shochu in his vacuum still (which is probably the only one in America). The still allows him to distill at a lower temperature, as low as 85 degrees, which results in less bitterness and no burning.*

Don is a great model for wannabe distillers, because he is adventurous and talented. The place itself is perfect, too, because in addition to the vacuum still (which opens people's horizons) he's got a Jacob Carl German-style column/pot still and a Vendome he designed himself. It's more variation than one would see at a typical distillery.

We'd use Stillwater as our base. We'd spend the week drinking, touring distilleries and bars, and distilling. Bill had even arranged for someone to cook for us, and he turned out a series of excellent, family-style meals. There were frittatas and coffee for breakfast, and a mountain of Dungeness crabs one afternoon. There was always beer on tap, and an endless supply of wine. Not to mention the booze on a folding table in the middle of the floor. People had brought samples: there was a crushed Dasani bottle full of brown liquor and a boiling flask and some bottles that came from a craft store. There was Jack Daniel's and a few Leopold Bros. products. Lance Winters from St. George had left a bottle of their dazzling Blue Agave. There was a

---

* Shochu, the low-proof distillate made mostly in Japan, is the largest-selling alcoholic beverage in the world (although I've heard the same for cachaça, and, for that matter, vodka). Don was working on a product called Twenty Four, which as of this writing is just rolling out. Twenty Four will fall, just, into the alcohol percentage allowed for beer and wine licenses. His shochu will therefore have a lower tax rate and be easier to sell.

whiskey with no label that everyone liked, which had been sealed with wax set with a piece of string styled to look like a fuse. There was grappa and cachaça and Willett bourbon. A couple of absinthes. Some limoncello that people drank as an eye-opener out of cordial glasses before they moved over to beer—a switch which took place, for the most part, well before lunch.

The class was invaluable. Not only did the students mash grain and work on the mashes and washes, they worked the stills, distilled some grappa, distilled the very mashes they'd begun. Lynne Carmichael, a beverage industry attorney, gave a workshop on legal procedures. Lance Winters gave a talk about production. Steven Wright, a profoundly knowledgeable spirits industry consultant, gave a two-day presentation that took the students from mashing to barreling. There were workshops on proofing and a workshop on barrels. Dave Pancoast came and demonstrated his small-scale labeling machine.

Everyone agreed that for someone starting a microdistillery, the class was money well spent.

"This class has saved me *thousands*," came from all corners like a refrain.

The first night, as some of the students mashed grain (Bill and I made a run to the grocery store to buy 8 pounds of sugar and spiked the grainy moonshine mash with it), others chatted and sat around. The talk turned to the economy, as talk was wont to do in December of 2008, and a recently unemployed Wall Street type relentlessly demonstrated not only that he felt he had the answer to everything, but that the chip on his shoulder was cut with an ax.

There was a surprising amount of standoffish animosity in the air. People would proclaim throughout the week that they loved one another and that this group was wonderful, but I've been in wonderful groups, and these people were all trying to hide things from each other, suspicious of each other. What's more, they seemed to have their minds made up about much of their business.

"I'm just going to use city water," said the straightforward young woman with the skin as pale as Pinot Grigio.

Others (including myself) implored her to think about filtration, to think about reverse osmosis, but she stuck to her guns.

She came from so far up into Maine that Canada was east of her rather than north, and she was very far along on her project to fill that region with superpremium, youth-oriented vodka, made from Maine potatoes.

It's not my place, in situations like this, to advise people or to criticize without invitation to do so, but there are moments when you just want to break something down for a person: superpremium youth-market? Contradiction in terms. Status-seeking youngsters purchase recognizable brands. Rebels spend money, but they want to be associated with something crafty, crazy, local, or obscure, rather than superpremium.*

The problem for new products is that there is a lot of competition, and a lot of money. Even the guys who generate some momentum find themselves smashed under the high heels of a battalion of slinky-dressed, cleavage-baring, sales reps from the big companies like Absolut or Diageo.

Still, most people looking to get into the microdistilling game plan on supporting themselves with the sale of white, unaged spirits while their whiskey ages, and in many cases it works.

---

* Furthermore, if you're going into the vodka market with nothing more than a marketing plan, prepare to be smashed to bits by the prodigious marketing budgets of the supercorporations. Vodka is not a quality-driven product. I don't mean that there isn't good vodka and bad vodka, there is. Legally, vodka is an alcohol without attributes. The better it is, the fewer attributes it has. It's a great irony. If someone starts talking about the flavor characteristics of their vodka, what they are really talking about are the attributes that make it bad vodka. (It needs to be said that one of my favorite spirits, the Tuthilltown Heart of the Hudson vodka, has a stripe of concentrated apple candy flavor running right through the middle of it which makes it at once incredibly delicious and by any plausible standard "bad" vodka.) Since vodka is, *by definition*, without taste or aroma, only two things really set one vodka apart from another: price point and image. Among the vodkas with a clean palate, it breaks down like this: Tito's is a vodka with a hand-crafted image and a low price point. Hangar One has a slicker, but still hand-crafted, image, and a superpremium price point. Grey Goose has a luxury image and a high price. Absolut or Stolichnaya are the "standards." Other vodkas attempt to differentiate themselves by being organic, or made from a certain grain, or from a certain region. Basically, it's a graphic design project—what's the label going to suggest to a potential consumer? How many people are there who like that sort of thing?

House Spirits has made money on Aviation gin, Medoyeff vodka, and Krogstad aquavit while their whiskey ages. They also sold barrel futures to help pay for the storage. The strategy was viable, and it's gotten them to the brink of very big things. In the summer of 2009, they harvested 52 acres of barley that they will malt themselves. Much of that malt will be used to produce a new product, a light, refreshing, and incredibly cocktail friendly blended whiskey. They believe that people want to know where their spirits come from, and while their locavore bent might not be enough on its own, the fact that the whiskey will be cheap and delicious will change the landscape of microdistilling in America.

House knocked it out of the park. They realized their visions perfectly, and their aesthetic is one that people dig.

There are other ways to achieve tremendous success. One of the best American whiskies—Hogshead—is made at Edgefield Distillery. These days it's made by James Whelan—he also has a white pear liquor sitting in a vat waiting to get bottled that I am anxious to taste again.* What sets Edgefield apart—aside from their quality, which is outrageously good—is that they are a part of the McMeniman's empire based in Portland, Oregon. McMeniman's owns microbrew pubs, movie theaters, restaurants, and music venues. Outside the Edgefield distillery there is a 3-par golf course, horseshoe pits, and picnic tables.

Thanks to this, James gets a lot of freedom. There is no pressure to float an entire start up business. The booze is another ingredient in the mix.

What these two distilleries do, more than they do anything else, is make unbelievably good liquor. They do that by experimenting, pushing the envelope. They take incredible care in what they do.

They listened to the advice that people gave them, too. On the doorframe at Edgefield, for example, you can still see the numbers Booker Noe wrote down when he visited their distillery. He gave

---

* Most of what we get to drink of the Hogshead was actually distilled by Lee Medoff before he went out on his own and formed House.

them a recipe for a rye that he'd wanted to make at Jim Beam, but he'd never had a chance. McMeniman's made it. When James looks out his door at a small stand of pear trees, he finds the time to pick them and distill them, so he can make a special run of Edgefield pear eau de vie from Edgefield pears.

Of course, these are the hallmarks of genius. House Spirits, Edgefield, Stranahan's, Peach Street, and Stillwater Spirits: these are the geniuses of the microdistilling world. (This isn't a complete list, of course, but it's close.)

Here at Don's distillery, I saw a roomful of headstrong individuals, and as I watched them, I didn't trust that they were going to turn out to be the next batch of genius distillers. There were some that I was *sure* were not. Of course, everyone who takes piano lessons doesn't play Carnegie Hall, either. In fact, most of them never perform at all. They all start at lessons, and they weren't good when they showed up.

The first night, we mashed three grain bills. One of the students had contributed a vat of smashed and fermented cabernet grapes. The room was pretty evenly divided: Some folks got right into it, learned where all the valves were, grabbed a shovel, asked questions. Others leaned on the bar and chatted among themselves.

Some of them had hobby-distilled, some had a rudimentary knowledge of a still. Even among the smart ones, there were huge gaps in their knowledge—"You said an infusion chamber for gin botanicals? Um, what's that?"

Obviously, this is specific knowledge, not the sort of thing you pick up, but it struck me, as the question was asked, that the person asking it had revealed a lacuna that contradicted their attitude about the class. It seems to me that if you don't know how to make gin (or what part of the still does it), maybe you shouldn't be leaning against the bar with a beer making jokes with the cook.

There were some good ideas flying around, too. Surely there's room for an artisanal Tennessee whiskey, and surely there's room for infused grappas from a young Sonoma winery.

But why would anyone go through what Rory was doing to do it?

He hadn't been paid in three years. His credit card debt was astronomical. He was hand-delivering product around the state.

Then I remembered what Jim Murray had said at his tasting. He asked how many people were making whiskey, and about half the class raised their hands.

"Because I think that this conference is gonna go down in history for absolutely changing the way things happen in this country. Because I can see a massive explosion." He said: "You guys who have put your house on the line, you've put your lives on the line for whiskey." He told them they should take amazing pride in what they are doing. That they shouldn't get lazy, they shouldn't take their foot off the gas.

This is why you do this. This is why you give it a shot. Because now is the time.

Small-scale distilling was a part of America that was lost along the way. When Jefferson and Hamilton headed off against one another, the little guy lost. The tide is turning. The movement is toward the local, the small. These folks are changing the way things happen in this country. Some of them are changing the way whiskey is made. Others are changing the way the law is written. Zac Triemert of Lucky Bucket Brewing and the Solas Distillery in Omaha, changed the legislation so he could sell his spirits at his pub, without distributing them first. Don Poffenroth and Kent Fleischmann of Dry Fly Distilling, in Washington State, wrote the laws that allowed microdistilling.

For American distilling, this is a watershed moment. We're at the peak of the Red Mountain Pass. Clearly, everyone isn't going to make it to the other side. But it doesn't matter. They're giving it a shot, and it's worth it to hear Jim Murray stand at the head of a room and say, "Guys, I'm absolutely honored to have had this tasting with you today."

Housegemacht

There lurks, perhaps, in every human heart a desire of distinction, which inclines every man to hope, and then to believe, that nature has given himself something peculiar to himself.

—JAMES BOSWELL, LIFE OF SAMUEL JOHNSON

THERE WERE EIGHT OF US AT THE TABLE IN THE BACK OF the restaurant, a few crooked and crumbling blocks off the river, in the warehouse district of New Orleans. At the head was Bill Owens. At the foot of the table Mike McCaw, who with Mike Nixon (together they are referred to as the Mikes) founded the Amphora Society, authored *The Compleat Distiller*, and designed the PDA-1. The PDA is a distilling column that breaks down and packs into a briefcase like a sniper's rifle. Its ingenious design allows for exacting separation of heads and hearts and tails. A home distiller who sprung for it would produce a glasslike vodka from the heart of the run. Mike explained to me that if you can really separate all the pieces of the run, you can blend them back together as you like, creating more aggressive flavor profiles and ending up with whatever you want. Add more of the heads, for instance, and you get a grainier whiskey. He sells hundreds of PDAs a year.

Flavor-positive distillates aren't Mike's thing, however. Those are the strong suit of the man who was seated next to Mike: Ian Smiley, the author of *Making Pure Corn Whiskey*. He has sold about 20,000 copies and is the most sought-after man in hobby distilling. Ian can fix your problems, steer you in the right direction, answer your questions, and set you on the path to nanodistilled perfection.

Across from us, Matt Rowley, champion of the scene, author of *Moonshine!,* the best primer I know on how to get started in the small-scale hobby of making your own hooch.

Three innocent bystanders were along for the ride.

Some of our party had known one another for as long as it had taken to get our first round, but we were leaning in, laughing, talking fast, and raucously ordering more food. Most of us were sharing our plates, and we had ordered braised pig's cheeks, fried pig's ears, three plates of their house-made charcuterie (exquisite head cheese, rillettes, terrines, and a sausage), two plates of fried rabbit livers on toast, a boudin ball, a ham hock, a sliced brisket, and two plates of fried alligator. Cracklins were arrayed in metal milkshake mixing cups and cones of paper, and we'd ordered one small ramekin of fava beans and potatoes.

I was drinking 144-proof George T. Stagg bourbon and Anchor Steam beer. The table was littered with bourbon glasses, most half-drunk. The waiter brought a steady stream of drafts and bottles.

Above us, on a sill of the window that afforded a view of the hearth from the dining room, was a copper Georgia Ridge moonshine still fabricated by Colonel Wilson. There was a rumor going around that every once in a while they cranked it up.

I had tried to get some bootleg out of them at the bar.

Rowley shook his head at me, disapproving of my blustery style.

"If we had any, I'd give it to you," said the bartender. "We had a party. It's all gone. We don't sell it or anything, we just give it away." The bartender nodded sagely, as if giving it away made it legit.

People misunderstand the laws they break. It's irresponsible to break laws badly.* I can think of only one set of laws more generally misunderstood than the laws against distilling, and that's the old saw about how undercover agents can't lie and have to tell you that they are cops. For the record: Undercover cops are lying with every word that comes out of their mouth; they lied when they got dressed that morning, when they stopped shaving, and when they introduced themselves. They lied when they said they would like to buy drugs from you, or at least they misrepresented the meaning of the sentence—of course they'd like to, that's how they're going to make the case that lands you in jail. They don't have to announce themselves as cops after all this subterfuge just because some criminal *asked* them. Regarding distillation, lets be clear: It's the making of it that's illegal. Distilling alcohol—any amount of alcohol—is against the law without a registered still and a permit. You can't buy alcohol legally and then redistill it, because the action of evaporating alcohol and condensing the vapors back into alcohol is illegal unless it's done in a registered, permitted still. The still itself is illegal if it's set up, and everything that follows your use of it—the transporting, the possessing, the selling, the giving away—is also illegal.

Technically, if you're cooking and you put wine in the food and you put the lid on so that the alcohol that is evaporating condenses on the lid of the pot and beads and rolls back down, you are breaking the law. Absurd, unenforceable (and obviously, no one would desire to enforce it), but according to the letter of the law, you've engaged in the process of distilling alcohol. I had recently sampled some tequila that had been infused with strawberries (go, do it, it's fantastic) and when the maker had poured the tequila into a glass jar to infuse it, he was breaking the law. All those vodka infusions up on the back bar in the Russian bars of New York are against the law, because that's not the container the alcohol came in.

I had law on the brain: we'd talked a lot about legality that day.

---

* How to Be a Criminal, Item 4: Read up on the laws you are breaking.

Mike, Matt, and Ian had sat on a panel at the Tales of the Cocktail conference entitled "Making Your Own Spirits," and in some small way it was historic. For while the enthusiasm of home distillers is intense, it remains a black hobby. Incredible expense, hours of time, all toward an obsession about which we can only whisper, using pseudonyms.

As far as any of us knew, the nanodistilling hobby had never before been addressed in a public forum. We all agreed it was high time.

I half-expected a phalanx of officers to file in with the last of the audience, or a jackboot on the door and agents in full riot gear while everyone was shifting in their seats and getting out their notebooks. Would we be handcuffed? Interrogated?

How many gallons of liquor have you made in the last six years? Where's the moonshine? Bring us to the still!

You could make a real sweep of the hobby if you waterboarded Matt Rowley.

Silliness and paranoia—it would never go down like that. Perhaps they'd simply seize the attendance records of the event and get warrants to search our houses. All across the country, cops were breaking into empty homes . . .

Mike and Matt and Ian are all exceedingly careful. Mike doesn't even distill in the states, choosing rather to conduct his experiments in New Zealand, where home distilling is legal. They warned the folks in the room that they wouldn't answer a question if they'd been informed of an intent to break the law. Hypothetical questions are fine. Direct questions are aiding and abetting.

"Commercial distillers," declared Mike McCaw with disgust, "have as their foremost goal consistency. It is the artisan who chases quality and perfection." The hobbyist is not constrained by market forces or the maintenance of continuity, but is, rather, able to explore.

Mike looked like a cheerful science teacher in a white button-down oxford. He's a slightly soft, happy-looking man with a gray beard. He was a natural at the head of the class, and he spoke poetically of the clouds of vapor rising in the still, how they crossed over one another like Venn diagrams, and how it was the job of a distiller to tap the proper gases and gather only the right ones. I thought of my still, Billy Gibbons, often cross-threaded, always leaking, and how every product I made was a happy accident.

Ian picked up on Mike's analogy of the clouds of vapors and talked about blending them together, finding the perfect mix of heads and tails and heart, combining the various chemicals to make a carefully impure beverage with perfectly tuned flavor.

Rowley, in a hepcat bowling shirt, divided home distillers into three groups: economic, technical, and artisan. Economically motivated distillers are motivated to drink more cheaply. One finds them making whiskey out of corn flakes and going for pure ethanol from sugar washes. They want purity, they want proof, they want a buzz. Technical distillers, he put forward, are gearheads, endlessly tinkering with their stills in their search for mechanical perfection. They take meticulous notes and keep perfect records. They are forever grabbing for the wrench, ready to make a small improvement. Artisan distillers are the foodies of the distilling world. They distill things they buy at the farmers' market, they distill fruit, they chase crazy ideas.

I wondered where I fit in on the spectrum of hobby distillers— certainly, I wasn't much of a gearhead, but then again I wasn't much of an artisan either. Clearly, economy was off the table: my distillates were the product of mountains of time and money. How did I fit into this world?

The answer came at the Carousel Bar in the Hotel Monteleone that night. We were talking about distilling, and I was trying my best to keep up and ask questions that were not inane. A young man who had been at the panel nabbed Ian's attention, interrogated him, and passionately scribbled the nuggets of wisdom Ian tossed his way.

The boy was towheaded and wide-eyed and when he left, he thanked Ian profusely.

Groupies, I kidded.

Ian smiled and said, "Just wait."

I'd been promoted, and with that promotion I saw my place. I wasn't an artisan or a tech head, I was an apostle.

I was exploring the faith.

I was bringing the news.

I'd already helped one soul along. Eckhard is a magazine writer of some real renown, a well-respected author, and a New York intellectual. He'd written about moonshine, and I had seen through his pseudonyms. We'd covered a bit of the same ground. I called him for advice about a source I felt sure that we shared, a semiretired moonshiner who mixed a strange brew of flattery and insult. I couldn't figure him out. Burk agreed he was an odd character and sent me his notes to prove it.

"But listen, I'm really glad you called."

Oh?

"I've been walking around Park Slope, and there's all these apple trees—they are *everywhere*. Nobody picks the apples, they just fall off the trees and rot. So I went in with someone and we bought a press, I'll e-mail you a picture, it's a beauty—"

I was already yessing and encouraging him before he got to the part where he paused and started with: "Do you think . . ."

Oh, yes, I said, I thought he could. A flurry of e-mails followed that initial discussion. I recommended a still to him from the Hoga Company—having denied myself one, I thought *someone* ought to have one. It'd be perfect for his job.

He read while he waited for the still to arrive, and we kept in touch. He was intimidated by Mike and Mike's book. He felt the whole thing was too technical, he'd never get it right. He'd also read some diary of a calvados maker, and he thought that he would never live up to that level of expertise.

I talked him down. I told him not to worry about what calvados makers do, not to worry about anything. Mike and Mike are very technical, and most of it would make sense later, but none of it mattered right now. I told him about the folks in the basement of the apple-processing plant in Winchester. If they could do it . . .

Eckhard hit the streets in the mornings with his teenage son and gathered bushels of apples from the unlikeliest of places. They'd found McIntosh apples at 18th Street and 8th Avenue. They picked yellow and red apples from the three trees in front of the shelter for battered women at the armory on 8th Avenue until the security guard shooed them off. They harvested from the trees in front of a local church. Intermittently, they'd set up the Happy Ranch cider press on the sidewalk.

"The juice is pretty great," said Eckhard, "brighter, fruitier, and less musty than any cider I've ever had."

A few weeks later he wrote to say: "The alembic has arrived! It's absolutely beautiful: all shiny, curvy, and beaten copper." He set the still on a Toastmaster hot plate. He was nervous but excited.

"I did it on our porch, here in Park Slope, under a picnic table covered with tarps. The smell wafted over a wide area, but I'm sure the neighbors just thought I was mulling wine . . ."

In New Orleans, I thought about Eckhard. I had a convert. He might have gone through with it anyway, but I had urged him, pointed him in the right direction, and encouraged him.

I'd never know as much as Ian, I'd never be as scientific as Mike. It wasn't my job. I'm not a distiller; I tell stories.

We were all together one more time, eating softshell crabs and drinking Abita beer at the Acme Oyster House.

Ian leaned back into the corner, flushed and grinning: "What you are looking at," he said, "is an inebriated man. And a very happy one."

We all laughed and I gave Ian a fraternal slap on the shoulder.

The Halifax Hunt Club

The end of man is knowledge, but there is one thing he can't know. He can't know whether knowledge will save him or kill him. He will be killed, all right, but he can't know whether he is killed because of the knowledge which he has got or because of the knowledge which he hasn't got and which if he had it, would save him. There's the cold in your stomach, but you open the envelope, you have to open the envelope, for the end of man is to know.

—ROBERT PENN WARREN, *ALL THE KING'S MEN*

I FLOATED ON MY BACK IN THE HOTEL POOL WITH MY ARMS out, bobbing and feeling the breeze and looking up at the blue, blue sky in Roanoke, Virginia. The moon had made a midday appearance and it was almost full. I floated and tried to be peaceful and to drift, empty and thoughtless, but the information rolled on, like the rush of a big river breaking over the rocks, or the churning of great machinery. The information: I had hundreds of facts and impressions; I'd witnessed hours of testimony. I'd watched surveillance video and seen photographs. I'd suffered through financial analysis. I'd listened to the surreptitious recording made by a police informant.

The recording had been made by Jarman Johnson as he rode with Jody Alton "Duck" Smith and some others to meet their accusers at the grand jury. They were facing thirty odd counts relating to operating a still without a license, money laundering, conspiracy, and Social Security fraud. What was it, really? Messy audio, the whoosh of automobiles, idle chatter punctuated by the sharp coughs of the rat with the recorder in his shirt pocket.

"Hell, I don't remember where I was yesterday!"

"Uh-huh."

"Half the time I can't read my own signature!"

Some laughs, and the smoker's hack.

"I just scribble!"

The grand jury had validated the charges. We were a week into the trial.

The information had led not to knowledge, but toward obfuscation, bewilderment, and possibility.

I had arrived in Roanoke and seen in the paper that four of the six accused had pled guilty late Friday afternoon. They were, according to the indictment, the employees, the still hands. Most of them had a previous liquor violation. The case against the two holdouts seemed conclusive.

I suspected that I was about to witness a very short trial, in which perhaps the remaining two defendants would simply stand up, revoke their plea of not guilty, and lay themselves at the mercy of the court. Federal court, after all, has a 95 percent rate of conviction, though that is slightly misleading, since only 8 percent of the cases ever make it to trial—92 percent take a plea agreement. Deals had been offered. Sharon Burnham had offered Duck two years and no forfeiture. He'd turned it down. Jesse Tate of the ABC had written me to say "They ought to add a count of 'stupid' on to the charges."

Somehow this slam dunk of a case had gone on for a week, and every day we'd spent in court had brought nothing but doubt and mystery.

I'd read the indictment compulsively, amazed by its precision, its scope. I couldn't imagine facing down a thing like that. The government knew when and where they'd bought the sugar. They knew when and where they'd bought the jugs. They knew that on January 26, Duck and his son had bought surveillance cameras, a splitter, and a time-lapse VCR. What's more, they'd intensified the case with numerous money-laundering and perjury charges. They were accusing Duck of defrauding the Social Security Administration and directing the proceeds toward a criminal enterprise (this is illegal in two ways, it's illegal to get disability to which you are not entitled, but it's extra-illegal to structure money so that you can conceal the criminality of what you're doing).*

Duck was, to listen to the agents and to read the indictment, the key player, the so-called kingpin. They had pictures, they had video, they had a still site: they had their man.

Margaret Smith stood accused of conspiring and of a string of money-laundering charges for paying the mortgage on the land where the stills had been found. It seemed, from a distance, open and shut: here were the stills; here were the money orders she'd written.

Margaret's attorney had pushed her to plead.

"He didn't believe a word I said," she told me.

She told me that at one point, in an attempt to drive a spike between her and Duck, he'd positioned a copy of Duck's telephone records in such a way as to allow her to see it. Did she see all these calls? All these women? You know he runs around on you, Margaret. Don't go down with him.

She'd resisted. She and Duck would have their day in court. Their pertinacity was paying off.

---

* How to Be a Criminal, Item 5: It's important to understand that criminal justice attends not only to the crime committed but to every ancillary activity involved in the perpetration, and especially perpetuation and concealment, of illegal activity, and that those acts, because they suggest intent, because they are part of a scheme, often carry heavier sentences than what we would normally think of as the illegal act. If you view it in a forgiving light, the law could be seen to forgive reckless impulse ("I was lonely and drunk and I picked up this hooker") and punish a pattern of concealment and manipulation ("I set up this bank account so that I could withdraw cash without my wife noticing and pay for hookers").

From my hotel room I called Morris to ask about Duck, and as usual he answered the phone already laughing: "Maxwell Smart! How're'you *doing*, my friend! What's the news from big trial?"

I told him things were confusing. Sharon was prosecuting and I wasn't sure she was making the case. (Morris was surprised—that didn't sound like Sharon. I agreed.) What did he think? Was it possible . . . could it be . . . is Duck actually *innocent*?

"He very well could be. I've known Duck for years." Morris reminded me again that he'd spent seventeen years out of the county. "But I've known him ever since I got back, and he's always seemed like a good guy to me." He went into a long digression about a restaurant he use to hang out in, but I'd learned not to try to steer him back, he never forgets the point, he just likes to fill in a whole lot of backstory.

"Well, one time I remember the story went that Duck hit it big, and I mean big, up there in a casino in New Jersey, and he came back with something like $250,000, and he bought that joint and renovated it. Well, it used to be a bootleg place. They had a trapdoor behind the bar, and you'd go in there and ask for some liquor and they'd go down the trapdoor, get you a pint or a quart or whatever it was, and they'd sell it to you. When Duck bought the place, he renovated it really nice, put a lot of money into it, and he closed that door up. I told him he was crazy! That was a piece of history, man!"

So you don't think he's interested in selling liquor?

"He wouldn't have closed it up if he was, right? 'Bout the only thing I know bad about Duck is that he likes to drink a little too much."

I heard he likes women a little too much, too, I suggested, going out on a limb, extrapolating from a throwaway comment someone had made.

"You might be right about that, too, you might have it there. I tell you what, he's a hustler, you know? But he's a good guy. I've seen him 'bout stoned, and I've seen him sober, and he's always seemed like a good dude to me."

I showered and dressed and followed Route 116 out of Roanoke through Vinton and toward Smith Mountain Lake, over the mountain switchbacks and through the curves that threatened a safe speed of 15 miles an hour. I had vague directions—take a right at a bar, look for a trailer that's for sale—but I found the place: a barn and stables tucked back in a hollow. I could see the smoke rising from the barbecue grills; I could see half a dozen trucks parked in the red dirt.

I drove down the hill and into the hollow toward where the hamburger smoke was pluming and parked behind a truck with a sticker on the back windshield that read I'M NOT SPEEDING, I'M QUALIFYING. There were trailers all around—a little one like you'd find at a construction site, and a bigger one—and a series of corrugated roofs propped up on poles, stacked to the brim with round bale hay on the far side and closer to the driveway covering a tractor, a backhoe, a Bobcat, and a John Deere riding mower. At the end of the gravel road there was a barn behind a covered porch, and inside the barn I saw someone raise their hand and wave at me, welcoming me, assuring me that I'd hit the right spot.

On the porch, tables were laden with chopped onions, deviled eggs, bottles of ketchup, and a jar of Duke's mayonnaise—the best mayonnaise by far—made at the old C. F. Sauer spice plant on Broad Street in Richmond. Just seeing it brought a flash of sweet tea memories: walking the Easter Parade down Monument Avenue in Richmond with a fried green tomato sandwich slathered with Duke's and a flask tucked into my tattered poplin blazer.

I smiled at the people arrayed on the folding chairs and drinking Pepsis and Rolling Rock beers. There were children about, and lots of country women reclining in their chairs with their mouths gaping slightly, as if the heat of the day had defeated them, their long hair blowing in the weak breeze of the box fans randomly deployed about the place. There was a pack of eight or a dozen little hounds snuffling and licking in the corner, and there were flies everywhere. As I walked past a pudgy child who looked to be three and a half, shoeless in a tie-dyed shirt and playing with a squirt gun, I heard a horse neigh and watched a couple of proud looking Rhode Island Red hens scamper across the yard with their combs quivering.

Duck Smith got me a stool and a cold beer, and I shook hands all around. I felt as if I'd joined the game in the back room.

Duck has a ruddy, kind face and a close-cropped beard. He wears gun-metal glasses and dark, well-tailored suits. He's of average height, with a slight paunch that suits him. In the courtroom he was hard to read. Sometimes he came across like a beatific reverend, peaceful and well meaning, but other times he looked like he was raising the bet in a high-stakes game of no-limit poker. Facing him across a table in the back room of a barn on a hot day, he resolved into a simple country man who looked like he worked hard and liked his friends and family.

Many of the folks gathered around the picnic tables and swatting at flies were supporters and kinfolk and intimates, and a key few of them were character witnesses, here to be interviewed by Greg Nawn, legal aid on the defense team. Greg's a big man with short hair; in court he scowls with intensity and looks at times as if he were standing behind a mobster with his arms crossed; he looks like the muscle. He sat at the table in a white t-shirt and blue jeans, drinking a can of beer with a legal pad in front of him and a Sharpie with which he took scrawling notes in a loopy, loose hand. He was exhausted already, a week into the trial, but he soldiered on, despite his swollen eyes and lack of sleep. They were in the shit, and there was no time for rest.

It went like this: a man with a bill cap cocked back on his head would sidle up to the table, hike his pants up at the crotch, and perch on the bar stool.

"Spell your name for me?" Greg would ask. "And do you know anything about Duck Smith having anything to do with moonshine?"

They all seemed to know how to say no.

Taking a break, Greg and I watched the animals and kicked the dirt.

"I love chickens," he said. "They're so beautiful."

I'd been headed toward this barn since I first visited Randall Toney and Jay Calhoun at the offices of the Illegal Whiskey Task Force in

August of 2007. Randall is a quiet man, shy until you get to know him (and then exceedingly funny and dry), with kind eyes and a gray mustache. Jay is more outspoken, a farmer, a country boy. They were both wearing shitkicker boots and blue jeans. Jay was wearing a camouflage t-shirt and a hunting cap. Randall tucked himself into a small chair by a filing cabinet and sat through the whole interview facing Jay, instead of me, with his knees pressed together as if he were wearing a skirt. Jay rocked back in his boss's chair and slapped his big boots—manure crusted into the treads—up on the desk.

"You know," said Jay, "there's a case at the grand jury right now. Should come back next week."

I asked who it was and was told that I'd have to wait and see. I asked if it was anyone I'd know already.

"He's been at it for a while. He's one of the ones that slipped through the cracks. Didn't get him on Lightning Strike."

"Didn't get him a bunch a times," added Randall.

You've been trying?

They nodded.

Have you got him now?

They looked at each other, and although the chorus didn't exactly ring out that their man was dead to rights, they both seemed to think so.

The grand jury didn't come back the following week. Or the following month. In October, I visited Sharon Burnham in the Federal Building and mentioned that I'd heard there was a moonshining case before the grand jury.

"Obviously, I'm not going to answer that question."

If there was a case, had the people involved been arrested? (Arrests are a public piece of information, and sometimes precede grand jury indictments, therefore allowing for a reasonable insight, or at least a searchable record.)

She didn't take the bait.

● ● ●

Jay Calhoun would later tell me how the investigation had progressed. The Illegal Whiskey Task Force had busted a guy. He wouldn't tell me who it was or what they'd caught him at, but they threw him a lifeline and offered a deal because they were suspicious that he was working as a still hand. He was resistant. They said they knew he had something to give them, and finally he broke down and said there was a still. He'd been there. You could see two smokestacks from the front door.

"Man, it's always like this," said Jay, shaking his head over the cat-and-mouse aspect of his job, no doubt remembering a long string of clues that led nowhere. "You get some little tip . . . somebody calls and tells you there's foam in the creek."

They found some smokestacks in Franklin County, and they looked around, walking the woods in circles and searching the deed records. They found nothing.

"Hell, I didn't know if we were in the right county. We just gave up. Then, one day, I was driving through Halifax, headed to Richmond on 360, something else entirely, and I saw these two smokestacks side by side. You know, it's worth a shot. So I called the Halifax County deeds office and asked if there was any land around here in the name of Jody A. Smith, or Margaret Smith, and there was."

Jay walked a power line clear-cut easement that bordered the property deeded to Margaret Smith until he found a building. He was about 125 yards away, but he could smell a "warm liquor smell," and he could hear clanging and moving around. "Sounds I associate with a distillery in operation."

I asked him why he didn't raid it then and there.

"I knew Duck wasn't in there."

The team started their surveillance. Don Harris would drive them out there and wait in the car, since he was between law enforcement jobs and didn't have a right to be traipsing around on other people's land, and Jay would walk the woods with Bureau of Alcohol, Tobacco, Firearms, and Explosives agent Don Underwood or Randall Toney. Across the road from the gate to the property, they set up a video camera in a tree. Soon they replaced it with a unit built by the ABC's own tech guy—a First Witness zoom camera (which looks like a camouflaged video camera) connected to a camera case with a power plug, a video in, and a spot for a 2-gigabyte SD card. What was special about the setup was that it detected motion, so it wouldn't record when nothing was happening. It waited for a change in the pixels, backed up 5 seconds, and then recorded until everything was again still. No more reviewing empty videotape, and they wouldn't have to slip out to the still site to change the tapes. They could just drop by every couple of weeks and change the SD card.

On May 16, 2006, they went out to change the card, and the camera was gone. They'd been made.

On May 17, they got search warrants.

On May 18, they executed them.

At 8:45 A.M., Special Agent Terry Henderson approached the door of Smith's Auto Sales, on Old Franklin Turnpike, in the tiny municipality of Redwood a few minutes east of Rocky Mount. Faded vinyl siding covers two white buildings, and there's a chipping sign that reads 20 YEARS IN BUSINESS, NO CREDIT, NO PROBLEM, WE FINANCE. The lot is full of cars and trucks. Duck owns it, and he runs a tack and feed room out of it, too, although he sells everything at cost.

"You can come in there and buy an Australian saddle for $250 that would be $800 somewhere else. The dog food I sell is cheaper than you can get it at Target." The plan, apparently, was a sort of grand, huge-margin loss leader setup: get people in the door to buy their tack and feed, and once they are regular customers of the place, they'll think of Smith's Auto Sales next time they need to buy a vehicle.

Margaret Smith was working that morning, covering for her daughter, who worked the desk as secretary and office manager. Agent Henderson made eye contact with her, announced himself, and entered.

She stood up from her desk, flustered, and said, "There's something I need to show you." She scurried to the back kitchen, opened the refrigerator, and produced a quart Mason jar, three-quarters full of moonshine, with about a pint of strawberries floating in it.* "It was on the porch when I got here this morning."

In his driveway, Duck met Don Underwood.

"What's going on?" asked Duck.

"You know why we're here," answered Underwood.

At which point Duck said Underwood wadded the search warrant up in his fist and threw it at him.

The agents testified that Duck was helpful and not overly distraught as they searched his house, hauling out financial documents, paper sacks with keys, and boxing up his computer. He gave them consent to search the shed (it was on an adjoining property that he owned, but which was not on the warrant). His mood changed as the agents announced they were going to search the attic, where they dug through the insulation and found $70,000 in fresh $100 bills and a black plastic bag with hydrometers.

In a drawer in the kitchen they found a black wallet, and in the wallet they found a scrap of paper with the address for CKS Packaging in North Carolina, which makes plastic jugs. In a grocery bag in the garage they found a milk jug full of moonshine, and in the refrigerator in the basement, a Mason jar full of moonshine.

The law also served a warrant on Jarman Johnson's white trailer with red trim on Long Horne Road, where they found a Turkish-made MKE pistol, a High Standard pistol, and a Glenfield rifle. They also found a small model of a submarine moonshine still and some bootleg liquor.

They raided the distillery in Halifax County and found the stills partially disassembled. There were boilers for four 1,200-gallon black pot stills. One of the boilers had been struck with an ax and "key-holed," rendering it inoperable. When the operators of a still know they are going to be caught (they found the camera, after all), they

---

* To read this on the inventory of the search warrant as it was returned is a bit of comedy. "Two blue receipts books and one plastic sleeve containing receipts . . . 3 Rolodex, misc. financial documents and one CD . . . Approx. 85 hanging files containing financial documents . . . One quart containing clear liquid and strawberries."

take the things from the still that are most valuable. The copper caps, which are handmade, were missing, and so were the oil burners that had been used to heat the still. The copper worm coils were found in the trees behind a fence.

The barn was a simple structure, a post-and-beam building clad in metal with a dirt floor and naked bulbs for lighting. The stills were big and made of stainless steel. Corrugated metal piping led to an industrial fan. A platform had been built, like a catwalk, to better reach the stills. Bales of hay were stacked under the platform as insulation to keep in the heat. Hoses were hung from the walls, and there was a plastic tub for proofing.

Two gallons of moonshine were found in a trailer on the property. In the still building there were 1,728 empty gallon jugs, 600 pounds of Domino sugar, 50 pounds of barley, 500 red Nepco caps (the kind that screw onto a milk jug), and 125 empty bags of Domino sugar.

The ABC brought out a Ford backhoe and destroyed the stills.

That was in May of 2006. In November of 2007 the grand jury returned the indictment as true. In September of 2008, I pushed through the revolving doors of the Federal Building in Roanoke and loaded my wallet, my keys, and my mechanical pencil in the dish by the metal detector.

"Where're you going?"

I said I was headed to Judge Turk's courtroom, courtroom number two.

"Are you a lawyer?"

I said I was a reporter. By the end of the week I'd have sacrificed every shred of objectivity. I'd have formed friendships and opinions. I'd be in too deep. That September morning, however, I was still just a reporter walking into a courtroom.

The marshals slipped my cell phone into an envelope.

The trial began, as I imagine most trials begin, with a discussion of technicalities. The defense moved to dismiss charges 31 and 32 of the indictment, which were witness tampering and obstruction of justice regarding the conversation in the Lincoln on the way to grand jury testimony. Jarman Johnson had recorded it. He was up against serious time, already a felon, in whose possession had been found firearms, and who was facing another liquor charge. Three strikes. He didn't want to go to prison.* He'd walked around with a tape recorder, trying to corner Duck, trying to get useful information out of him, something to give the feds, anything to lighten his load. Substantial assistance, they call it. The defense wanted the evidence of that recording blocked, the charges dismissed, and Jarman Johnson kept out of the witness box. How important an idea that would prove to be, I had no way of knowing, but I could tell they were playing hard.

Judge James Turk was rocked back in his leather chair, scowling as the lawyers argued back and forth. Finally he interrupted: "But it's done all the time, iddnit?"

All those in the vehicle had lawyers, the defense argued, and those lawyers were not present. "And a secret mole, a codefendant—"

The judge rocked forward and put a hand up to stop the arguing. "I'm going to deny your motion to dismiss, but I'm going to sever [the charges] and try the moonshine case."

Duck's lawyer, indicating the possibility of an appeal, and that the judge would be reversed, said, "If he gets convicted, we have another out if we go to Richmond . . . But that's not the way I practice law."

"We're here to try the moonshine case," said the judge. "That's what we're gonna do."

United States v. Jody A. Smith et al., Opening Arguments

There were the evidence boxes, piled up behind the counsel tables and stuffed with three-ring binders, paper bags, hanging files, and

---

* How to Be a Criminal, Item 6: Do not hire as underlings people whose next strike will be their third.

photographs. Collections of ephemera—receipts, scraps of paper, padlock keys, bank records—transformed and given a new weight. Someone once noted that everyone looks guilty when you watch them on a surveillance camera; there you are, in the 7-Eleven buying a Slurpee, but your motions are all jumpy, and the video is grainy, and you're wearing some sort of strange hat, and you never make eye contact with the camera. Why are you slouching? What are you trying to hide? The same is true of bank records and receipts and sticky notes when they are dragged out in court: they don't look right anymore. Sharon had piles of the stuff.

In a gray suit, her skirt just hitting her knees, she faced the jury.

"On July 26th, 2007, Defendant, Jody Smith, answered these questions under oath before a Roanoke grand jury: 'Did you ever see an operating moonshine still on the property?' Answer: 'Never.' Question: 'So you were never involved in operating a moonshine still on the property at Halifax?' Answer: 'That's correct.' "

"This," she continued, "is the key that unlocked the door to the building that held a large distillery, an illegal liquor still on property in Halifax County. This key came from the pocket of the defendant, Jody Smith, along with the keys that opened the two gates on the property. You see there, a picture of Jody Smith opening the gate that was locked and opened by this key. This is a picture of Jody Smith driving one of the trucks used to conduct the illegal liquor operation. The evidence will show that he owned the Halifax County property and the distillery that he built upon it."

She implored the jury to use their "six senses."

"You will be looking at a lot of documents, a lot of pictures, some videos."

She showed them pictures of Duck driving a truck, Duck unlocking a gate.

"You'll be hearing evidence from the witnesses. You can actually use your sense of smell, this liquor stinks, it smells. And the process of making liquor smells. The sense of touch, you'll have the keys, you'll have the locks that these keys fit. You'll be able to use the keys and try them out."

"Now, you won't be able to use your sense of taste. As I mentioned, there's lead in this and I don't think the judge would appreciate you tasting any of the evidence. But you do get to use what we call your sixth sense, your common sense."

He didn't do it alone, she explained. He paid men to break the law. They were industrious moonshiners, they made 100 cases of moonshine per mash-in out of four 1,200-gallon pots. They did it every week. She said they bought thousands of pounds of sugar in Richmond.

She showed the jury a plastic jug and said, "They had to use a tractor-trailer to haul 9,600 jugs, and that tractor-trailer was seen on Jody Smith's property."

She showed the jury the cap that sealed the jugs and said, "This is a Nepco cap. And Nepco's address was in Jody Smith's wallet."

It was a compelling argument, but Sharon was looking angry. I knew that one of the tasks she saw before her was convincing the jury that a law had been broken, that the defendants were criminals. Perhaps she was trying to put across some sort of righteous fury, but instead she looked cranky. We were in court, and she looked like a scolding teacher driven to angered distraction by the misdeeds of her miscreant charges.

What's more, she didn't look like the Sharon I knew before. Her hair, rather than sun-touched and light, looked frizzy and limp. Her smile was gone. She was stumbling over her words and referring back to her notes too often, even losing her place for a moment.

I wrote in my notebook, "Is this clumsiness staged?"—thinking that perhaps I was seeing the performative aspect of the job. Perhaps she didn't want the jury to think she was beating up on the defendant.

Judge Turk had told me in his chambers that such a thing was possible. "It's possible to overtry a case. They [the jury] may think that the government is pickin' on this person."

This is especially true in moonshine cases.

Judge Turk has been sitting since 1972, and he used to try a lot of moonshine cases. He's not sure if there's any less moonshine, or if there's simply less enforcement, but he doesn't get a lot of moonshine cases in his court anymore. Mostly he tries drugs.

He speaks with a thick country accent, and it's easy to imagine him duck hunting or sipping a Coke at a UVA football game. He is a jovial, human, and solicitous authority figure. Once a week, he brings his dog to work with him.

He explained that juries are very sympathetic to moonshiners.

"I know, back, it's been a long time ago"—he stretches out the word "long" not quite all the way to lawong, but close—"they found a still over here in Franklin County, and it was these young boys, 'bout eighteen and nineteen, at the still." Steeul. "So they arrested them, and they charged them, you know, with bein' in the bidness, and they testified—they were represented by the Davis firm in Rocky Mount—Andrew Davis used to represent 'em all the time. They said that they got this letter in the mayull, tellin' them that there was a job for 'em, and that they'd get so much an hour or something, and just to show up at this place and begin to work, and they did that, and they never saw anybody there, they said, and they didn't know who it was, and they got their money, on every Saturday I believe it was, in the mail, in cash. And they didn't know who they were, didn't know who the still was. And the jury found them not guilty."

"That was nullification," he said. "They were guilty of operating the still."

It was comfortable in Judge Turk's chambers, with little statues of airplanes on the shelves, leather chairs and leather books, and a nice chiming clock on the wall. Every day for thirty years he has played a crossword puzzle with his stenographer, Clara Whitlock. She kept a small note taped to the maple near her keyboard in the courtroom that said "Each person who passes thru this courtroom is a child of God." She was retiring; this case would be her last.

"The biggest difference between a drug case and a moonshine case," Judge Turk said, "is that ninety-nine times out of a hunnerd they'll want to cooperate with the government, tell them where they got the drugs and who they can bring in, and I've never known that to happen in moonshine, not ever that I know of. It's just sort of a moral code of the hills or something."

He told me that moonshiners always take the stand, and they never turn on each other. They're moral.

I asked him if that makes them a different kind of person than those who typically appear before him.

"Well, other than making moonshine, I think most of them are," he paused, "real good people." They are only criminals, he explained, in this one aspect. "Juries are right sympathetic to them. Well, they're good people. Hard workers, good to the wife, good to the family."

In fact, one of the public defenders initially put on the case explained to me on the telephone that if it were up to him, he would *always* go to trial with a moonshine case.

Even so, if Sharon's tactic was to diminish herself so she didn't come on like a steamroller, she was overplaying it. As she went on, I became convinced that she was truly unhappy about something. Something was not going right for her. There was the possibility that it was something else entirely—her husband was in Iraq trying to build and codify a justice system there, and he'd been gone for over a year. Perhaps she'd argued with him. Perhaps she had a cold. Perhaps she hadn't slept. Or perhaps something wasn't going the way she'd planned.

Or perhaps she didn't have the case she ought to have.

Public Defender Phillip Lingafelt represented Margaret Smith. He's a softspoken man not given much to courtroom theatrics. His opening statement was restrained and straightforward. Margaret was sick, her mother was sick, the government had no evidence of Margaret having ever set foot on the property, and in fact, she'd rented it to a man named J. B. Jones.

Then came the show.

Gilbert Davis (no relation to the famed moonshine defenders, the Davises of Rocky Mount) was representing Duck Smith. Gil rose to national prominence when he represented Paula Jones in her suit against Bill Clinton for sexual harassment. He argued that case in front of the Supreme Court. His presence in the courtroom has always been commanding, and he was described, back in those days, as a swashbuckler. He's changed his tack somewhat. For one thing, he's more or less going blind from cataracts. His heart is not good. He began slowly, and there was a lot of him holding documents four inches from his face and being a likable, bumbling, old fellow. He's a big man, and he breathes heavily, and he looks as if he is very sorry to be wasting your time with such silliness.

He had a poster with the rules of a criminal trial: (1) The defendants are presumed innocent. (2) The indictment is not an admission of guilt. (3) To convict, the burden of proof is on the prosecution. He explained the difference between a preponderance of evidence and the burden of proof. In a civil case, he explained, the prosecution needs only a preponderance of evidence.

"Imagine a scale, equally weighted, perfectly balanced. In a civil case you just put one feather on the side of the prosecution, just enough to tip the scale, and they've achieved their case."

He reminded the jury that this was not a civil case, and a preponderance of evidence was not enough to convict. The government needs to prove their case beyond a reasonable doubt. This was a criminal trial, and the burden of proof was on the government.

"And they won't prove it, because they can't prove it."

As he got going, all the bumbling melted away, stuttering and forgetfulness disappeared as he amplified his rhetoric. He was like an incredibly subtle pool hustler who gets better with each stroke of the cue, and you never notice it, but somehow, somewhere along the way, he has started running the table. That was Gil in action. By the end of the argument we were in church, we were listening to a master.

"They won't prove it, because they can't prove it. The government claims, *wrongly*, that this man operated a still. Four defendants in this case pleaded guilty on Friday. They were the ones who operated the still. Jody Smith had ties to this property, it was used as a hunt club. He knows some people who do make this stuff, you can't live in

Franklin County and not know someone who does. The government will say, *wrongly*, that Jody Smith took money from Social Security to pay for this still, but they found money in his attic. A lot of people don't like banks, and that's not a crime. He cashed his checks, and he hid the money in the attic. Is that smart? Maybe not. Is it a crime? No. There are a lot of charges here, it's a big indictment, but it all comes down to one charge. Moonshining. And the only evidence the government has to tie Jody Smith to the still is the word of a man convicted of this crime, a man who said he didn't want to go to prison. A felon who knew that if he gave the government something on Jody Smith, he wouldn't have to go to prison. The government claims, *wrongly*, that it was Jody Smith who made the moonshine. They won't be able to prove it. Because they can't prove it. Because it isn't true."

I had assumed that the defendant's best shot was that the jury would nullify the law and, despite the obvious guilt of the parties, refuse to convict them because this was, after all, southwest Virginia, and they didn't want to send a man to prison for making moonshine. Now, I saw another possibility. With a lawyer like that, Duck might just flat-out win.

After a short recess the real trial began, and the prosecution called its first witness: Jay Calhoun.

Jay cleans up well. I remembered his shitkicker boots propped up on the desk. Here, freshly shaven, in a button-down yellow oxford, a jacket, and black-rimmed oval eyeglasses, he looked downright professorial. He possessed a winning combination of expertise and accessibility, and he operated as a sort of bridge between Sharon and the jury.

One of the problems with prosecuting a moonshine case—although I'm sure it's not specific to moonshine—is that the entire process must be explained. For the government this allows them to draw a distinction between whatever preconceived notions the jury has brought to the case and the reality of the situation. They need to dispel the old-time mystique of the thing; they need to play, in a sense, exactly opposite of everything people have heard, and get rid of all the straw-chewing, Mason-jar, copper-pot, sippin'-whiskey stereotypes. They need to convince the jury that moonshine is made in vast quantities, in ugly stills, by people intent on making a whole lot of money. They also need to give the jury a crash course in distilling, for if you don't know what it means to mash in, and you don't know what it means to mix liquor in a proofing barrel, you'll never understand what's going on. To this end, they'd brought a model of a black pot still into the courtroom. It was a gorgeous little thing, a very well-made model with a tiny copper cap and little plank walls. Jay demonstrated the dollhouse still for the jury.

"You turn the heat on, and then when it's up to seventy degrees or so, you add the yeast. When it's ready to go—"

"When you say 'ready to go,' you mean that the mash has fermented and that there is alcohol in there ready to be distilled out?" asked Sharon.

"That's right. You affix this piece here." Jay daintily fitted the cap to the top of the boiler. He went through the parts, the process, and when the imaginary run was trickling out of the spout, he placed a tiny paper model of a 5-gallon bucket at the money piece.

"This is where the alcohol comes out, and they catch it in a bucket, here, and then they either pump it, or move it by hand to the proofing barrel." At which point he acted it out, in miniature, clasping the little model bucket between his thumb and forefinger and carrying it over to the tiny model of a proofing barrel they'd set up on a folding card table. He pantomimed dumping liquid out of the bucket, turning the little paper tube over at the edge of the proofing barrel.

Somehow the jury maintained their solemn looks and watched the proceedings with interest. They had been painstakingly plucked from a thirty-two-member cross-section of society that seemed weighted to the idiosyncratic. They had sat in the pews of the court—grandmothers, boxers, immigrants, couriers, gas station attendants, retired jailers—wearing borrowed blazers, sideburns, and in one memorable vision, a muumuu. Among the fourteen who remained: a garden club grandmother, a couple of men who looked like they spent most of their time under cars, a bluegrass musician. A woman who looked Indian sat dead still. She had straight hair that fell to her shoulders from the point of her head and she looked like a sand-castle pyramid. I don't think she even blinked. There was one young man with a modern, executive haircut and slacks who had presented as an intelligent fellow but had stood up, when asked by Judge Turk whether he'd ever sat on a jury before, and announced that he had.

"What was the case?" asked the judge.

"I believe it was a homicide."

I'd have chucked him off the jury right there—not only for the overzealous use of the terminology of the criminal justice system ("homicide"?) but also for the "I believe." Could he not remember?

The jury leaned forward in their chairs and watched Jay try to put the still together, and they concentrated, trying to understand what he was talking about.

As we moved from studying the model to studying the photos of the still site, I began to suspect that Sharon was pushing the wrong buttons. It seemed as if she was trying to prove that there was a distillery there at all, and at this point, with four defendants already convicted of that crime, that was public knowledge.

The question was not "Was there a still in Halifax County?" but rather "Was the still in Halifax County owned and operated by Duck Smith?" She was not answering the latter.

Perhaps she knew it. Perhaps the late change in the pleas from the other four defendants had caught her off guard and she'd been stuck with only a weekend to change the main drift of her arguments.

The jury was shown pictures of the still being torn apart by a backhoe.

"And that's not some sort of miniature backhoe or somethin'?" asked Sharon.

"No," answered Jay, with his eyebrows raised, incredulous.

Either from exhaustion or from a subconscious parroting of Jay's down-home speech patterns, Sharon had taken to dropping all her g's. Or, perhaps she was purposefully trying to seem like a country girl before the jury. "And when you're distillin' liquor . . ."

The distillery tour should have been fun. Here we were, after all, being shown around the dark side, seeing things that we wouldn't normally see. But it dragged on and on. It had been a tremendously long day, Sharon was visibly tired, but she managed to bring her presentation of evidence to a close by ringing some good bells.

In pretty rapid succession Jay disclosed that they found liquor under the sink at the mobile home in Halifax (which was near the distillery), that there were hydrometers in Duck's attic, and that there were more jugs in the shed next to Duck's house.

With that, the day was done.

We'd only just started, and yet everything had changed. Judge Turk's wisdom about the moonshiner's code had been disproved—for there was an informant. He'd worn a wire for the law, and he was going to testify.

Further, Duck's guilt was not predetermined. His lawyer was good. A case that had looked like a slam dunk on paper, a trial I had expected to last twenty-five minutes, was looking like a cliff-hanger.

United States v. Jody A. Smith et al., Day Two

Despite the country drawls of the witnesses, the poplin blazers of the attorneys, the southern wisdom of Judge Turk, this trial did not match the stereotype. There were no ceiling fans. The courtroom was modern and clean, with bird's-eye maple on the walls and an HVAC system that kept the room as cold as a meat locker until someone complained about the chill, at which point the AC was turned off and we all sat in pools of sweat until one of the clerks would decide that it was better to freeze than to cook. The whole thing was a little like having a fever, and during every recess throughout the trial the bailiff and the clerks and whoever else lingered would discuss the temperature of the courtroom in the fashion of old men on a Main Street bench talking about the weather.

Judge Turk sat, elevated, before a wall of wooden slats that looked like a gigantic Danish Modern coffee table nailed to the wall, with a brass seal floating over his head. I don't mean to discount the effect—he was imposing. A judge looms over a courtroom the way a man on horseback looms over infantry.

There were sixteen video screens (not counting computers) in the courtroom, and they were in almost constant use.

Jay Calhoun's testimony continued, and he talked the jury through what they saw on the television screens.

"Do you recognize this video?"

"Yes, ma'am, this is the video taken from the camera we set up across the road from the gate to the Halifax Property."

"And what do we see here?"

We saw trucks coming and going, we saw men in flannel shirts open and shut the gate. We saw Duck in a Ford truck, and Duck in another pickup, and Duck in a red Aerostar minivan. We saw Jarman Johnson open the gate and let a truck, being driven by someone else, into the property. We saw Duck driving the red Aerostar again.

Watching these clues felt like watching the beginning of an avant-garde film: things were happening, and we were struggling to piece together a narrative. That's what a trial is, really, the slow, obscure building of a narrative from a pile of facts. The lawyers aren't allowed to summarize, there are no primers, no exposition. The jury faces facts and must deduct the patterns for themselves. All context is implied.

Sharon tried to connect the dots before she ended her questioning of Jay by asking him what had brought him to set up these cameras in the first place.

He said that he had investigated the parked trailer of an eighteen-wheeler at another site, a piece of property in Pittsylvania County owned by Duck, and found plastic jugs there. He told the jury about the first night he'd walked the woods in Halifax, heard the sounds of an operating distillery, and smelled the telltale "warm liquor" smell.

It felt like a bombshell. There was no doubt but that Jay was qualified to discern whether or not a distillery was operating at a given place, and all that coming and going and switching of trucks . . . what else could they possibly be doing?

The jury sat stone-still, dead-faced, as if they'd been instructed not to react to anything, not to give a clue as to their state of mind. They hadn't, of course, received any such instruction, but they maintained their inscrutable demeanors throughout the entire trial.

Gil Davis rose, sighing, from his seat. Jay was apprehensive—he'd told me that he was, he figured Davis was going to go after him, and he was right.

"Who owned the land where the trailer was parked in Pittsylvania County?"

"Jody Smith."

"And how did you know that?"

"It's just common knowledge."

"You didn't ask anybody?"

"No, sir, it's known in the community that he owns it."

"What do you mean? You just walked onto someone's land, assuming that you knew whose it was? Couldn't he have sold it? Couldn't you have been wrong? Did you check? Did you do any sort of title search at all to determine the ownership of this land?"

"It's just known in the community who owns that land."

"How do you know?"

"I've been invited there before."

"Invited there by whom?"

"Jody's son, I believe, Jody Jr., invited me to a party there."

"I see, when was that?"

"I wanna say it was four years ago."

"And did you go to that party?"

"No, sir." Jay laughed a little.

"So you assumed, because Jody Smith Jr. invited you to a party there four years ago that you knew who owned the land and that you were free to walk onto that land without a warrant?"

"I had reason to believe there were jugs in the trailer."

"This trailer, however, it has doors? It was shut?"

"Yes, sir."

"You couldn't have seen anything from the road, is that right?"

"That's right."

"And how did you see the jugs?"

"There was a small hole in the lining of the door, the gasket, and I could peek in there and see."

But he couldn't see much, and it became clear that he'd gone back out to the trailer on a second date with a scope, a bendy gooseneck thing with a light on the end and a lens, and poked it in through the gasket and looked inside the trailer. Davis let it rest; he'd knocked a hole in the prosecution and he moved on.

He took off his glasses and let them dangle from his fingers, pinkie out like he was holding a teacup, and, holding a legal pad 6 inches from his face, scanned down his notes with his other finger. He knew how to take his time.

"This video, here, you say you've got sixty days of video?"

"I'm not sure, maybe six weeks."

"And over the course of this video, is this all the activity that was recorded?"

"Yes, sir."

"And what would you say the total time of the activity on this video was? Half an hour?"

"I don't know."

"But we saw it, we just watched it, was that about all the activity that you recorded, what we just saw?"

"Yes, sir."

"So over the course of six weeks or so, however long it was, everything that happened at the Halifax property would have been on this video?"

"We had the camera on the gate; anything that happened at the gate, we'd have recorded."

"And we've seen Jody Smith in one frame of that video?"

"I believe it's more than that."

Again Davis paused, and again he looked over his notes.

"These trucks . . . wouldn't a truck hauling liquor ride low? Liquor is heavy, isn't it?"

"Well, I don't know what they've done to these trucks."

"But if they'd modified them in some way, wouldn't they ride high when they were empty?"

Jay evaded the answer, stating that he wasn't a mechanic and didn't know, but it was a clear blow, and his evasiveness on the stand did nothing to discount the doubt inserted by Davis into what we'd seen.

Although these statistics were not available to Gil on the fly in the courtroom, he was right—where were the creaking springs? Six hundred gallons of liquor (if we assume it's 100 proof) weighs 4,762.5 pounds. A new Dodge 1500 four-wheel drive with a Quad Cab (which is what the truck looked like) has a curb weight of 5,201 pounds and a gross vehicle weight capacity of 8,510 pounds. The truck would have been about 1,500 pounds over its payload capacity. It would have looked like a loaded-down truck, riding on its axles.

Davis asked the judge for a moment. He was keen on this through-out the proceedings.

"Your Honor, could I have a moment?" and he would approach Greg Nawn at their table, and they would shuffle paper and whisper. Davis would continue his close-reading act, and after the witness had squirmed alone on the stand for longer than he could bear, Davis would return.

Davis showed the jury a picture of the top of the still, and Jay agreed that it'd been keyholed and rendered inoperable.

"Is it fair to say that at the time y'all went in, this still was not op-erational? Could somebody come in at that time and have operated that still? The keyhole on top makes it impossible to put the cap into it? Is that correct?"

"Yeah, but I would think if you had a couple men could go in there and hustle, you could get everything back together in about a day."

"To do that, you'd have to do a lot of soldering and other things would you not?"

"That would probably—I would just replace either the piece of metal or you could do some type of patch work. But it wasn't insur-mountable to get it back operating."

"But I think you said there's significant work to accomplish."

"Yeah, I mean, sure."

"And for somebody who would be in the business or had operated that, there's a lot of destruction that had already taken place. It would be pretty expensive or at least some decent sum to put it back so it was in the condition that it was before. Would it not have been—don't investigate me, but if I had a still—"

"Sure."

"—and I did those things to that still, it would be kind of costly for me to put it back. Putting it back so it could be operated again would take some time, and effort, and cost."

"I mean, yeah. I said probably a day with some hustle and I think you could get it back. And some money."

"And some money."

"And some money, right."

"Alright. I want to turn now to the night you say you walked the power line. Whose property was that?"

"I don't know."

"You just walked onto someone's land? Did you ask them?"

"No, sir."

This went on for a while, with Davis chasing Jay around the con-cept of whether or not he had a right to be standing on someone else's property, until it came out that Jay had been 125 yards away from the distillery building when he smelled the still and heard the noise.

"Could the smell have been anything else? Could it have been manure?"

"Manure? I don't think I'd confuse the smell of manure with the smell of a still. It's more like silage."

"Silage?"

After Jay explained what silage was—it's a fermented mix of plants and grains used as feed—Davis asked him if he'd seen any farms nearby. He said he wasn't sure.

The defense had no further questions, and we broke for lunch.

I wandered downtown Roanoke, wondering how much Davis had accomplished, and whether it had sunk in. He'd systematically called into question every piece of evidence offered by the government, casting doubt on the narrative and the actions of the agents. Was it working? It had to be working.

I ducked into the Texas Tavern. This little dive, a white concrete building with red paint advertising cheap hamburgers and bowls of chili, has been flipping patties—and owned by the same family—since 1930, and the prices haven't changed much. It's the kind of place you show up at three in the morning for a sloppy bowl of chili smothered with onions and relish and cheese. They seat 10,000 people, they like to brag, 10 at a time.

I ordered a double burger, set my notebook on the counter, and watched the classic, surly-but-friendly short-order cooks move with speed and precision. I tapped my fingers on the counter, looked around the room, and felt my heart leap into my throat.

There, just a few stools down, sat the defendant. He was by himself, spooning up a bowl of chili. The first thing I wondered was if I, too, should have ordered chili instead of a burger. It looked so good.

He was solemn before his two empty packets of oyster crackers, running the edge of a tablespoon around his heavy stoneware bowl. Was it legal to approach him? It had to be. Did I care? Would he talk to me? Why would he? Should I wait, go through his lawyers? Do the comfortable thing?

He was counting money. He was getting up.

I spun on my stool as he walked by and stuck out my hand. He took it, warmly, and held it.

I told him my name.

"I'm Jody Smith," he smiled, still holding my hand.

I told him I knew that, and that I was writing a book, and that a chapter of the book would be on this trial, and I tried not to laugh, even though I was nervous.

"Where are you from?"

I told him where I lived and wondered what he'd meant: Where did I work? Who sent me? I offered a card. He let my hand go and I gave it to him. If you ever want to talk about the trial, please get in touch, I'd really like to talk about this. Touching his sleeve: I don't know if it's appropriate, but good luck.*

He smiled and thanked me, then he was gone.

Trials are slow and laborious, and things got dull for a bit after lunch, with testimony about the land itself and who had bought it, and how the payments were made, and it was all relevant to the money-laundering charges, and certainly spoke to whether or not Margaret Smith was conspiring to conceal the fact that Duck actually owned the land, but it made for slow going.

We heard brief testimony from another agent who had ears like G. Gordon Liddy, a crew cut, and a bad case of police-speak: "At approximately 8:43 A.M. we observed a white female entering the premises," and so forth.

He was the agent who had been given the quart of strawberries in moonshine.

"Do you recognize this?" asked Sharon.

"Yes, ma'am."

He told her it was the quart of moonshine Margaret had produced, and there it sat, on the witness stand, for as long as they could keep it there. I noticed, too, that the little model still had not been dismantled. In fact, it stayed on its card table, right in front of the jury, throughout the proceedings. The jury had to look over and past it to see Duck.

Paula Jayson, known as PJ, swore that the testimony she was about to give would be the truth and sat down in the witness box. If she could have curled into herself, or rolled up like a potato bug, she would have—she was terrified and upset. She looked like a perfect coal miner's daughter, twenty-seven years old, with a streak of gray above her wide forehead like Susan Sontag's, a strong jawline, and a little ski

---

* My card has a picture of a whiskey still on it, which has led to many small moments of discomfort, though this one takes the cake.

jump of a nose. She pulled her charcoal cardigan tight around her, soft armor against the world, and faced the questions with obeisance.

Sharon asked her if she worked at Smith's Auto Sales, and she said that she used to wash cars there and ultimately became a manager. She doesn't work there anymore; she's a machine operator now.

"Besides being an employee of Jody Smith, did you have a relationship with him that extended beyond work?"

"Yes, ma'am."

"During what time period was that relationship, please?"

"Approximately 2003 to 2004."

"Have you since that time continued to—since the time that you last worked at Smith Auto Sales, have you continued to have contact with Mr. Smith?"

"Yes."

"Can you tell us kind of what the nature of the ongoing contact has been?"

"Just . . . friendship."

Clearly, they'd dated.

"Do you have any animosity towards him?"

"I'm sorry," PJ said, choked and halting, "I don't understand what that means."

Judge Turk asked, "Are you mad at him?"

"Thank you, Your Honor," said Sharon.

"No, sir."

"Any ill feelings towards him?" asked Judge Turk.

"No."

PJ started to cry before Sharon could get to her next question. Sharon urged her to have a glass of water and asked, "It's difficult for you to be here, isn't it?"

"Yes."

PJ had a very bad year in 2006. She was arrested for drunk driving, and at her trial, after she'd been convicted (and lost her license and therefore her job), agents approached her and handed her a warrant. She had been observed selling two Xanax pills (for $5 and a pack of cigarettes), and on a separate day they'd watched her sell someone a pint of moonshine.

They told her that they would not press the charges if she'd talk to them about Duck Smith.

They didn't know that she'd found out that day she was pregnant.

Judge Turk interrupted.

"Did you have the baby?"

"Yes, sir, I had twins."

"Are they identical twins?"

"No, sir."

"Well! You'll have two personalities then! How old are they now?"

"They're two."

He smiled at PJ, and she smiled back.

Sharon returned to the entering of evidence, which included mostly receipts for money orders she'd gotten for Danny Davis, one of the four defendants who had already pleaded guilty, and who owned the Halifax property until Margaret Smith took it over from him. Money-order receipts written at Smith's Auto Sales felt like real evidence at least—it seemed like something that really tied Duck into the web— but it also felt weirdly underwhelming. I waited for the bomb to drop. They must have her here for a reason . . . they wouldn't put a weeping girl on the stand, scare the hell out of her, just to talk about receipts?

But it never came. Sharon thanked her and asked her to answer whatever questions the other attorneys might have.

Gil rose, introduced himself, and smiled. Again, he held the legal pad to his nose and scanned it. He asked her if it was only Danny Davis for whom she wrote money orders, and she answered that no, it wasn't. In fact, it turned out, Smith's Auto Sales operated as a sort of Kinko's for the little community. If you needed something faxed, you could send it; if you needed something typed, the girls would do it for you. If you couldn't figure out the proper wording of a letter to the power company, PJ would write it for you.

She was born in Kentucky and dropped out of Franklin High School in Rocky Mount when she was sixteen. For money, she had refurbished motorized wheelchairs, worked at Advance Auto Parts, and she worked for Duck twice.

"How did you know Danny Davis?"

"I met him at the Hunt Club."

The "Hunt Club" was a party cabin and a loose confederation of friends, and many in the courtroom seemed to have a hard time understanding its existence.

"What did you hunt?" asked Judge Turk. "Not foxes?"

"It was just a place to go," answered PJ. "It was a social-type thing."

Gil decorously added, "It was a place you could go and relax, is that right? You could watch TV, or have a beer, and be with friends, is that right?"

"Yes," PJ nodded, and you could see in her eyes the sort of drunken mayhem that must have gone on. The sweaty benders, the hillbilly heroin, the pills, the orgies of Budweiser.

"And while you were at the club, did you have any indication of any kind of skullduggery?"

"I don't understand . . ."

"I'm sorry. Did you have any idea there was anything criminal going on?"

"No."

"And all the time you've known Jody Smith, have you known him to be involved in moonshine? Did you ever know of a still operated by Mr. Smith?"

"No."

"And did you talk to Mr. Smith about testifying here today."

"Yes, sir."

"And what did he tell you?"

"He told me the same thing he always told me." She was tearing up again. "He told me to tell the truth. He always said that you never get anywhere by lying."

"Did you benefit by testifying here today?"

"I like to think that my daughters benefited."

She walked off the stand and out the door, staring at her feet and pulling her sweater tight. Her beauty faded as she neared; her skin was ravaged, pocked, and creased. She hunched forward and took short, fearful steps, tears streaming.

I couldn't believe it. I couldn't see what the government had gained at all. They'd put a sad, broken waif on the stand, under duress. It made them seem desperate to make their case. They obviously didn't care if she sold two Xanax: they hadn't even arrested her for it. They'd used the potential charges as leverage. They'd shown PJ that they could bring despair and ruin down upon her; they made her see that she could have her babies in prison.

It had backfired. I remembered what Judge Turk had told me in his chambers: "It's possible to overtry a case. They [the jury] may think that the government is pickin' on this person." I certainly felt they were.

She'd never seen a still, never heard about any moonshine.

"He always said that you never get anywhere by lying."

"I like to think that my daughters benefited."

Duck was not going to be sent to prison on testimony like that.

United States v. Jody A. Smith et al., Day Three

First thing Wednesday morning, the case broke hard toward the defense. Margaret Smith had testified throughout that she had rented the Halifax property to a man named J. B. Jones. She had described J. B. Jones to the grand jury as a big man with a white beard who always wore a baseball cap and bib overalls. He looked, she said, like Uncle Jesse from *The Dukes of Hazzard*. Gil had picked up the J. B. Jones story as well, inserting it here and there. If they could establish the existence of J. B. Jones—or even the possibility of his existence— they could lay the whole thing on him.

The man who sells the sugar at William R. Hill in Richmond took the stand, and when asked to identify who he had sold sugar to, he said that there was no one in the courtroom he recognized.

When he was asked to describe who, then, he had sold sugar to, he said that there was a big man, always wore bib overalls, looked like Uncle Jesse.

I'm not sure if I actually gasped, but I might have.

Margaret's lawyer reached over and nudged her. She said that was the turning point. He hadn't believed her at all, was trying the case out of a sense of duty alone. For up until now we'd had no external assurance that J. B. Jones existed. If Margaret and Duck were conspiring, after all, they could simply have agreed to invoke this outside man, this character. Now we had testimony that indicated J. B. Jones was real.

The trial marched on: we heard from the lady who sold the jugs in North Carolina; she couldn't recognize anyone in the room, but she identified the fax number and it matched the fax machine at Smith's Auto Sales (which PJ had established was a more or less public fax machine). Margaret Smith's taxes were examined. A forensic scientist, an Indian, took the stand. He was impossible to understand, not only because of his accent but because he was so concrete that it seemed as if he were having another conversation altogether. George Thomas took his oath and testified that he'd sold Duck and his son $1,000 worth of cameras.

The evidence was underwhelming, and circumstantial, and Sharon looked as if she were drowning. Everything seemed to add up to nothing. Gil kept knocking her down. She walked to and from the witness stand and her podium with her head bent forward and down. She talked in fits and starts, and verged at times on the apoplectic or vaguely palsied, like Katharine Hepburn at the end of her life but without the suavity. She maintained her anger, but it was no longer clear on what it was focused. Was she angry at Gil? The case itself?

Even when Sharon had something good, Gil discredited it.

The cameras: Duck had said there was vandalism, which the shopkeeper said was, in fact, the reason people typically buy cameras.

The manager of the Rocky Mount Lowe's took the stand. Amazingly, they can scan the UPC code of a product and find out when it was sold and at which register. They can then, if the time frame is right, go through the surveillance video for that register and show who bought the item. There was Duck, buying a sump pump for cash at Lowe's.*

Gil asked the man to unpack the box.

"Does this look like the manner in which it is originally packaged?"

"It's hard to tell, but yes."

"Has this pump ever been used?"

"No."

Exhibit 14 was a sump pump that had never even been used? This was ridiculous.

The prosecution had a key witness in the wings, however—Jarman Johnson.

He walked into the courtroom looking uncomfortable, and he stayed that way. He wore black jeans, a short-sleeve Western shirt with the sleeves cuffed, and he walked with a splay-footed swagger. His hair was greased and styled into a ducktail. It was a cinch that those were Lucky Strikes in his pocket.

Sharon flipped photographs on the screens, and asked him to identify people. He cocked his head and looked at her sideways. It might have been more due to his failing hearing than his temperament, but it made him look suspicious of everyone.

"Why were you at the Halifax property?"

"To make moonshine."

"Were you paid?"

"Yes, ma'am."

"Who paid you?"

"Duck Smith."

Sharon was gaining ground.

"Have you worked for him before?"

"Yes."

"Have you been caught?"

"Yes."

---

* How to Be a Criminal, Item 7: Buy equipment at tiny mom-and-pop hardware stores with no computer systems and no video.

"Why hasn't Duck been caught?"

"I dunno, maybe he's smarter."

"Who gave you the money to buy the sugar?"

"Duck Smith."

There were eight or a dozen sharply dressed lawyers loitering in the court, and the judge explained that he needed to meet with them. A short recess was called.

Sharon beamed at Jarman as he came down from the stand and told him he was doing great. She asked him if he wanted a smoke and arranged for the bailiff to take him outside. She was smiling for the first time since the trial started.

Margaret's attorney was chatting with friends in the back of the court.

"Oh, are you the defense on this case?"

"Part of, I'm one of the defense attorneys. My client is the innocent one."

One of the agents came back and asked me how I thought Jarman was coming across, and I told him it was going well.

"We were nervous about him. We didn't know how he was going to play."

I told him he'd brought them neck and neck. He was doing very well. I didn't follow that with the qualification that he was doing very well for a deaf felon.

When the trial resumed, Jarman watched video and commented on it.

What a feeling that must be! What must it be like to watch a video of yourself committing a crime you thought you were getting away with? It must be fuel for a hundred paranoid fantasies. It must feel like the first ten seconds after a car accident, when all you want to do is rewind and realign the world to make what just happened go away. Jarman didn't seem like the reflective type, but was he, perhaps, looking back on those halcyon days? In the video he was leaning against a farm gate on a nice spring day with his pockets full of money and the truck full of liquor. He must have been having a good time. Getting ready for a night out. He hadn't any idea that what he was really doing was building a case against himself, and yet there it was on sixteen video screens in Judge Turk's court: Jarman Johnson breaking the law.

Sharon asked him about the Hunt Club, and he said he wasn't a member; as far as he knew it was just a place to crash when you were making liquor.

"And how often would you stay there?"

"Every week."

During Gil's cross-examination, Jarman denied any knowledge of J. B. Jones.

Gil successfully painted Jarman as a snake by coaxing him through an explanation of his presence at the wedding of Duck's granddaughter: he'd worn a wire and hovered around Duck like a puppy, trailing him everywhere, trying to get more on tape. Duck's granddaughter doesn't have a single picture of Duck at her wedding in which Jarman isn't looming.

Gil pushed the point that Jarman had made moonshine before, and that others at the still had as well, trying to establish that they wouldn't have needed a kingpin.

Sharon's redirect was short.

"When Duck was at the still, who was in charge?"

"Duck Smith."

"And when you mashed in, was Duck there?"

"Yes, ma'am."

"And when you loaded the liquor, was Duck there?"

"Yes, ma'am."

The 16,000 gallons of moonshine that the government was claiming had been made at the Halifax still had been sold, as usual, on the streets of Philadelphia. One of the great mysteries of the moonshine business is how all these good old boys in their feed-store hats ever got hooked up with Philadelphia in the first place. What did they do? How did they do it? Some lily-white, Wonder-bread-eating farm boy with shit on his shoes drives the Ford up to North Philly, gets out of the truck, and says *what?* The connection is almost inconceivable. The moonshiners I've met are a lot of things, but city-smart isn't one of them. Every once in a while, an agent (usually retired) would offer up some idiotic assertion.

One of them said: "Black people know black people."

You have got to be kidding: the secret network of negroes is the reason that these country bumpkins have figured out how to sell millions of dollars of liquor into the roughest areas of Philadelphia?

Jay Calhoun suspects it happened in prison. Or more specifically, he heard a story about a bust, where a bunch of moonshiners were thrown into prison together, and after they got out, the trade expanded, which is clearly more appealing than the Secret Negro Network but still smells like fish to me.

The next witness elucidated the issue. In this case the connection proved to be very simple and hinged upon coincidence rather than design. I recalled Buddy Driskill's invocation of the lieutenant in moonshine operations, and the structure that law enforcement lays upon what often turns out to be a loose series of opportunities and happenstance.

John Taylor Jr. is a soft-faced black man. On the stand he was quiet, nervous, and polite.*

He'd been the buyer for the still out in Halifax, and he'd trucked, by his own admission, six or seven thousand gallons of liquor up to Philly in his Dodge.

John Taylor's father, John Taylor Sr., had worked with Duck and lived in Virginia, and they'd become friends.

"I loved him," Duck told me. "He was a good man, one of my best

---

* He wasn't the first person to have demonstrated anxiety on the stand—it seemed that a preponderance of witnesses believed that if they said the wrong thing, or admitted something, that they'd be led off to jail by the bailiff. Duck's accountant had seemed downright defensive of his business practices, stressing that he relied on the information proffered to him by his clients. One woman, a secretary, seemed to think that she'd be not only jailed, but also fired if she couldn't properly explain the notes and doodles she'd made on a square of paper.

friends. I know it, he's black and I'm white and so what? They want to say we can't be friends? Hell."

By his son's admission, both on the stand and on the courthouse steps, John Taylor Sr. ran a lot of liquor to Philadelphia.

John Sr. died, and Duck went to the funeral, where he told John Jr. that he'd do anything he could for him. John Taylor got sick, couldn't work, and burned through his inheritance, so he called Duck. Then he started running liquor.

Both of those things happened. John Taylor called Duck, and John Taylor ran moonshine. Whether or not they were connected depends on whose story you're buying. That he filled his truck with liquor at the Halifax property was not contested.

It is what he said about what happened while he was there that changed my mind about everything.

Taylor described the pickup: He would drive to a spot, and he'd leave some money in his truck. Someone would take his truck, and he'd wait. The truck would come back full of liquor—fifty or sixty cases each time.

We watched again as trucks went in and out of gates in stop motion; there's Jarman, leaning on the fence. Then John Taylor said that Duck had stayed with him while the truck was being loaded with hooch. They'd sat by the river and talked about John Taylor Sr.

I was stunned.

By the river?

Jarman, in his testimony, the very testimony upon which the prosecution's case hinged, had said that Duck was at the still when they loaded the liquor and that he was in charge.

SHARON: And when you loaded the liquor was Duck there?

JARMAN: Yes, ma'am.

Suddenly, I saw, it all came down to Jarman's word versus John Taylor's.

If I believed Jarman, Duck was a ringleader, the man with the plan, funding the whole operation. If I believed Taylor, a different picture coalesced.

My mind was racing.

What about the hundreds of phone calls between Taylor and Duck?

Perhaps Duck hooked it up, perhaps his hands were a little dirty, but was he guilty of the charges levied against him? Greg Nawn said of the case: "To be born in Franklin County is to be guilty of one kind of conspiracy or another." There was something to that. Did Duck know both John Taylors? Absolutely. Did he know Jarman Johnson? He knew him very well; they rode their Harleys together and Duck had employed him at the car lot. Was Duck therefore the kingpin of a continuing criminal enterprise?

The government was asking for a leap of faith.

People should not go to prison on faith. That's what Gil had meant when he theatrically paraded a poster board around the courtroom floor. A man should not go to prison because of suspicion. The government needs proof beyond a reasonable doubt.

I had doubts, and I felt they were reasonable. When I had first walked into the courthouse, I had assumed Duck was guilty. As the case progressed, I had come to think that he was probably guilty, but that he might win his case. Now . . . well, now I didn't know what to think.

United States v. Jody A. Smith et al., Day Four

Don Harris has floated from agency to agency, with a heavy focus on enforcing liquor. He was on the stand when I arrived at court. His testimony was a summation of the business allegedly conducted by the distillery, and suddenly nothing seemed to add up.

My notes changed tenor. Instead of strictly recording the goings-on, the notebook is full of challenges and contradictions. John Taylor's testimony had fired something in me. I was no longer a reporter.

I was arguing the case. So far, I was only arguing to myself, in my notebook.

The government had alleged that the output of the distillery at Halifax was 100 cases per mash-in, but where was the rest? If the distillery had been paid $9,800 from Taylor, the rough total of all his alleged trips to the still, how could that possibly cover the expenses? They'd spent $1,000 on cameras alone! They'd spent thousands on electricity, sugar, diesel fuel for the oil burners, the mortgage—it didn't add up!

I saw an innocent man facing years of prison.

Again, the real nature of a federal trial revealed itself and we slowed to a crawl as more accountants testified. Never was it clear what was being established as we staggered through analyses of bank records, tax records, and receipts. We were all getting sleepy. Judge Turk leaned heavily on his elbow and then jerked back to attention when it slipped off the arm of his chair. The jury was drowsy, too. The day closed with a brutal, lengthy, analysis of financial records seized from Smith's Auto Sales. Hours of testimony amounted to the fact that Duck had pocketed—or used as petty cash—something like $20,000 a year out of the total take of his business, which made about $350,000 a year. Certainly, he should have reported it to his accountant.

Back at my hotel on the fourth night of the trial, I grabbed the indictment. I went through the charges one by one, exploring my doubts.

Was I just rooting for the outlaw? I didn't think so. I had drunk that horrible sugar jack out of the Danville nip joint. I harbor no romance for the greedy industrial moonshiner. Further, I like the Illegal Whiskey Task Force—both personally and as an agency of enforcement. In a world where most police action takes place after the crime has been committed, it was wonderful to see that a few guys were actually out there investigating things, trying to stop the illegal activity they were charged with curbing rather than simply mopping up after the fact.

With a seething brain I worked late into the night, drinking beer and combing over the indictment. It had looked irrefutable, iron-clad. Now, I hurriedly found refutation for every count. Nothing added up. The case against Duck was in shambles. The reason Duck had stubbornly gone to trial was that he was innocent.

I was losing touch with my responsibilities as a reporter. I was only going to get in deeper.

United States v. Jody A. Smith et al., Day Five

Gil Davis has a bad heart, and he was exhausted. When I arrived at the courthouse on Friday morning, everyone was standing around on the steps—we were recessed for the day so Gil could rest.

I talked briefly with Greg Nawn and Gil, and they said they were going to be out by Smith Mountain Lake that weekend, interviewing character witnesses. I asked if I could come, and they said they'd ask Duck.

While I waited to hear from them, I drove down to Rocky Mount and out Route 40 and took a few snapshots of Smith's Auto Sales. I swam in the hotel pool. I read microfilm in the Rocky Mount library. I obsessed over the case.

It was hot and the full moon floated pale in the sky during the day and I floated in the pool and considered the information. Sharon had introduced over two hundred pieces of evidence. She had set two hundred gears spinning. She had built this gigantic machine that rushed and chugged along, but to what purpose? Had she made her case? Was the machine just some sort of folly, a system of weights and levers and gears that did absolutely nothing?

Nothing, that is, except work toward the incarceration of Margaret and Duck.

Greg called—I could come out.

When I got there, Greg introduced me as a friend of Junior Johnson's.

Oh, no, that's crazy, I protested, Junior has a lot of friends, I only just met him. I was, in fact, down there on his farm just a month ago—and Duck caught my eye. He managed, with a wink and a little nod, to tell me to shut up. I know how to stop talking.

We talked about the case, and we interviewed the character witnesses, and we chewed through some hamburgers and potato salad. One of Duck's friends pulled me over to the side and offered up a Mason jar of moonshine out of a cooler. I pulled off it; it was sweetened, I think, with damson; it was delicious.

"It's been so long I been facing this," said Duck. "I can't stand it. It's tense. Two years I've had this hanging over me. You want to see the donkeys?"

Duck has a small herd of miniature donkeys, and he whistled for them to come in from the pasture. We went out to the field and tried to put a rope on one—Duck wanted one of the kids to ride him—but the donkey had lost his halter and we couldn't catch him. Anyway, the big horse, Rock, wanted all the attention, and he'd nip at the miniatures and chase them away. A neighbor held on to Rock, giving him sips of beer, while Duck walked out into the field.

The neighbor was a blue-eyed country man wearing a straw hat that said John Deere (which Rock eventually ate). He was the father of a ten-year-old boy named Eathan. Greg was thinking about putting Eathan on the stand.

Eathan had walked down to the barn the day before the trial, and he'd given Duck a small statue of a horse. He said that Duck had always been good to him, and he loved coming down here to ride the horses and work in the barn.

"I thought it might bring you luck."

"I just reached out," said Duck, "and grabbed him around the neck and I hugged him." He shook his head a little. "Ain't that something? He didn't have to do anything like that."

Duck had wanted to keep the little statue on the table at the trial, but the lawyers had told him not to.

● ● ●

That night I worked with Gil and Greg at the house that Gil had bought on the lake after he'd won a mineral rights lawsuit for something in the neighborhood of $40 million. The walls were bright white, and the air-conditioning was cranked. Gil was puttering around in a t-shirt and shorts (both Washington Redskin red). He had some softshell crabs defrosting on the counter. There were piles of paper everywhere, sticky flags, binder notebooks. Lawbooks were stacked high on every table. We were combing the evidence. We were building time lines.

It's hard to be a lawyer. You have to think on your feet, and you have to react to what's going on. I think they were relieved to find that I had taken notes throughout and that I could piece the case together as a narrative. What's more, my narrative ended with Duck's acquittal.

We worked together, and I was thrilled and more than a little honored to have been taken up so quickly. I grew up fantasizing about being a lawyer. I imagined myself surrounded by papers and books in the woody nook of a law library, valiantly defending justice with my intelligence. The evening was heady, thrilling stuff. I was happy to volunteer my time, although it meant the complete sacrifice of my last shred of journalistic integrity. They paid me in compliments. Greg was convinced that I could set up a business as a trial observer.

Eventually, Gil started rehearsing. It started slowly, but you could tell that he'd shifted. He would take our points, whatever we'd just built up, and he'd start speechifying. Within a few hours, he was including the "Ladies and gentlemen of the jury." It was powerful. His argument was profound.

We were going to win.

United States v. Jody Smith et al., Day Five, Take 2

In the courtroom Monday morning the gloves were off. The arguments were more heated, more antagonistic. The lawyering was looser, bigger points were being made, and bigger liberties were being taken to make those points. We were coming to the end.

Everything was different for me, too. I'd joined the team, and the moments before court were filled with handshakes and smiles and pats on the arms of the friends and family. I conferred with Gil and Greg; we whispered about strategy. I encouraged Duck, and he shook my hand and looked me in the eye and seemed full of gratitude and friendship.

Bureau of Alcohol, Tobacco, Firearms, and Explosives Agent Underwood was on the stand, and his testimony took up the entire day.

Sharon seemed stuck. She was like a comedian without any punchlines. She struggled along, pushing out setup after setup—where was the resolution? Where were the climactic, final points? There were none.

Out at Gil's lake house we'd broken it down. The only thing tying Duck to the still was the testimony of Jarman Johnson, and Jarman Johnson was a liar and a felon. Gil was going to hammer it home.

He worked on Underwood. First, he reestablished the possibility that J. B. Jones could have been the sugar daddy. He reminded the jury that, although the government was claiming that the still site was a flurry of industrious activity, they had only two days over the course of six weeks of videotape during which anyone was there. Gil established the idea that the moonshine they'd found at the trailer could have come from somewhere else. Plenty of people used that building. Just having moonshine in a building doesn't make you a distiller.

Then, the key: "And would you say that the only evidence you have tying Duck Smith to the still at Halifax is Jarman Johnson?"

"Yes, sir," answered Underwood.

That was it. The baseball was soaring over the fence, the Hail Mary pass had found the hands of the receiver. We were going to win.

Gil approached me after his cross-examination, called me over to the rail.

"How'd that go?"

"You nailed it, Gil."

He smiled and nodded. He asked me if I had any ideas, and I told him again that he had nailed it.

The government rested.

The defense case was nothing much, a series of character witnesses and some small points of evidence. Past employers and friends and preachers testified to the trustworthy and wonderful nature of the defendants. It's an absurd thing, really, and I can't imagine it carries much weight with the jury. Although I suppose if you skipped it the jury would surmise that you couldn't even find anyone to say anything good about you at all.

Jarman Johnson's brother-in-law—he goes by the moniker "Fuzzy"—took the stand and expressed that he credited Duck Smith with saving his life. He'd been a drunk and Duck had rehabilitated him. He testified that he wanted to move, because he lived right next door to Jarman, and Jarman burned every friend he ever had. It was only a matter of time until someone came around to shoot him, and he didn't want them to shoot up the wrong house and get him by mistake.

"Would you trust Jarman Johnson with money?"

"I had once. He's still got it."

United States v. Jody A. Smith et al., Closing Arguments

Certain strange behaviors had spread through the court during the course of the week. Duck's family and friends, who arrived in force for the closing arguments, seemed to have decided that the seating was like a wedding. They sat behind the defense table, as if they were the bride's family. Also, the audience had taken to standing for the entrance of the jury. At the start of the trial, only the defense team offered up this honor. Whichever agents or court employees happened to be in the pews didn't rise for the jury. But Duck's friends and family did. It was spontaneous, and it was heartfelt, I think. They were putting Duck's fate in the hands of this dozen, and they would have brought flowers and cakes and paid for their parking if they'd been allowed. Instead, they stood.

I had talked with Greg, and we were sure we were going to win. We all agreed that Margaret's case was 100 percent. There were some doubts about Duck; we had to trust the jury to have really understood the discrepancies in the case.

"I think God is on our side," said Greg. "Or the Constitution."

It wasn't over yet.

Sharon had tightened up. Her clothes were nicer, her hair was styled, and she brought her full game to the closing arguments. She stood up straight, and no longer did she stammer or look frustrated. I don't know where she found her reserves, but she was back. This was the Sharon I'd interviewed. This was the woman you did not want to face in the courtroom.

She explained what it meant to be a part of a conspiracy. Even if Margaret didn't want to do this stuff, if she willfully blinded herself to the true activities out at the Halifax property, she was guilty. Margaret had known Duck for years. They'd slipped away and gotten married in the Bahamas (their marriage wasn't legal). She knew what Duck did, and if she knew what he did, and she helped him to run this business, she was guilty.

"And you better believe that making liquor is a business."

With that she flipped to Duck's case. She took us through a tour of the evidence.

"What about this J. B. Jones? This Uncle Jesse character. Could he have been real? Sure. Did he help buy the sugar? Sure he did. Does that release Jody Smith of responsibility? No."

She was on a roll.

"Even if all you believe is that Jody Smith called John Taylor, he's still guilty. The defense will say that we have not shown that Jody Smith was present at the distillery. Well, you don't have to catch the bank robber in the bank to know that the bank was robbed. Some of you probably have children, but I think this example will make sense to you even if you don't. Imagine a child took a cookie out of the cookie jar. What does he say? He says, 'I didn't do it.' But we know. The cookie is gone, after all. And even if he's eaten it, and cleaned up the crumbs, and he tells you 'I didn't do it!' can there be any doubt?"

When you handicap a horse race, you measure all the odds, look at the horses, you look at the conditions of the race, and you narrow it down. You remain serious and focused, and you come to a conclusion built not on passion, but on something close to science. Every once in a while, however, you are overwhelmed. The third race of the Triple Crown, for instance, the Belmont Stakes, and there's a horse going to the gate that has won the first two legs. You want it so badly. You want him to win the last leg. I had been hurtled down this highway before. In love with an outcome, I threw away science, I discarded reason, and gambled on passion. As Sharon built her case, I began to feel the slippage. The horses were in the gate, and I had $100 on a horse that suddenly didn't look as strong. The story had carried me away. My desire had overwhelmed the truth.

Sharon's argument was a piece of art.

Would Gil overcome this?

Lingafelt argued his closing case for Margaret first, and he made it clear that he would not lie down and simply give the case to the government. He explained that she was on muscle relaxers and anti-depressants. She has fibromyalgia. Throughout the period when the Halifax distillery was operational, she was caring for her dying mother, two hours away. The irregularities in her testimony before the grand jury were the irregularities of a human being without a grand scheme.

"If she was a criminal mastermind, if she was party to a conspiracy, she'd have her story straight. But she didn't. And that's because she's innocent."

This was high drama. I wanted to applaud.

It was Gil's turn. We were on the home stretch.

"Did Duck Smith know people who made moonshine? Course he did. But we don't convict people because they know people."

He covered the sugar salesman: wouldn't he have recognized Duck?

He paused dramatically and said, "If Margaret Smith is not acquitted, there is no justice in America. Not only did they not prove their case, their case is absurd.

"Jody Smith cooperated with the investigation, because if you're innocent, you want the investigators to do all they can. Because you want them to work hard. You want them to find the truth. Because the truth will set you free.

"It comes down to one person you have to believe," he intoned. "Jarman Johnson. And Jarman Johnson lied to the agents. He lied about the existence of J. B. Jones. He lied to his own brother-in-law. And he's lying now."

I watched the faces of the jury. They were opaque.

"Today, in this courtroom, you are the nation. Give the United States a fair trial. There are doubts in this case. I have not drawn any unreasonable inferences from this evidence. There are doubts. If they are reasonable, you must acquit."

Sharon had one last bit of argument, which amounted to nothing more than reminding the jury that the United States was not, in fact, on trial. The task before them was simple. Look at the evidence, and find Duck guilty.

The arguments over, the jury retreated to deliberate. Jay Calhoun and I sat by the marshal's offices and told each other stories. At five the court adjourned. The jury would finish tomorrow.

In the courtroom, while people packed up, Gil said to me: "I don't know." He shook his head. "What did you think?"

I told him it was rough. They were even, fifty-fifty.

"Sharon," he said, "she did a great job. That was a really good closing argument. And Lingafelt nailed it, too. I wish I'd done better. I'm just so tired."

I told him I thought he had made the points that needed to be made, and that if the jury was sharp, they'd figure it out.

He looked morose.

He was right.

When the jury came back the following day, they found Duck and Margaret guilty on all counts.

I Always Go to Sea
as a Sailor

My behavior began to worry me. I began to wonder if my
absorption was absolute ...

—GEORGE PLIMPTON, PAPER LION

DUCK AND MARGARET WERE SENTENCED IN JULY OF 2009,
almost a year after the verdict. In the interim, Phillip Lingafelt introduced a fascinating motion to dismiss the money-laundering charges
on the basis that funds used to operate a business, even if that business is illegal, are not proceeds or profits, and therefore do not qualify
as money that is laundered. Judge Turk overturned those convictions.

As I slid my pencil and my wallet into the dish by the metal detec-
tors, I was, again, hopeful. There were real arguments to be made:
The production claimed by the government seemed to me (and to
Gil and Greg) unsupported by evidence. Sharon based her numbers
on the still running every day, but if it was running all the time, why
wasn't there more action caught on camera? If it was running all the
time, why were the jugs empty?

Margaret Smith was sentenced first. She didn't present any character witnesses. Lingafelt simply stood at the podium and gave a statement. He said this was a sad day, a tragedy. Margaret was fifty-eight years old, and had lived a good life, and now found herself convicted as a felon. To incarcerate her, claimed Lingafelt, would be "like using a sledgehammer to kill a gnat."

"I don't think this is a gnat," said Judge Turk.

"While the operation might have been substantial," said Lingafelt, "her role was more gnatlike."

Lingafelt put forward that Margaret had been used. It was her tenderhearted nature that got her, she was a person prone to being taken advantage of, she was depressed, insomniac, and still suffered from fibromyalgia. She had been caring for her dying mother while the still operated and was now caring for her daughter and grandson.

Sharon argued that Margaret had been a willing conspirator.

Margaret herself stood up and in a shaky voice said, "I want to tell the court I'm sorry. Out of love I believed in people I shouldn't have."

Margaret's family started to cry in the pews.

Judge Turk explained that according to the sentencing guidelines, she was facing twenty-one to twenty-seven months, and he agreed that this was a tragic event. She had no prior convictions, and she posed no threat of future violation. There was no evidence that she had gone to the still site and no evidence that she had profited.

We held our breath.

She was sentenced to a year and a day.

Her family wept broken, defeated sobs and held one another. Judge Turk came down from his bench to shake hands.

"You know you'll be out in ten months," he said to Margaret, "you can do it. You're a strong woman."

I couldn't help but think that her sentence did not bode well for Duck, for while it was a downward departure from the sentencing guidelines, it was real time.

Duck's witnesses were wonderful. Veterans, preachers, and young mothers he'd helped out all spoke of his miraculous conversion, his recent epiphany, and his many good works. He was a pillar of the community, and he was a church-going man.

Glen Cooper took the stand, and Judge Turk asked if he was related to a certain group of Coopers.

Cooper exclaimed, "I campaigned for you!"

Judge Turk remembered that indeed he had.

Bobby Lee Scruggs took the stand. He and Duck had traveled together to play poker, before Scruggs found religion and quit drinking, smoking, and gambling.

Gil asked, "I heard you won a lot?"

"I didn't lose."

The judge asked if he had reported all that income to the IRS.

"Oh . . ."

"Don't answer that."

Throughout his testimony, the judge would return to the poker.

"So, you quit playing poker all together?"

"I'm a changed man."

"You can't play poker?"

"You've got to be perfect to get to heaven."

Throughout the proceedings, Sharon contradicted the portrait of Duck as a man occupied only by good works by reminding the court that he financed cars at 18 percent and repossessed them when the customer couldn't make the payment. She put forth that he landed all these people in court. He cheated on his taxes. He skimmed from his business. Sharon argued that there was a public Duck Smith, who was a good man, and a private Duck Smith, who was greedy and would do anything he could get away with. He was greedy and he made liquor. The equipment he made it with was dirty, filthy; there were *rats*.

"Don't we care about the people in our communities?" asked Sharon. "Alcohol is a scourge."

Duck stood and said that he hadn't been a perfect person in his life, and he asked that he be allowed to go somewhere where he could help people.

He was sentenced to forty-eight months.

Four years, plus $217,000 in restitution, plus thirty-six months probation: a substantial sentence based upon an evidentiary narrative that was not at all straightforward. After reviewing hours of testimony and hundreds of pieces of evidence, I felt that we still didn't know what had happened out there in Halifax. Whether or not Duck Smith was a big-money moonshine operator had been resolved in the legal sense, but had it really been proved?

Equally troubling, I found, was that I had yet to resolve the moral ambiguity of moonshining. After years of studying the illicit production and sale of whiskey, I have come to no decisive conclusion. In parallel, I can suggest that a man who grows marijuana so he can smoke it, and sells some to his friends, is very different from a man who purposefully sets out to create a marijuana-farming business.

My friends in law enforcement will no doubt disagree.

My predisposition is permissive. If you want to get drunk, I have a hard time imagining that someone should tell you not to.

But I drank that wretched poison out of a nip joint, and that's not stuff that needs to be celebrated or set free. Dr. Brent Morgan conducted a study in an Atlanta hospital and found that a substantial percentage of undiagnosed illnesses in the emergency room could be linked to moonshine consumption. Researchers studied 25 of the 200 lead-poisoning deaths across the nation in the past twenty years, and found that 20 of them could be linked to moonshine. This might make your chances seem pretty good, but Dr. Chris Holstege of the University of Virginia found that 60 percent of the moonshine he analyzed had unacceptable levels of lead. The federal standard for drinking water is that it can contain 15 parts per billion. One sample analyzed at UVA contained 599 parts per billion. Of course, this could be regulated separately. I can only imagine that if I was found to be painting carrots with arsenic and selling them at a farm stand, there would be legal repercussions that would not hinge upon the legality of the carrot.

The illegality of hobby distilling is a simpler nut to crack. It should be legalized. We are allowed to produce 300 gallons of beer or wine at home every year. (We aren't allowed to sell it.) It seems perfectly reasonable to suggest that we should therefore be able to distill the alcohol out of that 300 gallons and produce 30 gallons of spirit per year. I would suggest that if the government fears the potential tax loss—although this loss seems unlikely, I have yet to meet anyone who distills their own hooch and doesn't also go to the liquor store to buy gin and tequila—they should ask that home distillers send in a fee, $150 a year or something, to cover the taxes on the distillate.

Distillate is often required to be secured, and is frequently cited as a fire hazard, but there are no restrictions on the securing of my liquor cabinet. I have dozens and dozens of bottles of spirits—currently a shelf creaking under the weight of something like seventy-five bottles I've accumulated from microdistillers and in the pursuit of the perfect cocktail. I am not required to keep it locked in a bonded space, and I am not required to build an explosionproof room.

Could people hurt themselves? Well, they can also poison themselves canning tomatoes. I would love to see the change, and if home distilling were legalized, it would help the microdistilling industry in the same way that hobby brewing helped microbrews. I have seen the industry blossom in the past few years. Stranahan's has quadrupled its capacity and took over its own fermentation. House Distillery is on the verge of launching its most important product and has just harvested its first crop of barley. We are at a watershed. Hobby distilling gets people interested in an industry that is creating jobs, preserving flavors and traditions, and offering a new revenue stream for farmers across the country.

That said, I am done with it.

For it is one thing to go to sea as a sailor if you are, in fact, a seaman. Ishmael had several voyages in the merchant service when he signed on to the *Pequod*, after all. It is another thing entirely to borrow a costume and get on a boat just to see what happens. There will come a time when the decision must be made: sailor or tourist?

I am no outlaw. My experiments were over; Billy Gibbons was going to have to go. It is time to get back on dry land where I belong.

Acknowledgments

I started chasing the white dog when Kris brazed together the first worm, years ago.

Thanks to Peter McGuigan and Hannah Gordon at Foundry Literary + Media, who worked hard to make this book a reality. Thanks to Denise Roy for loving it and Colin Fox for seeing it through.

Stefan Beck read every word, including many that were misspelled and thousands that didn't make the cut. Mark Elliott pretended that the VCU libraries hired him to be my research assistant. Josh Meissner read it through at the end, long after I had lost my eye for detail.

Thanks to Jess Graber and Jake Norris of Stranahan's Colorado Whiskey. Rory Donovan of Peach Street Distillers told me to drive over the Red Mountain Pass and was waiting for me in Silverton after I did.

Gil Davis and Gregory Nawn did far more than open their files, though they did that, too. Jody Alton Smith Sr. was gracious despite the pressures upon him. I wish him luck, and I can only hope that I've recorded his ordeal accurately. My thanks go out to Jody's family and friends, too.

This book wouldn't be half as much as it is were it not for the excellent tour guide capabilities of Joe Michalek, Junior Johnson, and the man I will continue to refer to as Skillet.

I've talked to Bill Owens more or less every week since he first told me there was no such thing as moonshine. He's a great friend.

Jesse Tate of the Virginia Alcohol Beverage Control met me in the woods and took a liking to this project. He worked hard on my behalf, was always ready to drive me around, make an introduction, or go for a beer. I appreciate it.

A lot of people have to say yes for a book like this to work. Thanks to Jimmy Beheler, Burkhard Bilger, Sharon Burham, Jay Calhoun, Amanda Clapp, Chuck Cowdery, Dino, Buddy Driskill, Jay Erisman, Kent Fleischmann, Mike Gangloff, Ibby Greer, Don Harris, Andrew Faulkner, Fred Hay, Daniel Hyatt, Christian Krogstad, Matt Laferty, Larry, David Mahaffey, Mike McCaw, Lee Medoff, Don Payne, Jack Powell, Christine J. McCafferty, Jen McCaffery, Robert Messenger, Brendan Moylan, Don Poffenroth, Timothy Rives, Jesse Roverana, Matt Rowley, Jorg Rupf, Laura Ruttum, Allison Schneider, Kyle Sinisi, Ian Smiley, Bill Smith, Tim & Shelby Smith, Morris Stephenson, Bruce Sterling, George Stranahan, Randall Toney, Zac Triemert, Anne Tuennerman, Judge Turk, Rene Uhalde, Thomas Waugh, Chris Weld, Brendan Wheatley, and James Whelan.

Thanks to the students of the inaugural ADI Whiskey Seminar for letting me shadow their class.

For hanging out with West when I couldn't, and allowing me to use their houses as if they were remote office sites: Maggie Benmour, Sara Link, Jennifer and Roland Engelhardt, Barbara and Jack Thomas. Rob Link, for being game. Will and Carrie Watman for all of the above and for their inexhaustible patience for my ramblings.

My son, West, was far more helpful than he could have known. He and I spent hours talking about this book when he was one and two years old, and I'm sure he would have rather been talking about something else.

And Rachael, *sine qua non*. Without her I wouldn't know what to do or why to do it, and I certainly wouldn't have as much fun.

About the Author

Max Watman is the author of *Race Day: A Spot on the Rail with Max Watman*. He was the horse racing correspondent for the *New York Sun* and has written for various publications on books, music, food, and drink. He was raised in the Shenandoah Valley and has worked as a cook, farmer, silversmith, tutor, greenskeeper, warehouseman, and web designer. After many collegial adventures, he earned a BA at Virginia Commonwealth University and an MFA at Columbia University. The National Endowment for the Arts awarded him a literature fellowship in 2008. He lives in the Hudson Valley with his wife and son.